THE ASIANS

Their Heritage and Their Destiny

Revised Edition

Paul Thomas Welty

J. B. LIPPINCOTT COMPANY

PHILADELPHIA   NEW YORK

Drawings by Cy Ferring, from OLSON'S ORIENT GUIDE *by Harvey S. Olson. Copyright © 1962 by Harvey S. Olson. Published by J. B. Lippincott Company.*
Maps by William Gray

FOREWORD

A number of American universities have for some time been the leading centers in the world for the study of Asian societies. Work on Asia at the graduate or more advanced undergraduate level has been sufficiently widespread to produce a considerable demand for suitable textbooks and has been going on long enough to produce a number of highly competent scholars to write them.

Interest in the study of Asia at less advanced levels is more recent. People have come increasingly to feel that Asia is so important in the modern world that a good general education should give some knowledge of Asian societies as well as of Western societies. Consequently, courses on Asia are being started at high school and beginning college levels. For this it is much harder to find suitable textbooks, partly because the demand has existed for a shorter time and, more important, because a textbook at this level is harder to write. A suitable book needs to discuss some rather profound issues briefly and in simple language. It has to convey to a student brought up in a highly industrialized society the very different conditions of life which prevail over most of Asia, and it has to deal with some fundamental problems of cultural differences in order to overcome widespread misconceptions among people who have not thought clearly about these problems—a category which has included some men in responsible positions as well as high school and college students.

The failure to understand cultural differences leads to a pair of fallacious beliefs. On the one hand, people start with the correct assumption of a common humanity and jump to the false conclusion that the differences between Western culture and the various Asian cultures are superficial, that the social sciences as worked out for Western societies can be applied with comparatively little change to Asian societies or that their political problems can be discussed in terms of comparatively simple analogies with the West. On the other hand, people start with the correct assumption that there are quite profound differences between Asian and Western societies and jump to the false conclusion that Asians are fundamentally different in nature from people of European descent.

In fact, the wide differences between the ways in which people behave in different societies can be explained by differences in their institutions and forms of organization and by the differences in their traditional systems of belief. There may be some real differences in predominant temperament between different races but a large part of the differences in patterns of behaviour between different societies can be explained in terms of a common human nature influenced by different social institutions and different ideologies.

It follows that the most important task of a book introducing Asia to the American student is to give some understanding of the social and economic environment in which most Asians live and of the various systems of thought which influence their approach to present-day problems, just as the thinking of people in a Western culture is influenced by their environment and traditions. (It is, of course, important to keep clear the distinction between saying that certain factors influence people's thinking and saying that these factors determine their thinking. In many Asian societies the educated elite has taken the lead in rejecting important parts of the traditional system but, even so, the form of the reaction has been influenced by the tradition it was reacting against.)

A book which has succeeded in this task will have given the student a foundation on which he can build an increasing understanding of Asia as he acquires more detailed information. A book which has not provided this foundation may impart a lot of miscellaneous knowledge about Asia but will not have given any real understanding.

It is the great merit of *The Asians* that it puts its main emphasis on this most important and most difficult task, while also giving the main outlines of geography, history, politics and government, for the main areas of Asia from Pakistan round to Japan. It is, perhaps, not too difficult to give an American student some understanding of the daily life of a typical Asian in various areas, but it is extremely difficult to give in clear and simple language a short account of a complex system of religion or social philosophy. However, the reader will find such accounts of Islam, Hinduism, Buddhism, traditional Chinese social philosophy, and Japanese Bushido and Shinto. Though such short accounts can obviously only give the outlines of their subjects, they do give these outlines clearly and correctly. (I checked the section on Buddhism by asking a friend from a Therevada Buddhist family to read it and he reported that it was a good summary of basic Buddhist beliefs as held and practiced in his part of Southeast Asia.)

Thus, students who use this book to start their study of Asia can obtain not only an outline knowledge of history, geography and politics but also the basis of a background knowledge of Asian ways of life and ways of thought which can make it possible for them to turn their knowledge about Asia into a real understanding of Asia.

LINDSAY OF BIRKER
Professor of Far Eastern Studies
The American University
Washington, D.C.

CONTENTS

PROLOGUE

This book has been written to introduce the people of Asia. It is not possible to tell the complete story about a people so numerous, so diverse, and so ancient, in one relatively short encounter, but perhaps this introductory survey will stimulate those unfamiliar with the non-Western world to want to know the people of Asia more intimately and more fully. I have tried in the following pages to give some insight into the forces that have made the Asians what they are today. I have broadly sketched the landscape where they live and work, discussed their ideologies and ideals, emphasized certain aspects of their social and political life, and conveyed, I hope, some appreciation of their aspirations and destiny.

To counter any preconceptions which might prevent the Western reader from responding to what follows with a sympathetic and receptive mind, I have first called attention to the Asians as people. I have then commented on some of their attitudes toward Americans which, I believe, will reveal something of the high barrier of stereotype and misconception separating the two peoples. Too frequently, when we first meet others of another race and culture, many of us become preoccupied with the differences which distinguish us from them and tend to ignore the fundamental humanness that we share with them. I have long believed that many Western minds have been closed to an understanding of the Asians by the feeling, conscious or unconscious, that they are too alien to be comprehended and too strange ever to become familiar. It is a natural human reaction to exclude the unfamiliar and incomprehensible. If there is anything I want you to underscore most heavily in my presentation, it is that I am writing about people, people who are seeking in their own special way for that better life we all desire here and hereafter. I would not want my words on their dissimilar approaches to truth and happiness to obstruct the perception of their questing humanity.

1

Engaged in a mighty effort to find alternative patterns of life, the Asians of this century are not a static people. New ideas and institutions from elsewhere have been introduced into Asian life and are compelling them to uproot, review, and change treasured conceptions deeply rooted in the past. This process is necessary but torturing, and change and conflict are often found together on the Asian scene today. Sometimes the Asians are able to resolve these conflicts through compromise and adaptation. At other times they protest fiercely in an attempt to preserve the integrity of their own revered traditions. I have tried to show the dynamic character of a people in transition.

I have stressed those qualities of the Asians which in my opinion best illuminate them on an introductory level. For example, I have pictured the external unity which links the Asians together with physical and spiritual bonds, but I have also shown the diversity which distinguishes Asians from one another and is apparent even among those living within the same areas. The Pakistanis and the Indians both live in South Asia and were closely associated for centuries upon a common land, but there are radical differences in their religious viewpoints and in their approaches to life on earth. The Japanese of East Asia borrowed extensively from their Chinese neighbors, but it will become evident in what follows that there are characteristics of the Japanese social and political life which sharply differentiate them from the Chinese of yesterday and today.

I have presented the Asians on a regional and topical basis. Since it has become customary to group the Asian people into the three regions of South Asia, East Asia, and Southeast Asia, I too will introduce them in this order. But there are more cogent reasons for presenting them in this order. The great religions of Hinduism, Buddhism, and Islam went forth from South Asia and shaped the minds and cultural landscape in many Asian lands. The human, earthly philosophies of Confucianism and Taoism, originating in China in East Asia, have sometimes played a major role in molding the cultural, social, and political systems of other Asian countries. Culturally and ethnically, the people of Southeast Asia continue to reflect the deep and pervasive influences of the South and East Asians upon their way of life. By knowing something about these people we can better understand the Southeast Asians. In terms of international politics it is also desirable to meet the people of South and East Asia first, for the largest and most powerful nations are found in these two areas. Their political and military activities affect the lives of all Asians and, for that matter, all mankind.

Within these Asian regions I have focused on topics which I feel are important for an understanding of most of the people in these three areas. Thus, because the vast majority of South Asians live on the Indo-Pakistan subcontinent and developed there conceptions and practices which have influenced multitudes of Asians, I have treated in some detail the ideologies and the social and political life of these people. I have chosen, for example, to underline the development of Pakistan into an independent state and to elaborate on the ideology of Islam which gives meaning and purpose to the life of the Pakistanis and many other Asians. In the case of Ceylon, on the other hand, I have elected to point out briefly some of its more important problems and the significance of its location, for most of the Ceylonese are of Indian origin, hold the religions of Buddhism or Hinduism, and are related to the Indians by many social similarities.

In considering East Asia I have commented in some depth on the ideologies and social and political life of the Chinese and Japanese who are the largest groups in this region. The civilization of the Koreans, though possessing its own distinguishing features, was substantially shaped by the Chinese and, to a certain extent, by the Japanese. I have, therefore, confined my remarks about the Koreans to their unhappy history of invasions and to the economic and political problems that beset them today.

The region of Southeast Asia is partitioned into a variety of countries whose citizens share numerous ethnic, social, and economic characteristics with other Asians but also differ from South and East Asians and from each other. Their concentration on the good earth near the life-giving waters of the river and the sea, and their deep involvement in raising food are typical of the entire Asian scene. But most of them are not driven by the spectre of starvation which is the feared comrade of so many of their fellow Asians elsewhere. Millions of them share with other Asians the name of Buddhist, but their interpretation of Buddhism demands more of man than does the interpretation accepted by their neighbors. They, like other Asians, stir restlessly when the cry of colonialism resounds among them, but the emotional appeal of nationalism has widened the cleavages which keep them apart.

I have surveyed Southeast Asia on a regional basis rather than country by country. There are too many of them to introduce individually and with justice within the restricted space of this introduction. Consequently, I have dared to attempt a brief regional synthesis of their religious, social, and political life. This method of treatment will necessarily result in omissions, but I will be more than satisfied if it stimulates a search for a more detailed knowledge of these people among the interesting and informative books that have been written especially about them.

Indeed, in my efforts to achieve the great value of simplicity in this introduction, it is possible and probable that I have appeared to overemphasize and omit. I am aware that objections may be made to some of my statements, for this is always a likelihood when one is concerned with the presentation of a general picture rather than particular cases. In the light of my purpose it is impractical and most difficult to document adequately every statement or to include everything pertaining to the complexity of the Asian scene. My observations flow from the personal and priceless experience of living, working, and sharing pleasures and sorrows, successes and failures, with the Asians over a long period of time. Although complete knowledge of them can never be mine, I have related what I think is significant in their way of life, in their thoughts, and in their yearnings. My words are intended to be preliminary rather than final, and I trustfully write with the expectation that those seeking a deeper and greater knowledge of the Asian people will find in this beginning a helpful introduction to other and more profound commentators.

It is my strong conviction that all of us should have some fundamental knowledge of the Asians. It is important because of our common humanity. It is frequently profitable and always stimulating to contemplate and savor alternative approaches to happiness. But more immediate and compelling is the goading fact that their fate is inextricably involved with ours. Their ideas, their feelings, their tensions, their struggles, in one way or another impinge upon our daily lives with a vigor and impact undreamed of only a relatively short time ago. I call upon the Japanese, Chinese, Koreans, Laotians,

Vietnamese, and other Asians to witness to the truth of this statement.

For more than a hundred years the nations of the West influenced the policies of most Asian nations, and their fate was to a large degree dependent upon the Westerner. In earlier times Asian powers had been at least as strong as those of the West. The Mongol invasions reached the Adriatic in the thirteenth century, the Turks besieged Vienna in 1683, and Chinese naval expeditions reached East Africa in the fifteenth century. But from the sixteenth century on, Western society started to change and by the end of the eighteenth century had gained vastly greater power. During the period beginning in the sixteenth century with the sea journeys of the adventurous Portuguese and ending with the Second World War, the nations of the West struggled to dominate Asia. Portugal, Spain, Holland, France, England, Germany, Russia, and America vied with one another on that continent. By the end of the nineteenth century the great mass of Asia was under their guardianship. It was only natural, then, that Western interests should prevail, overriding the desires of the governed Asians. Their destinies lay in other hands.

The conclusion of the Second World War brought radical changes for them and for us. One by one Asian nations became independent and Asian statesmen became exclusively occupied with advancing Asian interests. Policies formulated on the basis of Asian interests do not always harmonize with Western conceptions of a good Asian policy, and many of us are often left confused, groping, and upset, by the outcomes of these policies. Our reaction stems in large measure from a lack of knowledge of the feelings, needs, and desires of the Asian people and from a misunderstanding of reality in Asia. Ignorance of Asian realities can lead only to continued antagonisms and possible bloodshed; a comprehension of these realities is essential if conflicts of interest are to be minimized.

These thoughts have spurred me to record something of the heritage and destiny of the Asian peoples. I have sought to write with clarity and simplicity, for my task is to inform, not to confuse or to mystify. I have divided the total picture into manageable parts which lend themselves to careful scrutiny. I have also endeavored to present a synthesis by reuniting the parts and giving meaning to the total scene.

CHAPTER 1

THE HUMANITY OF ASIA

The need today is for philosophers and scholars—whether in Asia or Europe or Africa or the Americas—who will address themselves to the human situation. The need now is to talk not about geographic destiny but about human destiny.
—NORMAN COUSINS

Asia is people. People till Asia's earth, write Asia's poetry, make Asia's laws, fight Asia's wars, and dream Asia's dreams. Asians are people with a destiny. Few Westerners grasp the meaning of this destiny, because few outside Asia fully comprehend the humanity of Asians. They think of them first as inhabitants of a region called Asia, and only second as fellow human beings.

The humanity which Asians share with the rest of mankind and which nourishes the seeds of Asian destiny is overlooked by most foreigners in their preoccupation with the cultural differences which distinguish Asians from themselves. This preoccupation with eye-catching differences blinds them to the basic human needs, human drives, and human aspirations of the Asian people. They do not see the dynamic human forces which move Asians to act. They see only the acts, and these are acts Westerners would not normally perform. The Asian mother who sells her daughter, the Asian laborer who smokes his pipe of opium, the two Japanese lovers who commit suicide together, the Indian who wanders off to become an ascetic, leaving his family behind—these are some of the acts often headlined in Western minds as the peculiar substance of Asian humanity.

Most people cannot imagine the anguish of this Asian mother pushed to a decision by the spectre of famine. They do not understand the harshness of the laborer's life relieved only by a better world given him by the opium pipe. Many cannot appreciate the despair that grips those Japanese lovers when they find every avenue of a future happiness together closed to them. Few people in the world outside of India comprehend the spirit that moves an Indian ascetic to live a life of constant sacrifice. Thus, most Westerners are led to think of Asians in terms of the mysterious and the inscrutable. People who act so differently seem alien, even frightening.

It becomes easy to reduce Asians to stereotypes. Indians are "mystical," "cow-worshippers," and, until recently, "a peaceful people." Japan is a land where all men have buck teeth and all women wear beautiful kimonos. It is also the land of the cherry blossom festivals, peopled with soldiers who always fight fanatically and make suicide charges. Two prominent writers about Asian people have commented with insight upon these stereotypes with regard to Japan. Frank Gibney in *Five Gentlemen of Japan* writes: "It is hard to pour them [the five Japanese individuals he is describing] into the rigid casts of 'Japanese character' which foreigners at different times have constructed. . . . It is hard to fit them into the land of Madame Butterfly and never-ending cherry blossom festivals, faithfully and gullibly described by generations of Western tourists." James A. Michener in *The Floating World* states: "About the only generalization I could accept about the Japanese is that they will all have black hair."

Thinking in terms of stereotypes has influenced Americans—and others—to draw a line separating "Eastern" man from "Western" man. On one side of the line there is an "Eastern" way of life—alien, quaint, and mysterious. On the other side of the line there is a "Western" way of life—human, normal, and understandable. This belief is classically expressed in Kipling's statement: "East is East, and West is West, and never the twain shall meet."

Kipling, like many today, was unfamiliar with the process known as cultural diffusion. Both "Easterners" and "Westerners" have borrowed material products, as well as ideas, mores, and other intangibles, from each other and adapted them to their own cultures. Many non-Asians have learned to taste and like the many spices that come from Asia, enjoy the coolness of silk pajamas upon the skin, and delight in the green depths of their jade rings. Pajamas are a cultural import from India, while silk and jade rings originated in China and Southeast Asia. The carved teakwood chest, the patterned hand-woven rug, the small, exquisitely carved ivory statue have been familiar Asian objects in American homes for generations—so familiar

ASIAN
CONTINENT

that they often go unnoticed now. The clean functional lines of contemporary homes and furniture are distinct influences from Japan. Chinese ideas about education and government have influenced both French and American scholars, and Buddhist philosophy has found a home in many "Western" countries.

"Eastern" products and "Eastern" ideas have become an integral part of the "Western" way of life. This is because they are products made by *human* hands to meet *human* needs and *human* wants, and humanity knows no geographical boundaries. They are ideas formulated by *human* minds to satisfy *human* aspirations, and "Easterners" and "Westerners" share a common humanity.

Products and ideas fashioned by "Western" hands and "Western" minds have been welcomed and adopted in all the countries of Asia. There is nothing incongruous about Buddhist monks chanting thousand-year-old scriptures in new air-conditioned buildings. Do not Christian monks chant thousand-year-old scriptures in new air-conditioned buildings? There is nothing unreasonable about Asian soldiers fighting with modern weapons in Vietnam. Do not modern soldiers elsewhere fight with modern weapons? There is nothing unusual about the modern Asian agricultural agent urging the peasant to adopt more efficient farming practices. American farmers, too, had to be prodded to adopt modern practices. In the East today, a steel mill stands beside a field in which a man is pulling a plough; trucks share the streets with men and women bent under heavy burdens; modern air-conditioned apartment buildings shade small stifling huts crowded with people and vermin; jet planes swish over an Asian farmer pushing a squealing wheelbarrow in which sit a man and a pig, and the farmer looks up, wonders, and accepts this latest creation of humanity. In each instance the goal and function is the same, only the method differs.

There is no longer, if there ever was, an "Eastern" or "Western" destiny—there is only a human destiny. The destiny of the Asian people can be comprehended only by those who know that Asians are moved by the dynamic forces of human needs, human wants, and human ideals, that they are conscious of the shape and magnitude of their destiny and are determined to mold this destiny to meet their needs.

CHAPTER 2

ASIANS LOOK AT AMERICANS

Why do Americans know so little about India, when we Indians really understand the United States?
— INDIAN MEMBER OF PARLIAMENT

Many Asians are convinced that they can recognize an American anywhere, that they understand the American mind, and that their conception—and, sometimes, abhorrence—of many American practices and principles is correct.

Asians often have a feeling of affection for Americans. Until recently they thought of America not only as a vigorous, youthful country, but as a country where a new and shining way of life was practiced. They considered the United States their friend among the great Western powers and the only great nation where Asians could find a sympathetic understanding of their revolutionary ideals. Was not America born of revolution? Was she not a colony that had successfully cast off the greatest colonizing power of that time? Did she not live by a Constitution that guaranteed freedom and the opportunity to pursue happiness in one's own way? Was this not the land of Washington, Lincoln, Jefferson, and Wilson— American statesmen still venerated by Asians as great, living supporters of their dreams of freedom? Educated Asians know American history well. It has inspired many Asian statesmen to strike out against colonial chains. No American awakened the latent nationalism of the Asian people more than Woodrow Wilson when he promulgated his famous fourteen points and proclaimed the right of all peoples to self-determination. Probably the greatest modern friend of Asians, in Asian eyes, was Franklin D. Roosevelt. They felt that he embodied the revolutionary traditions of early America, and some Asian students wept in their rooms and on the streets when they heard of his death. It was as though they had lost a kind and warmhearted friend.

11

Many Asians believe that they draw with Americans on common sources of strength. Thus, Madame Pandit, the sister of Nehru, quotes the words of Lincoln to describe the source of India's strength: "What constitutes the bulwark of our own liberty and independence? It is not our frowning battlements, our bristling seacoast, our army and our navy. These are not our reliance against tyranny. All of these may be turned against us without making us weaker for the struggle. Our reliance is in the love of liberty which God has planted in us. Our defense is in the spirit which prizes liberty as the heritage of all men, in all lands everywhere." A recent official Pakistan document, *The Constitution, A Study* (new constitution) begins: "Democracy, in the classic phrase of Abraham Lincoln, is 'government of the people, by the people and for the people.' "

Prior to the Second World War Asians did not associate America with the resented nations of Europe. America was a former colony. What did she have in common with the empire-inspired countries of Western Europe? America was not given to colonizing, at least in Asia—the Philippines were acquired as a result of war with a colonizing power and more in the way of an accident than an intentional grab of Asian land—and American statesmen had stated over and over again that they were utterly opposed to the imperialistic practices of the Western powers in Asia. America stood like a giant in the West, the embodiment of all that was good and fine in the Western Hemisphere.

"THE GREAT AMERICAN TRAGEDY IN ASIA"

Only since the Second World War have Americans come to be regarded with wary eyes by many Asians. American strength has become suspect. American technology has become a symbol of materialism, and American economic help has been interpreted to mean the entrance of a new exploiter into Asian fields. Some view Americans as possible obstacles in their path to national independence and dignity, whereas a few short years ago America was the one country most Asians counted on to help them in their climb to national greatness.

These Asians have begun to think of America and the nations of Western Europe in the same terms. They state that during the war America showed herself ready to sacrifice Asia, provided that Europe could be saved, and that America reserved the atom bomb for use on Japan rather than on Germany. After the war they felt themselves forgotten on their war-ravaged lands, while American billions were poured out to bolster the tottering economies of Western Europe. NATO was formed, and American troops and treaties guaranteed the borders and independence of Western European nations, and even of Greece and Turkey, from outside attack. Some Asians felt that Americans guaranteed nothing in Asia except occupied Japan, South Korea, the Philippine Islands, and the vast seas that washed their coasts.

Thus, in a number of Asian minds, America gradually became associated with Western Europe. When this happened, America came to be regarded with all the old hatreds, antagonisms, suspicions, and fears with which Asians had long viewed the nations of Europe. Also, since America was the greatest Western power, she became to some Asians the leader and main supporter of those whom they resented as the old exploiters of Asia. Thus, slowly, inexorably, almost unnoticed, at least in the United States, America took over Britain's role as the whipping boy for all the ills of Asia. By a tragic historical irony, a great segment of the world's people, who had never really experienced any American imperialism, cast the United States in the role of cohort and champion of Asia's former Western governors. This changing role from one of friend to enemy in the minds of many Asians might be called "The Great American Tragedy in Asia." The aftermath of this tragedy will be with Americans for a long time; it is so easy to destroy, and so difficult to restore.

Much of this changed attitude is the result of propaganda put out by Communist and neutralist sources; Asians have been influenced by slanted books, magazines, and newspapers in which Americans are caricatured as militarists and warmongers. Although most of these caricatures are found in left-wing publications, they have managed to convince an amazing number of Asians that Americans are too ready to embark upon military adventures. Asians are, for the most part, extremely desirous of maintaining the peace of the world. They realize that any war must inevitably draw them in sooner or later, and they prefer it as late as possible. Asians need generations of peace to solve their enormous economic, political, and social problems. To have the greatest power in the world poised on the brink of war, as they picture America, frightens and angers them. Of course, Americans do not want war either, but too few Asians know this.

To the peasant, laborer, teacher, intellectual, and housewife in Asia, the word "American" conveys the idea of money, vast sums of money. Not so many years ago some Asians believed the story that American streets were paved with gold. The Chinese had received fabulous reports of the gold strikes in California, and they called this state the "Golden Mountain." They still do. This conception of the abundance of gold in California came gradually to be applied to all of the United States. Most Asians still believe that Americans are very, very rich. In many areas of Asia there is a special price reserved for Americans who want to buy Asian goods. They reason that it is only fair that those who have so much should pay more and share a part of their great abundance with them. Movies, books, and even official propaganda put out by the United States itself have helped to reinforce this attitude of the Asian people. What American is not himself staggered at times by the lavish display of living he sees in some movies? The mink, the sable, the wonderful, comfortable house, the magnificent furnishings, the great spread of food, the long gleaming cars, arouse the yearning and envy of Americans as well as Asians. The difference is that Americans know that only a very few of the people in this country live in such luxury, while the Asians believe that most Americans live this way. All over Asia the male definition of paradise runs something like this—"a Japanese wife, Chinese food, and an American home." Communist propaganda describing the "poor American worker" has failed to make an impression. Western propaganda which tries to connect a well-fed look and luxurious appearance with a democratic way of life merely compounds their misconception of Americans: the blood, the labors, the self-denials that are inevitable in the birth and growth of any real democracy are not a part of their American image. They believe that, to an American, making money is the most important occupation and that his main goal is to become wealthy. Frank Moraes, editor of India's largest newspaper, *The Times of India,* reports that "In many Eastern eyes America mistakes the means for the end. By exalting private enterprise and the individual she makes the acquisition of wealth for wealth's sake an end in itself."

Some Asians have transferred this conception of Americans to the Asian scene. Disregarding the number of schools, orphanages, and hospitals Americans have established overseas, they think that Americans look upon Asians primarily as objects which may or may not contribute to their materialistic advancement as a source of labor, and as pawns in the game of war and politics who are less important than the strategic areas they occupy. In other words, these Asians believe that the materialistic bias of the American people blinds them to the humanity of Asians. The Americans are accused of seeing only a dollar bill when regarding the Asian scene; they do not see the human being paying the bill. It is ironic that the same dollar bill obscures the richness of America's humanity from these Asian viewers of the American scene.

Asian intellectuals consider the history of the Westerner in Asia marked only by economic exploitation and by political maneuvering with no thought to Asian interests. They describe it as a chronicle of wars fought with and without Asians, but never for Asians. They indignantly accuse Western entrepreneurs of having bulled into their lands accompanied by soldiers and gunboats and lured by Asian products and raw materials. They buttress their case by referring to the manner in which their magnificent cultures were ignored. That foreigners would overlook a culture built with such tremendous effort over the centuries was to have been expected of men obsessed by greed; but some foreigners went further and condemned, reviled, and rejected it with violence, and this was barbarous, uncivilized and inexcusable. They point to the growth of large merchant-sponsored cities on Asian soil which became the gathering places for foreigners and the centers of Western political and economic power in Asia. The handicraft industry of Asia was almost ruined by the flood of cheap machine-made products from the West, and English arms even protected the smuggling of opium into China in order to produce a favorable balance of trade. They were convinced then that the only morality the Westerners possessed was a profit morality. This conviction is still stubbornly maintained.

In recent decades too many Asians have tended to associate Americans with the economic exploitation which was fashioned by Europeans, and not Americans, in the seventeenth, eighteenth, nineteenth, and twentieth centuries. Communist followers and sympathizers are industriously striving to reinforce and broaden this tendency in order that America may become in the eyes of all Asians the great modern symbol of a materialistic people with imperialistic goals and ideals.

American materialism is contrasted in Asian minds with their Asian "spirituality." Despite the prominent part played in their history and economy by the wealthy literati of China, the samurai of Japan, and the rajahs of India, Asians feel that they possess a more elevated spirit than the Americans. The Indians point to their religious practices and their teaching that all earthly things are ephemeral and transitory as evidence of their basic attitude toward material objects. They cite their saintly men who have given up all worldly possessions in order to bring themselves closer to the goal of spiritual freedom. The Chinese refer to their emphasis upon social relations and upon the necessity for individuals to play their appointed roles in the society. The group, the family, the society, is most important; the individual is secondary, and so is any profit he makes. The profit is for the family and, more recently, the state. The Japanese call attention to their divine ancestors, their Shinto shrines, their beauty-laden country, as reflecting the essence of their lives. Those who practice Zen Buddhism prefer frugality to abundance, simplicity to ostentation, and quiet meditation to the ceaseless search for material gain. During the Second World War the Japanese believed they would win "a victory of spirit over matter." American reliance upon material things was inferior to the Japanese reliance upon the spirit. Perhaps a war was started and lost because the American spirit was too well hidden from Asian eyes.

OTHER CONCEPTIONS OF AMERICANS

Some Asians have neatly catalogued Americans as "impulsive," "uncultured," "lacking in judgment," and "vigorous." They contend that Americans are overly quick to respond to actions which affect their individual or national interests. Sometimes such quickness creates a feeling of admiration and joy in Asian hearts, as when American generosity comes rapidly and lavishly to the aid of victims of a natural catastrophe. At other times such impulsive responses cause uneasiness, as when Americans seem too eager to offer military solutions in Asian disputes. They feel that this "impulsive" characteristic is associated with a "lack of judgment," and they caution Americans to wait and meditate awhile before taking action. They frequently feel called upon to advise Americans to study carefully all the pros and cons of a statement or a policy before publicizing it to the world, lest anything said by the world's most powerful nation disturb the peace of the world.

They look upon Americans as citizens of a very young country which has not yet had time to build an enduring culture, and they contrast American youth with Asian age. Asia is an old land of settled people. For them age denotes maturity and wisdom in both the individual and the nation. They prize the gift of time which gave them so many centuries to think, to err, to suffer, to experience, to change, to reject, to reform, to change again, and finally to piece together a civilization which worked and withstood the restlessness of man. They feel that this accomplishment—the creation of a host of years—has left them with a maturity of judgment and the perspective of age. They sorrow that Americans have not had this advantage, especially since they hold such economic and political power. It is interesting to note that one of the major criticisms often levied by Americans against Asians is that they are slow to act and to make decisions. It appears that too much time or too little time can also contribute to misunderstanding among men.

Asian newspapers generally play up incidents of discrimination against minority groups in the United States, and they resent the sense of racial superiority which this discrimination implies. The Indians were and are the victims of white supremacy laws in South Africa. Under the British they were discriminated against in clubs, employment opportunities, and promotions. The Japanese and Chinese have both experienced American exclusion laws, and during the Second World War the removal of Japanese Americans from the West Coast was well-publicized in Asia. Most Asians privately concede that discrimination is a universal human issue, for most Asian countries are also plagued by minority problems.

It is a characteristic of stereotypes that they do not convey a true picture of all individuals. Asians also find Americans baffling because they are continually meeting Americans who are religious, idealistic, and dedicated to humanitarian goals; interested in money as a means to an end; not given to using any means to reach a desired goal, but only those means which in their eyes are right; cultured, sophisticated, and courteous; tactful, forbearing, patient, devoted to working for peace.

For both Americans and Asians, the important and fruitful task of this time is to understand their common humanity and their common goals and aspirations. In the pages that follow an attempt has been made to advance this understanding by showing where and how the Asian people live and what they believe and by discussing selected aspects of their economic, social, and political way of life.

CHAPTER 3

THE PHYSICAL
AND ECONOMIC SETTING

Asia is not just the biggest and most continental or highest or wettest or most diverse of continents. It is interesting because it is the most human.

—GEORGE B. CRESSEY

The region called Asia in this book stretches from Pakistan on the west to Japan on the east and from the northern borders of China to the southernmost boundaries of Indonesia. Within these borders are included the countries and territories of Pakistan, Ceylon, Nationalist China (Formosa), Communist China, North Korea, South Korea, Outer Mongolia, Japan, Burma, Laos, Thailand, Cambodia, North Vietnam, South Vietnam, Malaysia, Indonesia, Philippines, and Nepal. There are also smaller areas such as Sikkim, Bhutan, Brunei, Singapore, Hong Kong, Macao, and some other small islands.

This region has a total area of about 7,815,000 square miles. Some of the individual countries within it are larger than many American and European nations. China, the People's Republic, rivals the United States in size. India is larger than any European country except Russia. Indonesia is more than three times the size of France and extends east and west approximately the same distance as that separating the east and west coasts of the United States. Pakistan is about three times the size of Italy.

From the western boundaries of Pakistan to the disputed eastern borders of Indonesia, the distance is about 5,200 miles. From the northern borders of China to the southern boundaries of Indonesia, the distance is slightly over 4,000 miles. The shortest route from New Delhi, the capital of India, to Peking, the capital of China, is

George B. Cressey, *The Patterns of Asia,* edited by Norton Ginsburg (Englewood Cliffs, New Jersey: Prentice-Hall, 1958).

Population of Asian Countries

	Area	Population (In Thousands)	
Brunei	2,226	88	(1962 est.)
Ceylon	25,332	10,625	(1963 est.)
Hong Kong	398	3,592	(1963 est.)
India	1,261,416	449,381	(1962 est.)
Malaysia	128,512	9,979	(1963 est.)
Pakistan	365,529	98,612	(1963 est.)
Sikkim	2,818	161	(1959 est.)
Singapore		1,687	
Burma	261,789	23,664	(1963 est.)
Cambodia	66,607	5,737	(1962 est.)
China (Formosa)	13,952	11,301	(1962 est.)
China (Communist)	3,691,502	700,000	(1962 est.)
Indonesia	575,893	97,765	(1962 est.) **
Japan	142,726	95,899	(1963 est.)
North Korea	46,814	11,100	(1960 est.)
South Korea	38,452	24,994	(1960 est.)
Laos	91,428	1,882	(1962 est.)
Mongolian Peoples Republic	604,247	1,019	(1963 est.)
Nepal	54,362	9,387	(1961 census)
The Philippines	115,707	30,241	(1963 est.)
Macao		161	(1960 census)
Thailand	198,455	28,835	(1963 est.)
North Vietnam	60,156	15,317	(1963 est.)
South Vietnam	65,948	14,900	(1962 est.)
	7,814,369	1,646,331*	

*(Over Half Of The World's Total Population)
**(Excludes New Guinea)

INDIAN OCEAN

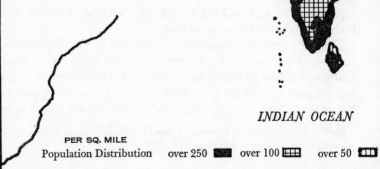

PER SQ. MILE

Population Distribution   over 250 ■   over 100 ⊞   over 50 ⊡

around 2,500 miles. From Karachi, the former capital of Pakistan, to Tokyo, is approximately 4,300 miles. It is about 3,200 miles from Djakarta, the capital of Indonesia, to Seoul, the capital of South Korea.

Over a billion and a half persons live in Asia. Of these more than a billion live in China and India. This means that approximately every fourth person in the world is Chinese; more than one out of every three persons is either Indian or Chinese.

Generally speaking, wherever there is arable land in Asia, there the land is also crowded. Population density in many areas exceeds 2,000 persons per square mile of arable land. The greatest concentrations of people are found near the rivers and the coasts. The Chinese live around the Yangtze, Yellow, and West rivers for the most part and along the eastern and southern coasts. The Indians group themselves along the Ganges and Brahmaputra river systems of northern India, and along the rivers and coasts of peninsular India. The deltas of these rivers also support great numbers of people in East Pakistan. In Japan, the densely settled areas are in the central and southern half of the island of Honshu and on the islands of Shikoku and Kyushu. Much of Burma's population is located in the Irrawaddy River Delta, and the Mekong River nourishes great groups of Cambodians and Vietnamese. In Indonesia, the islands of Java, Madura, and Bali contain most of the people. Most Asians are concentrated in small sections of their total land area.

In many Asian countries the birth rate is quite high. In Formosa, Malaysia, and Thailand, for instance, the birth rate is over 39 per thousand population; in Ceylon, 36.6; in the Philippines, around 29; and in India, 25.8. But 17.2 in Japan compares favorably to the birth rate in the United States which is 21.6, in France with 18.2, Italy with 19.1, and the United Kingdom with 18.5. It has been estimated, however, that the annual average birth rate in Asia is around 30 per thousand, as compared with 20 per thousand in Europe. These figures are approximations and subject to change.

The problem of overpopulation plagues every nation except rice-surplus areas like Thailand and Upper Burma. Elsewhere in Asia there is not enough arable land to feed the fast increasing population. With China showing an approximate net increase of 12–15 million per year, and India an increase of almost 10 million per year, to quote but two figures, it is obvious that the necessity to provide for these extra mouths harasses the people concerned with feeding them. Many observers believe that overpopulation is the paramount problem of all Asia.

THE QUEST FOR FOOD

For most Asians the quest for food is continuous and demanding. The unending search for food is the familiar and traditional aspect of Asian life, and agriculture has been the main occupation of Asians for thousands of years. They are primarily interested in obtaining a food supply for themselves and only secondarily in producing crops for a commercial market. Because their fields are generally small and subdivided into scattered parcels and there are many mouths to feed, they are forced to demand much of the land, and this intensive cultivation has encouraged a higher concentration of population in Asia than in other agricultural areas of the world. This system of cultivation required a greater population in order to produce more, which in turn required a greater amount of crops to feed the growing numbers of people. The arable land of Asia has filled up, and for many there is only the desert, the jungle, and the wastelands left to cultivate. But the system persists in much of Asia, and families continue to multiply, and the quest to feed them becomes even more exacting and arduous.

The Asian's pursuit of food is made harder by physical and social forces which are beyond his power to control. The rains might be delayed or come in too little quantity. Rivers sometimes overflow and destroy the crops of millions of peasants. Locusts, pests of one kind or another, fire, banditry, feuds, wild animals, any of a hundred calamities might afflict the peasant and destroy his food. Moreover, sickness and the social requirements of funerals, weddings, and other occasions may require an outlay of money so that if his crop is harvested, he must use it for the payment of debts he has incurred because of extraordinary expenses. He lives in constant fear that his food may give out before the next harvest, and the threat of starvation is an everpresent reality for him and millions of other Asians.

Many Asians live on the ugly edge of famine. No words can convey the scope and impact of the tragedy of famine. Perhaps it is better this way. Few people can stand the overwhelming shock, the unforgettable memories, and the revulsion that famine leaves with

China rivals the United States in land area. Its population is presently expanding by approximately 12 million per year.

those who witness it. The author can only give the reader some impressions. Row upon row of bodies lying on sidewalks and in gutters, bodies that were once recognizable individuals but now have lost their identity as persons and are merely the common face of hunger. Hopeless eyes and skull-like heads. A village at dusk and a child protesting with wrenching, breaking cries as it tries to suck milk from a dead mother's breast. Weak hands clawing at a few clumps of weeds. A dying man cursing heaven and his fate in a voice almost inaudible. A mother bargaining with one who has rice over the price of one small daughter—she has four other hungry children. She wants four and one-half pounds of rice; he wants to give only four. She receives four pounds of rice for one five-year-old daughter.

These pressures which spring from the physical and social environment cause the Asians to concentrate on the production of grains and cereal crops. Grains are eaten directly, rather than indirectly through the raising of animals, because cereal crops provide more food value if eaten directly than if given to an animal which could then be slaughtered for food. As a result there is little

The 3,000 mile sweep of Indonesia approximates the distance across the United States from east to west. Java alone contains 58 million of Indonesia's approximately 98 million people.

grass for animals. The water buffalo, cow, bullock, and other work animals obtain their food from the stubble they can find in the wastelands and on the small dykes separating the fields, a diet which is supplemented slightly with some cereal grains provided by the farmer-owner. In some parts of Asia even the work animal is dispensed with, and the ploughing and furrowing is done by man himself with the hoe instead of a plough. The food of a farmer takes less space than the food of the buffalo or cow. Thus most Asians eat grains and vegetables at their daily meals. Even in those parts of Asia where most families raise pigs, it frequently happens that when a pig is killed most of the meat is sold for cash, and only a few scraps are left for the family.

Rice or wheat is the basic food for the majority of the Asian people. They eat very little meat or eggs, and in the interior, very little fish. Many think of the Asians as being solely rice-eaters. Rice is the principal food for most of the Asian people, but wheat is preferred by many others. Rice is the principal crop south of the Yangtze River in Central China, but north of this river wheat, millet, and soybeans are the principal crops, and wheat is the favored food. Thus the saying: "He is a man who eats wheat flour every day, why should he not have a smooth face!" In South China, rice is the

The Indo-Pakistan subcontinent is larger than any country of Western Europe. The population of the Republic of India is approximately 450 million, compared with 53 million for the United Kingdom and 48 million for France.

principal crop, and it is the preferred food. With the exception of Burma, Thailand, and prior to the Second World War, Indo-China, Asian countries are forced to import rice and other food supplies to make up their food deficiency.

The Asians are always looking for ways and means to stretch their available food supply as far as possible. One of the means of making their rice last longer is by eating gruel, or *congee*, which is a soup-like rice dish containing much water but little rice, instead of a more substantial portion of ordinary cooked rice. Rice gruel gives a temporary feeling of repletion, but the feeling quickly dissipates when work is required in the fields.

Barley, millet, corn, sorghum, and sweet potatoes are common foods in Asia. Sweet potatoes have relieved more hunger pangs in China than perhaps any one single food. They grow in all types of soil and are prevalent everywhere. Where the American or European child is commonly seen and pictured chewing or sucking a piece of candy, a Chinese child is frequently occupied in nibbling at a cooked sweet potato. In North China the sweet potatoes are planted immediately after the wheat has been harvested. Millet is not the preferred grain for Asians, but it grows where wheat and rice cannot be planted and therefore is common where the soil is not good and where there is a lack of water.

For most Asians food is the center of their lives because they are never sure they will have enough of it to live. There are certain periods of the year when the Asian has a chance to eat his fill of good food, as at funerals or weddings and during the sacred or secular festivals, such as New Year's and on national holidays, but these periodic feasts are not a daily occurrence. It is not surprising that food is often the dominant topic of conversation in Asia. Asians talk about all aspects of food: how to produce it—the ploughing, hoeing, weeding, irrigating, harvesting, threshing, hulling, winnowing; the kinds of food to produce—rice, barley, sweet potatoes, wheat, millet, sorghum, soybean, and the hundreds of varieties of vegetables which are grown in Asia; the ways it should be prepared —broiled, steamed, fried, boiled, and the spices and sauces that should season it. Wherever Asians gather, there, sooner or later, either directly or indirectly, the conversation will shift to food.

Modern Asian leaders are striving desperately to solve the food problem besetting their people. Some are attempting to industrialize their nations and to introduce, in the fastest possible way, the new and unfamiliar machine into the lives of the people. But sometimes their goal may not be in the immediate interest of the people they govern. The money or capital to build modern plants and buy modern machines and machine tools comes inevitably from the peasant farmers who comprise the vast majority of the population. Since many of the farmers are living on the edge of famine and barely making enough to feed their families, any increased food tax inevitably pushes them nearer the starvation level. If priority is given to quick industrialization, famine may ravage many, as happened in Communist China. If, on the other hand, the farmer is permitted to keep more of his surplus food, his personal condition is improved but industrialization is delayed. China is stressing quick industrialization, while India has emphasized the expansion of agriculture.

Some Asian leaders argue that if they can industrialize rapidly it will be possible to take care of surplus people by channeling them into plants and other productive work. This may be true. But industrialization does not come fast enough to take care of the millions now living who have no land and no prospect of ever possessing land. These landless millions are the ones who suffer first when famine grips the land. Industry must grow at a very rapid pace if it is to absorb even a small percentage of the increasing number of people.

The land must be made to yield even more food with the use of modern agricultural methods and a more efficient use of artificial fertilizer. The Chinese Communists have communized the farms with the thought that larger farms using modern machinery and modern methods and worked by the co-operative efforts of all will result in greater productivity and more efficient use of the land. Recent reports indicate that the commune system has, in many instances, augmented rather than alleviated the misery of the people. The Indian leaders have not turned to this method of solving the land problem, but they have given the development of irrigation and power systems top priority, and they have recommended progressive socialization of agriculture marketing and of processing industries in rural areas through the introduction of co-operatives. The government policy is to create and foster co-operatives in all possible aspects of agricultural operations. But at the present time the people are still increasing at a rate faster than the increased productivity of the land.

Throughout a vast part of Asia, national leaders are supporting the plantation system first introduced by foreigners. The only countries in which this system is of no special importance are Japan, Korea, and China. In all the other Asian countries plantations, which specialize in particular crops, usually tropical crops for export, are common. These plantations produce such crops as palm oil, tea, coffee, rubber, and sugar. Since the plantation system depends upon a large labor supply working with a relatively small number of tools, it reinforces the Asian emphasis on human labor.

The magnitude and immediacy of the food problem in Asia varies from country to country. Some countries in South-East Asia, such as Thailand and Burma, are self-sufficient in food, and Japan is absorbing much of her manpower into a booming industry, but for most of the Asian leaders the question of how to feed a fast-growing population adequately is always paramount.

HEALTH

Most Asians do not starve to death, but most are victims of malnutrition. They get enough food to keep them alive and working, but not enough to keep them healthy and efficiently working. As a result, many Asians are susceptible to disease and are not able to ward off the epidemics and sickness which are prevalent in Asia.

Most Asians receive their calories through grains and vegetables rather than by way of animal proteins. This is in contrast with some Western nations where a great part of the diet comes from animal protein. Protein is essential for growth and life, and animal protein is of greater nutritional value than vegetable protein. The Westerner gets much of his protein from meat, eggs, milk, cheese, butter, and other foods. The amount of food consumed by the various Asian populations as compared with the amount consumed in the United States will give some indication of the inadequacy of the Asian diet.

In the United States, the average man consumes about 3,160 calories per day of which between 11 and 12 per cent are protein. The figures for Asian countries are much lower. The Japanese consumes around 2,310 calories of which about 5 per cent are animal protein. The Burmese consumes 2,150 calories per day but only about 5 per cent are animal protein, while the Indian eats about 2,000 calories per day of which less than 5 per cent are animal protein. These selected figures are approximations and may be rapidly dated. Of course, in Burma, India, China, and other Asian countries there are times of famine and disorder when the people eat less calories and less protein.

Most Asians at birth cannot expect to live much beyond forty years of age. The baby born in India and Thailand may expect to live to forty years of age, as can the Chinese on Formosa. The Japanese are more long-lived, and Japanese babies can expect to live to forty-five or more.

In the United States a citizen can expect to live beyond sixty years of age, and the average is rising every year. An American of forty is considered to have reached the prime of life and the most useful period of his life both for himself and his community. Many Asians at this age have died or are about to die. This is a tragic loss of talent and unreplaceable experience. Most Asians are aware of this loss, for they give an honored place to those who survive and live to ripe old age. Age is respected in Asia, perhaps because it is relatively rare; those few who attain the age of sixty, seventy, or beyond seem deserving of honor, praise, and attention.

The majority of those who die young in Asia are from the poorer classes. The wealthy, a small minority, have a much better chance of growing old. They eat better, they are able to afford doctors and medicine. They receive much better care from their children and relatives because the necessity to make a living does not drive their family to work with the same remorseless regularity as it does the poor.

The wife of a poor man cannot always take time to care for her baby. It may lie untended for hours, often bitten by mosquitoes or insects of one kind or another. Sometimes the baby is cared for by the younger children who are willing, but untutored in child care. At times the mother has too little milk and cannot afford to hire a woman to feed the baby for her. It is not easy for her to buy milk. The rich, on the other hand, do not require the mothers to work in the fields, nor at domestic tasks for that matter. They can afford to hire servants to care for the house and men to till the fields. The mother has time for her baby. Should the mother lack milk, the family can buy it and feed the baby from a bottle or hire a woman who has abundant milk in her breasts to nurse the child. This woman is usually of a poor family and is willing to give her milk for extra money or food, for she too has babies to feed.

A great many infants die even before they reach one year of age. It has been estimated that one out of every four dies before the age of five. Of course, many infants in every part of the world die before reaching the age of one or five, but a greater number of them die in Asia than elsewhere in the world.

In the United States, about 25.2 infants per thousand live births die before reaching the age of one; in the United Kingdom, about 22.1; in France, about 26.1; and in Italy, about 40.1. Some of the Asian countries show the following figures per thousand for deaths of infants before the age of one: Malaya 68.9, the Philippines 73.1, India 86.7, Ceylon 57.5, Thailand 47.1, and Japan 30.7.

Infants are peculiarly susceptible to disease during the first year of life. Many of the mothers of Asia have neither the time, the money, nor the facilities to practice the hygienic methods of some Western countries. Certainly they desire to follow the best practices, but they are prevented from doing so by their environment and circumstances.

Someday Asian mothers will be able to give their babies better care, and fewer babies will die. When this happens, the population of the Asian countries will take another leap upward. In this case, as in the other instances of raising the standard of living in Asia, there arises the threat of overpopulation. Already the land of Asia is thronged. What will happen if, through increased food supply and better medical facilities, more infants survive and more people live to an advanced age?

There are few health services of the Western variety available for the majority of the people, but the services of doctors versed in native medical lore and trained in the traditional Asian manner are generally available everywhere in Asia. This is particularly true of China where a monumental *materia medica* evolved over the many centuries of China's growth. Most Asians rely upon their own Asian medical services or upon home remedies. The average Asian must be quite sick before he goes to the expense of calling in a doctor, either Asian or Western. Doctors and medicines cost money, and the ordinary Asian does not have money to spare for such expenses. Doctors and medicines mean that somebody goes hungry and that they will all eat less this year.

From the viewpoint of sanitation and hygiene, Western medicine is more advanced than that of Asia. Also, preventive medicine is more advanced in the West. In many areas of internal medicine and in their *materia medica* the Asians have done some striking work for centuries. Many herbs used for medicine in Asia have been adopted by the West, although Western scientists have then isolated the substance in the herb which is medically valuable, while the Asians continue to use the entire herb. Hence, Asian medicines are often bulky and given in soup and serving bowls, whereas Westerners generally take small pills.

Doctors versed in Chinese medicine are still in demand by Chinese everywhere in the world, even by those living in the United States and Europe. London, Paris, Chicago, New York, and San Francisco have Chinese herbs and drugs available for those who desire them. One of the most fascinating and sometimes efficacious medical practices both in China and Japan is *acupuncture,* the practice of sticking needles of gold, silver, or steel into various parts of the body in order to relieve pain. Western observers, including the author, have seen patients suddenly relieved of severe pain by means of acupuncture. While many Westerners scoff at acupuncture as a nostrum, millions of Asians continue to use it as a means of relieving pain. In China and Japan the plant *moxa* is rolled into a small cone, set on fire, and applied to some part of the body as a cautery. The legs, arms, and backs of many Chinese and Japanese show scars from burning with *moxa.* It is believed to be a specific remedy for fainting fits, rheumatism, lumbago, arthritis, and many other ailments.

A comparison of inhabitants per physician in some Asian countries with that of the United States is illuminating. In the United States there are about 790 inhabitants per physician. In Indonesia it is estimated that there are over 60,000 persons per physician; in Pakistan, 15,000; in Malaya, 7,300; and in South Vietnam, 22,000. Japan, with 940 persons per physician compares favorably with France, with 930. Large Asian cities like Bombay, Manila, Hongkong, Peking, and Shanghai have hospitals and up-to-date medical services, but the great rural areas of Asia suffer from an acute lack of modern medical services.

ILLITERACY

Widespread illiteracy in Asia is a tremendous obstacle in the path of modernization and industrialization. Modern technology and social progress require a population who can read and write. An illiterate society is not necessarily a primitive one, and certainly Asian society and people cannot be characterized as primitive. A society where many have an appreciation for the opera and the classics, where exquisite courtesies are extended and expected, where many know the Vedas by heart and will sit all night watching the epics dramatized—this kind of society cannot be characterized by any term but *cultured*.

But the demands of an industrial society require that illiteracy be abolished. Asian nations are well-launched on a program of modernization which demands a reading and writing public. Thus, compulsory education is the law in most modern Asian nations.

Illiteracy is prevalent everywhere in Asia except in Japan and in the Philippines. When Japan started her rapid modernization program in 1868, a basic reform that was stressed rigorously was compulsory education. Japanese children of both sexes were required to take at least six years of schooling. The Japanese understood early that they could not create an efficient industrial society unless they had a literate people. The Philippines were made education-conscious by the Americans who governed these islands from the beginning of the twentieth century until 1946. Schools were established all over the islands and education was made compulsory.

Elsewhere in Asia the literacy percentage is low. In India it was estimated at one time that approximately 80 per cent of the population ten years of age and older were illiterate. Since the Indians entered upon their modernization program this figure is going down rapidly. There has been a significant decrease in illiteracy in the Asian countries in recent years, but the statistics on this decrease are not always available.

Everywhere, in India, China, Burma, Thailand, Indonesia, Vietnam, Malaya, and Pakistan the top priority is being given to the building of schools and the training of teachers. The goal of all these nations is the eradication of illiteracy. Nevertheless, the number of people who require teaching and the lack of teachers and facilities will delay the total eradication of illiteracy for years. A start, however, has been made, and there is no question that within a decade the great mass of young Asians will know how to read and write.

CITIES

Although most Asians live in the country, there are great numbers of people who live in cities. Cities are growing in number and size. The following selected cities have a half million or more population: Kobe, Tokyo, and Yokohama in Japan; Shanghai, Tientsin, Canton, Harbin, Hankow, and others in China; Karachi and Chittagong in Pakistan; Manila in the Philippines; Saigon and Hanoi in Indo-China; Djkarta and Surabaya in Indonesia; Colombo in Ceylon; Bombay, Calcutta, Madras, and others in India; Singapore, Hongkong, Macao, and still others not mentioned.

Most of these cities are ports and look to trade and to the sea for the preservation of their economy. These cities are the centers of political and economic control in Asian countries, and most of Asia's leadership lives in them. Many of these cities are Western in origin, attitude, and appearance. It is in the cities that the new ways of

life are practiced extensively, and from them the currents of change and reform emanate. The cities of Asia are assuming more and more importance in this modern period of Asia's history.

But although there are great cities in Asia and they are growing in number and importance, the hundreds of thousands of villages housing hundreds of millions of people are one of the most significant features of the Asian landscape.

To see these economic and physical conditions of the Asians in some perspective one should realize that similar conditions prevailed in the West a few centuries ago. Then, the European peasant, like the Asian peasant, lived at a level when a few bad harvests produced many deaths from starvation. And even in upper-class families a high proportion of children died. Up to the mid-eighteenth century many European visitors to Asia were impressed by a higher level of material civilization. The Asians are now trying to catch up with the changes which have revolutionized Western society in the last three centuries or so.

CHAPTER 4

THE ASIAN VILLAGE

Asia is a land of villages. It has been estimated that India has six hundred thousand villages; mainland China alone has somewhat more than half a million villages and towns. The majority of Asians live in villages because of the predominance of agriculture as an occupation. The village encompasses a man's life. The Asian is born, grows up, marries, begets children, grows old, and dies within the boundaries of some village. Some individuals do get an opportunity to travel, and even go abroad, but they belong to a very small minority. The male adult frequently journeys to the market town a few miles away which serves the needs of his village, but the Asian woman literally lives out her entire life within the confines of the village of her birth and her marriage.

Villages are the center of daily life for most Asians—Mahatma Gandhi spoke of the village as the heart of India—and the boundaries of the village are the boundaries of the individual Asian's life.

Villages in Asia are not planned; they just grow. For this reason a village is frequently a network of tiny winding lanes and alleys which lead to some courtyard and some door. These alleys and lanes are often filled with refuse and sewage and are seldom covered with anything but mud and filth. Sometimes cobblestones are laid, but they are usually uneven and irregularly spaced. The narrow avenues of a village permit only the passage of man and beast; there is no danger of a child being struck by a car as he plays and romps along the twisting lanes. Around the village lie the fields which the people of the village cultivate. During the working season, the villagers walk from their homes to the fields carrying their farming implements and often leading or driving before them a water buffalo, a cow, or a bullock. At dusk—sometimes later if they are very busy—they return to their village home with their implements and animals.

The social system is partly responsible for the haphazard growth and compact look of Asian villages. Most Asians have at one time or another practiced the joint or large family system and, even though the family may have divided the common property, the bonds of kinship still hold. When their common house became too small to accommodate the growing family, they merely built an extension to the house and moved in. Thus the village grew, with the closest kin generally living nearest to each other, and the houses were close together because they were extensions of other houses. This compact housing pattern served other purposes. In the first place, it provided better protection against theft and raids from bandits, deserters, and enemy villages. In some areas feuds start between villages over boundary problems, water rights, and fancied insults, and they can be very vicious and continue for years. The windows of the village houses were and are small and often barred, making entrance difficult for an intruder. Villages were thrown upon their own resources in protecting themselves because in the past Asian governments afforded little protection to the villagers. Moreover, houses built close together conserved land. Good land is scarce in Asia, and land that is used for housing cannot be used to produce food. The result is a cluster of houses built close together, identified by a name, and recognized as a social unit by the villagers themselves and others.

Some villages, particularly in Japan and South China, are stretched out like a string. They are laid out in rows on one or both sides of some natural or man-made phenomenon such as a river, dyke, or highway. Another type of village, found frequently in Japan, is made up of several clusters of houses. It is administratively one unit, although physically separated into several groups of houses.

The Asian village is primarily a group of farmhouses. Secondary activities, such as governmental work and manufacturing, are seldom carried on in the villages, though in some communities there are blacksmiths, weavers, workers in copper and metal, rope makers, pottery makers, and other artisans, and a number of villages have small markets where food, medicine, dyes, and other articles are sold. These village stores, generally very small, do not offer the variety and quantity or quality of products which are to be found in the larger market towns and cities. The villagers use their village stores in emergencies and for ordinary purchases. Some villages deliberately establish a small market section in order to keep money in the neighborhood. This market serves the neighboring village as well as the village of which it is a part.

Many of the shops of the market town in China are run by people whom the villagers regard as outsiders. Sometimes shopkeepers who have resided in the village for five or more generations are still regarded by the villagers as outsiders. When asked where their home is, they will often give their ancestral province, which they may never have seen. Cantonese merchants can be found in towns and cities all over China and when asked this question will invariably reply, Canton city or Kwangtung Province. Canton is the capital of Kwangtung, and the people from Kwangtung are generally referred to as Cantonese.

HOUSES

As a rule the villagers are poor and their houses are not pretentious. Many Asian houses are made of mud which is stamped and beaten into a tough consistency and then sun-dried and hardened. Sometimes mud bricks are used. The windows are generally small, barred, and frequently covered with thin paper rather than glass which is too expensive. In many villages the dwellings of the well-to-do and the ancestral halls, village centers, schools, and some shrines and temples are constructed of brick or stone. The roof may be either thatch or tile, depending upon the physical resources of the area. The distinguished and sensitive author Gertrude Emerson wrote in *Voiceless India* a description of the thatching of her bungalow in India.[1]

Two Tharus [the name of an Indian tribal people living on the border between Nepal and India] sat on the ground and made rope of the fine grass. They held lengths of grass firmly with their toes and twirled the strands in their hands, feeding the grass lengths as needed. Bundles of this twine were tossed to the man on the roof. A number of bamboos, previously soaked in water to make them resistant to rain, had been split into narrow strips. These the Tharus tied down horizontally across strips. Then they took bunches of coarse grass and tied them firmly to the bamboos, with the loose ends streaming down like hair. They worked in one long line, beginning at the bottom and progressing upward. When they had finished, the thatch stretched over the Happy House [the name she gave her bungalow] like a field of cloth of gold, eight inches thick.

Village houses differ in plan and room layout from country to country and from place to place within a country. In many parts of South China a house has three rooms. The front room is the largest and is used for a number of purposes. Rice is threshed in this room, guests are entertained and fed here, and traditionally the ancestral shrine occupies a prominent position in this multipurpose room, though farm implements may also be stored in the corners. The kitchen, which is behind the main room, is generally smaller and contains stove, chimney, and miscellaneous kitchen goods. Behind the kitchen or beside the main room may be one or more bedrooms which are usually small and crowded with simple furniture such as chests, beds, and chairs. Outside the house there is a privy and sometimes small storage huts and manure pits.

Human waste is used extensively in many parts of Asia as fertilizer. Since most Asian farmers do not have access to artificial fertilizer nor the money to buy such fertilizer when it is available, they resort to human fertilizer as the cheapest and most abundant organic material available for fields and garden plots. Pits to store human excreta and the penetrating odors which accompany this custom are part of the village landscape and atmosphere. Though the practice

---

[1] Gertrude Emerson, *Voiceless India* (New York: The John Day Company, 1944). Used with permission.

is highly unsanitary, some method of storing and using a cheap fertilizer is necessary if the villagers are to continue to reap a harvest from an old and much worked land.

In many parts of Southeast Asia a typical house rests upon stilts at heights ranging from four to seven feet above the ground. It often stands in the middle of a fenced compound and is shaded by fruit and palm trees. Although located in a village, the houses are not as crowded together as in other areas of Asia. The house may have a roofed verandah which is open during the day but can be closed at night with a screen or lattice arrangement. There is also frequently a large front room which serves as a parlor, work room, and dining room and, when necessary, a sleeping room at night. Usually behind the front room there are private bedrooms which vary in number depending upon the size and wealth of the family. Should there be more than one family in the household, each family is assigned a private bedroom. Animals generally occupy the space beneath the house, but this space may also be used as an additional work area or for other purposes. The roof is usually thatched. Privies, bath facilities, and storage huts are located in the compound outside the house. This type of house has certain advantages. It provides protection against floods and pests of various kinds. It is adapted to the warm climate of Southeast Asia, for it permits a good circulation of air. Certainly it makes feeding the animals easier because they can be fed from above with little effort. Even if the compound in which the house sits is small, the privacy and sense of spaciousness experienced by the occupants is unknown to the families living in the more compressed villages.

Villagers in Asia have few material possessions in their houses. What they do have is practical and useful; rarely beautiful or unessential. The poor Indian home has been described as having a stove, a bench, a rope bed, a few brass pots, and nothing else. However, hovels in Indian cities are often worse than homes in Indian villages.

The villagers spend much of their time outside their homes, working, gossiping, and playing. It is a common sight in Asia to see villagers gathered together outside their houses at dusk during the slack season, conversing, smoking, or merely looking at the scenes of daily life around them.

COMPOSITION OF THE VILLAGE

Asian villages vary in size and composition. In the north of India, villages average about 500 persons, but in the south, they average around 1,000. This variation in the size is true also of China, Japan, Korea, and the countries of Southeast Asia.

The composition of the village community ranges from a homogeneous group, all bearing the same surname and descended from a common ancestor, to unrelated individuals separated from one another by barriers of class and caste. The former holds true of some villages in China which may even be named after the family names —the Village of Wang, the Chang Village, the Li Village, and so on. More often the village is composed of individuals having several family names, with one or two or more families predominant.

In India the village may be made up of groups belonging to different castes. There are the cultivating castes, laboring castes, herdsmen, fishermen, basket and mat makers, blacksmiths, carpenters, washermen, barbers, and many others, all living together in a common village yet separated by the rigid barriers of caste. Outcastes live in the same villages, in a part separated by a strip of ground or a stream or some other demarcation. They are scorned by the other villagers and held in contempt. They live in hopeless poverty; to visit their homes is to visit a people condemned. Indeed, this is the way they are thought of—a people condemned to a life of hardship and pain by their sinful acts of a previous existence. They live as village scavengers and perform the filthy and degrading tasks that no other Indian villager or city dweller will do. They dress poorly, live in squalor, often stay at a distance from other castes, possess little land, generally have little to say about the government of the village, and regard the material future without much hope.

The government of India is trying to alleviate the wretched state of the scheduled castes, the official names for outcastes, but the Indian villagers generally continue to scorn them as inferior and insist that they live segregated from the rest of the village.

Although a variety of people live in the Asian village, and although caste and class barriers separate the villagers from one another, there is a feeling among all of them that this is their village and that they have something in common. The villagers may not care to eat, talk, or associate with other villagers conceived as inferior, but all are regarded as members of a single community and as having a stake in that community.

In the past the village has been described as a self-sufficient community. The villagers grew the food they ate. Rice, wheat, barley, corn, and other cereal crops surrounded the village, and many of the villagers had private gardens where they grew such vegetables as turnips, squash, sweet potatoes, peas, and beans. Salt, sugar, and cooking oil were among the few food items which the community did not possess, and although some villages possessed facilities for processing these foods, most did not. Salt was a government monopoly in some countries and a principal source of revenue. Villagers usually made their own clothes. The women spent long days and nights spinning the yarn, cutting, sewing, and finishing the clothes for their men and their children. But here also the village depended upon outside sources, for often the dyeing of finished garments was done by a specialist.

The villagers are practical in their choice of clothes. They usually wear cotton, but they also have dress clothes of silk and wool which they wear during some special celebration or when visiting or entertaining others. In northern Asia, wool and padded, quilt-like clothes are worn for warmth, and children sometimes wear layer after layer of their ordinary cotton clothes in an effort to keep warm in winter. Some observers have jokingly remarked, and with some truth, that the children of North China wear their entire wardrobe from the beginning to the end of the winter season. But for most Asians clothes are not a major problem. Farmers work in the fields stripped down to shorts or an abbreviated piece of cloth. Children run around naked. Many go barefoot or use cheap straw sandals which are cool, light, and not very durable. Few villagers use socks or stockings and what clothes they do wear are full and open to the air. Loose and full trousers, shirts, and skirts are the villagers' answer to the warm climate in which they live.

Many agricultural tools are made in the village. Simple ploughs, hoes, spades, and shovels are beaten out by the blacksmith. Sometimes he makes iron pots and cauldrons for cooking purposes. Workers in copper and pottery also make items for household and other uses. Weavers and dyers sometimes ply their skills within the village, especially if it is a large one and able to support them throughout the year. If the village is small, the villagers find it necessary to go elsewhere to buy tools, household equipment, and other necessary utensils. Sometimes the weavers, dyers, blacksmiths, and workers in copper travel from village to village as needed, much like peddlers vending their wares from house to house.

In the larger villages services are sometimes provided by the various crafts. Often in an Indian village the barber, the washerman, and the like receive a share of the village crop for their services. This is a co-operative endeavor and in a real sense symbolizes the community feeling of the villagers and the social unity of the village. In other parts of Asia the villagers frequently cut their own hair or go to the market town where barbers practice their trade on a permanent basis. Since barbers often go from village to village cutting hair, it is commonplace in Asia to see a barber at work on a squatting customer on the side of a road or street. In most of Asia the village women wash their family clothes by hand. A group of women at some stream or river bank pounding the clothes on flat rocks with wide short paddles is a typical village scene. Pounding the clothes clean reduces the durability of the clothing, but they find soap too expensive.

LENDERS OF MONEY

The bankers of the village are the moneylenders or pawnbrokers. These are among the most hated persons in Asia. They are considered parasites who have grown wealthy on the exhausting labor of the villagers. Without them, the villagers would not have facilities for borrowing money in times of emergencies; with them, the villager frequently finds himself enslaved for years and sometimes for life.

It frequently happens in the villages that money is needed for celebrations such as weddings and funerals. When a son or daughter marries, the villagers expect the parents to follow local customs. As all know so well, the force of public opinion, especially in small communities, is strong. The villagers of Asia ostracize the person who does not follow local customs, and as the village is their life, the great majority of villagers dare not depart too far from accepted usage. Thus, in the matter of weddings, the Chinese, Japanese, Koreans, Indians, Pakistanis, and others expect the family head to spend money rather lavishly on food, clothes, and other forms of conspicuous consumption. Since the villager has no reserve of capital or food, he is forced to turn to the moneylender for the required cash. The moneylender is usually happy to lend it, especially if the man is a responsible villager and this is the first time he has borrowed money. The interest required on this loan might run as high as 10 to 15 per cent per month. The villager may find himself in a desperate predicament when the time comes to pay off merely the interest on the loan, and it often happens that he must continue to borrow money even to pay off the interest which accumulates at a pace beyond measure. Finally, he becomes so deeply involved that he and his entire family can only look forward to a life dedicated to enriching the banker or moneylender. Funerals pose the same problem for the villager, particularly in East Asia where the concept of filial piety has penetrated deeply into the mores of the society. The son is expected to carry out the mourning rites for the parents or other older relatives. He must invite the relatives to a banquet, hire mourners for weeping, buy a decent coffin, invite priests to chant prayers, hire pallbearers, and sometimes engage musicians to play during the procession to the grave. These expenses are heavy, but if the villager does not fulfill his obligations to the best of his ability, he will find it difficult to continue to live among neighbors who expect this obligation to be met. Accordingly, he borrows money and the trap closes around him. It is ironic that the villager who follows the "good path" as indicated by his village culture should end up almost inevitably in the awful trap of debt from which he may never escape.

Most people think that Asians are in debt only because of starvation and lack of food; few realize that such common occurrences as weddings and funerals are also inescapable reasons for borrowing money. The force of public opinion may be as frequent a cause for borrowing money as the force of hunger. This is a condition which could exist only where poverty is so prevalent and need so great. The moneylenders argue that high interest rates are necessary since the peasant is so vulnerable to calamities that may prevent him from repaying his debts. However, most moneylenders appear to make out rather well.

NEW ECONOMIC FORCES

It cannot be said that the Asian village was ever completely self-sufficient, but it was relatively so in comparison with the cities and villages of today. This was evidenced in Japan, Asia's most industrialized nation, during and after the Second World War when thousands of city dwellers returned to the country to live with their families, relatives, or friends until the crisis was over. But with the coming of a money economy to Asia and the introduction of new Western-oriented ways of life, village self-sufficiency is lessening.

Cloth is available now at a price cheaper than the individual villagers can make it. It is also prettier and more colorful. The villagers now buy machine-made and machine-dyed cloth. Many no longer buy the raw cotton but thread made in mills, thus saving the women much work. There are still millions of women who have the skill and do make their own clothes, but more and more of them are depending upon machine-made products. The villagers are relying more upon manufactured farm implements than upon hand-shaped ploughs, hoes, mattocks and sickles. These farm tools are being made available to the farmer at cheaper and cheaper prices and are generally of better quality and more efficient than the tools made by hand. The blacksmith's place in the village economy is slowly decreasing in importance.

Asian villages are gradually being integrated into the economy of the entire country. They are no longer isolated from other villages nor from the cities and towns of the country. Fountain pens, locks, keys, pots and pans, combs, flashlights, batteries, nails, mirrors, and electric light bulbs are commonly found in many Asian villages, and the villagers are beginning to depend upon these imports. The price of their rice or wheat crop, the wages they receive from their farm labor, the fluctuations of the price of their main cash crop, are all now dependent upon the world and national market. A drop in the price of rice vitally affects each Burmese and Thai farmer. A drop in the price of peanuts alters the plans of a Chinese farmer who is dependent upon this crop for the cash he needs to buy various essentials. No longer is it the price set in one or two market towns that influences the price of rice or wheat in the village. New roads, buses, railroads, radios, newspapers, telephones, magazines, technical education, and an increasingly bewildering variety of communications are invading the villages of Asia and breaking down their intellectual as well as social self-sufficiency.

Villagers still remain more self-sufficient than their city neighbors, and in a pinch can get along much better than city people. But the process of the integration of village and national economies is accelerating.

CHAPTER 5

IDEOLOGY, SOCIETY, AND POLITICS

Most Asians are preoccupied with the search for food and constantly beset by natural and man-made calamities which demand their unflagging attention to avoid and overcome. But the Asian, like all men, has certain beliefs and lives in a community of his fellow men, often very close to them in the land of compact villages. He also lives within a political framework and atmosphere which is affecting more and more his individual actions and future. To understand the Asians it is necessary to have some basic knowledge of their ideology and their social and political life which must be viewed not only in terms of their traditional beliefs, social customs, and political framework, but also in terms of newer ideas and practices usually imported from outside Asia.

Modern Western ideas have not permeated all levels of Asian life, for underneath these new thoughts still remain many layers of traditional belief. Asian thought cannot be understood merely from the philosophic base of the West; it must be studied in the light of its tradition and traditional ways of thinking if there is to be any understanding at all. The people of Asia live in a modern era, but they think in an old era. They know that the thinking of the West has challenged their traditional ideologies, and accepting the challenge, many Asians are incorporating the thought of the West into their traditional thought. The educated classes in particular are guiding their actions on many of the principles laid down by Western philosophers. But the great mass of the uneducated and many of the educated still cling to the traditional thought their fathers and mothers taught them. Although their national life is directed by men who are often steeped in Western ways and Western thought, the great mass of people think much as their ancestors did.

Two civilizations of Asia have influenced the thought of the majority of Asians—the Indian and the Chinese. India gave to Asia Hinduism and Buddhism; China reinterpreted and extended Bud-

ISLAM   BUDDHIST   HINDU   CHRIST.   SHINTO

In India, Hinduism gradually prevailed over Buddhism, which also originated in that country. Still a major force in Japan, where it co-exists with Shinto, Buddhism is on the decline in China. Pakistan and Indonesia are the largest Muslim nations in the world. While Islam also spread to the Philippines, most Filipinos today are baptized Catholics.

dhism and also gave to Asia Confucianism and Taoism. Both
civilizations contributed other ideologies to their own national life,
but these remained national or regional, rather than international,
in character.

Islam has also had a tremendous impact upon millions of Asian
people. Pakistan and Indonesia are the two largest Muslim nations
in the world, and there are millions of followers of Islam living in
Malaya, China, Borneo, the Philippines, and other Asian countries.

The social life of the Asian people changed little over many centuries before the coming of the Western nations to the East. Their
way of life was based on custom and tradition peculiarly suited
to the agricultural base of the community. Classes were distinguished, roles well-defined, and for the vast majority of Asians the
family was established as the center of social control and social
activity. Today the social life of Asia is in the process of change. It
has been radically affected by the impact of foreign ideas, customs,
and social attitudes. By the middle of the twentieth century these
new ways of life have penetrated deep into Asian society. The traditional has not been completely given up, and many Asians still
cling tenaciously to the old social ways, but the change is obvious
and continuous. The social life of Asia today cannot be described
as exclusively traditional or modern. It is both, and something
else—a compromise.

Traditionally, the joint or big family system was found throughout the entire region of Asia. Under this system the father, mother, unmarried children, and married sons, together with their wives and children, lived under one roof and had a common budget. This family system is still found throughout Asia, but industrialization, urbanization, and the impact of outside ideas are increasing the number of small Western-style families, especially in the cities. Traditionally, women in Asia were subordinate to the men, who dominated the political, economic, and social life of the country. In many Asian families the female was often less welcomed, less cared for, and less respected than the male. She found it difficult to get a divorce, rarely picked her own husband, and was often ill-treated by her frustrated and jealous mother-in-law. The subordination of women is still prevalent in many parts of Asia, but education, enlightened ideas embodied in the constitutions and legal codes of Asian countries, and, most of all, the fierce determination of Asian women to better their position are rapidly modifying this traditional attitude. It was also a common custom in Asia for marriages to be arranged by families rather than by individuals. Marriage contracts were negotiated and concluded by the family heads, though the individuals concerned might be consulted at times. This practice is still common in many parts of Asia, but the youth of Asia are revolting against the custom. The struggle of modern young men and women to choose their own mates is another characteristic of Asian social life today.

Patterns of social life in Asia are changing rapidly. The old forms and relationships which were founded upon different values and ways of thinking are gradually being replaced and modified by newer forms and relationships founded upon more modern beliefs and philosophies. It is a time of social upheaval in Asia.

Traditionally, society in Asia was divided into the ruler and the ruled and their interests were rarely identical. The ruler did not regard himself as responsible for the welfare of the people, except perhaps in traditional China and areas governed by some Muslim rulers, and he never thought of himself as the people's representative. He was exclusively interested in preserving his position, maintaining control over the area he ruled, and increasing the wealth of his family and his favorites. The people existed for him, were not consulted about national and regional affairs, and were expected to obey his commands without question. The people did not think of themselves as members of a nation, that is to say, a group of people tied together by a common culture, common language, common tradition, and motivated by a desire to be politically independent. They were loyal to a village and a family, but not to any larger entity.

Today there is a difference. The people of Asia are thinking and speaking of *their* country and *their* policies and *their* political goals. In many areas of Asia the leaders and the people regard themselves as working together toward a common set of goals. Growing numbers of leaders think and speak of themselves as representatives of the people. The people, in turn, are coming more and more to look upon these leaders as their representatives. Moreover, Asian people are beginning to understand that it is *their* will that the government ought to express. Elections are being held in every Asian country, and although the choices are sometimes limited, the people do get a chance to vote in a formal manner. Frequently, they have responded enthusiastically and in India, Japan, Indonesia, Malaya, and other Asian countries have turned out in great numbers to express their opinion at the polls. Many of the new Asian leaders thus elected attempt to follow the will of the people in their legislative and executive acts. Of course, the people are still vague about the duties and functions of their representatives, and the leaders frequently act according to their own personal bent, but eventually the people will make their will felt in a more organized and decisive

Communist ▨ anti-Communist ▥ Neutral ▤

The countries of Asia are caught up in the power struggle be-
tween East and West. Following India's lead, some are striving
to maintain neutrality. Japan, Pakistan, South Vietnam, Thai-
land, and the Philippines are tied by treaties to the U.S. Although
Communist China, powerful and aggressive, looms over the
countries of Southeast Asia, North Vietnam is the only nation
in that area formally linked to the Communist bloc.

manner. The leaders today are interested primarily in raising the standard of living for their people and in making their nation a strong force in international affairs. At home and abroad, liberal democratic governments have awakened the people to a sense of their importance and the importance of their nation-state in world affairs.

Because this is still a new political phenomenon, the traditional way of life remains an integral part of the present way of life. The past has left a legacy and that legacy is evident in the way millions of Asians continue to think and live politically. The new has not been completely grasped and assimilated, nor the past completely forgotten, and to understand the Asia of today, it is necessary to understand the Asia of yesterday. Because the traditional and the new are both struggling to maintain themselves in modern Asia, critical conflicts emerge. The political problems that face the Asian people today are many and complex.

In the pages that follow an attempt will be made to outline the traditional aspects of Asian ideology and social and political life, as well as to describe the transitional complexities of the present.

In the following section the life and thought of the people of India and Pakistan in South Asia, and China and Japan in East Asia, are presented in some detail because these countries have had a great influence upon the life and thought of all Asia. A basic understanding of these civilizations is fundamental to an understanding of other Asian countries.

CHAPTER 6

SOUTH ASIA

South Asia includes the countries of India, Pakistan, Ceylon, and some small Himalayan states. The republics of India and Pakistan, the two largest nations, are located on the mainland of Asia, while Ceylon is separated from the southern tip of India by a few miles of water.

There is such a close physical unity between India and Pakistan that commentators writing about these two countries often treat them as one geographic unit. The republics of India and Pakistan were formerly one territorial area governed by Great Britain. For religious, economic, and political reasons this territory was divided in 1947 into three parts. Two parts, one in the extreme west, the other in the extreme east, became the Republic of Pakistan. The third part, located between the other two, became the Republic of India. The political divisions thus created cut across railroads, highways, power lines, and villages which were built formerly with one geographic area in mind. This neglect of geographic considerations has disrupted the relations and, to a certain degree, the economy of the two nations.

CEYLON

In terms of physical geography Ceylon is the southernmost part of India. Technically an island, Ceylon is actually an extension of peninsular India, since the shallow waters separating it from India are dotted with many small bits of land. Because of its advantageous position in the Indian Ocean it has been used since ancient times as a port of call for ships passing east and west. About 270 miles long and 140 miles wide, it is only slightly larger than West Virginia.

Ceylon has a population of approximately 10 million, the great majority of whom are Singhalese who are the descendants of the original Ceylonese colonists who came from the valley of the

Ganges River in north India around the sixth century B.C. The Tamils, who make up about 10 per cent of the population, came to Ceylon at a later date from South India, many of them in the past century to work as laborers on the plantations. One of Ceylon's most vexing problems today is the tense relations between these two groups. The Singhalese are lighter-skinned, are largely followers of Theravada or Hinayana Buddhism, and speak the Sinhala language which in 1956 was made the official language of Ceylon. The Tamils are darker, are predominantly Hindu, and speak the Tamil language of South India. In their drive to unify the country culturally, economically, and politically, the Singhalese aroused the alarm and antagonism of the Tamils, who are fiercely resisting assimilation lest their culture, language, and livelihood be endangered. There have been instances in recent years of riots, bloodshed, and violence between the two groups which have brought about adverse reactions on the social, economic, and political levels.

Ceylon achieved its independence in 1948 and is a member of the British Commonwealth of Nations. Formerly under Portuguese and Dutch control, it came under British domination in the eighteenth century. Since independence the political situation in Ceylon has been in a state of flux. Until 1965 the Prime Minister of Ceylon was a woman, Madame Sirimavo Bandaranaike, widow of a former Prime Minister who was assassinated in 1959. Madame Bandaranaike was elected in 1960 on the Sri Lanka Freedom Party (Socialist) ticket. It is interesting to note that the only woman Prime Minister in recent times was elected in Asia, where the position of the woman has traditionally been a subordinate one. Her government embarked upon a policy of nationalization. Insurance, public utilities, newspapers, education, to mention a few, were brought or were slated to be brought under government control. Madame Bandaranaike sought the support of leftist groups in the country and formed a coalition government with a Trotskyite party. After a no-confidence vote in December, 1964, Madame Bandaranaike dissolved parliament and called for new elections in 1965. She lost this election.

There is little industry in Ceylon because of a lack of essential raw materials such as coal. Tea, rubber, and coconut products are Ceylon's main exports. The mountains of Ceylon intercept the monsoons from the southwest and the northeast, thus bringing abundant rain which makes possible the rapid growth of tropical evergreen trees and the cultivation of tea, rubber, and rice. Ceylon is synonymous with tea the world over, but the country is dependent upon imports for most of its manufactured needs and a large part of its food supplies.

Friction between minority groups, rising costs of living, divided political parties, strong labor unions, often infiltrated and led by Communists, have too frequently given Ceylon's domestic scene a chaotic appearance.

THE UNITY OF SOUTH ASIA

South Asia is not only a territorial unit in terms of surface features; it also manifests a definite unity in terms of climate, religion, and politics. The countries of South Asia depend upon the early summer monsoon which brings needed rain. All of Asia relies upon the monsoon, but this area is peculiarly dependent upon the regular coming of the rain-bearing monsoon winds. When the monsoon fails to appear on time, or brings too little water to the thirsty land, famines frequently result. Culturally, the people of South Asia have much in common. They are a religious people. The great religions of Hinduism, Buddhism, and Islam have marked the land and the people. The Hindu temple, the Buddhist stupa, and the Muslim mosque everywhere give an otherworldly beauty to the landscape. The soaring simplicity of Muslim architecture is offset by the wonderful exuberance of Hindu art. The Brahmin, the Buddhist priest, and the Mullah are honored and respected. Politically, the three principal countries of South Asia have the same heritage and the same aspirations. They are all former colonies of Great Britain, and won their independence at approximately the same time. They all manifest the same nationalistic aspirations and all profess to believe in a democratic form of government based upon modern Western examples such as England and the United States. All of them are members of the British Commonwealth of Nations.

The location of the Indo-Pakistan subcontinent between Europe, Africa, and the Middle East, on the one hand, and the Far East and Pacific regions, on the other, early exposed it to many outside contacts. Northern India was convenient to the mainland routes between Asia and the West, while peninsular India lay actually astride the water routes between the Pacific and the Atlantic and Mediterranean areas. India was the eastern limit for Western trade and exploration, and the western limit for Far Eastern traders and travelers. Warehouses of Graeco-Roman pottery have been found near Pondicherry on the southeast coast of India. This location gave India and Pakistan the opportunity of receiving cultural and ideological contributions from many civilizations. India has often adapted these new contributions to fit her civilization and, in many instances, has passed them along in an Indianized form to the other civilizations of both Asia and the Western Hemisphere. Thus, Graeco-Roman art forms were carried by the Buddhist missionaries to China, and the Indian names for rice, ginger, and pepper were borrowed by the old Greeks. It is significant that today India also aspires to bring the East and the West to a better understanding of each other by interpreting one to the other.

CHAPTER 7

THE IDEOLOGY OF INDIA

The ideology of the people of India is the result of a long and continuing search for the origin and meaning of life. Answers that Indian thinkers and sages have found to the questions of what, whence, why, how, and whither man and the universe make up most of the content of Indian ideology. Meditation on these fundamental questions has played a decisive role in shaping the Indian way of life.

Indians gave primacy to that man or group of men who wrestled with these questions. Thought was more important than action; meditation was valued over the incessant search for material goods. Wealth and power were important goals, but spiritual realization and self-contemplation ranked higher in the scale of cosmic values. This attitude is demonstrated by the tremendous respect given to the ascetics and hermits who are found all over India; by the position of the Brahmins—the priestly group who have attained to knowledge and renunciation—at the top of the hierarchy of castes; and finally by the overwhelming appeal of Mahatma Gandhi, who was famed for his self-discipline, ascetic life, and renunciation of worldly goods.

Indian sages were puzzled by the transiency of existence and the universality of suffering; they were intrigued by the unity that appeared to be manifest in the diversity that was the universe; they were challenged by the presence of an intangible soul or spirit coexisting with a tangible material world. Accordingly, they sought to explore the nature of man and the universe, of matter and non-matter, of existence and nonexistence, and finally the ultimate reality of all things. Their findings form the substance of Indian ideology.

Philosophers in India dealt with the world of the spirit more often than with that of matter. Their thought assumed a spiritual and metaphysical character which has been a distinctive feature of

Indian ideology. It is for this reason that the ideology of India provides for a religious way of life and furnishes such a creed and worship for the people that everything an Indian does has a spiritual significance, and every act is for him, in a very real sense, a religious act.

One of the results of this search for the ultimate reality underlying the material world, this search for the ultimate truth and ultimate reason for existence, was the founding of two religions, two ways of life, which have influenced the beliefs and acts of countless millions living on the mainland and islands of Asia. These two religions are Hinduism and Buddhism.

Other religions arose in India, such as Jainism in the sixth century B.C. and Sikhism in the sixteenth century A.D., which continue to have a number of followers, but their influence is not comparable with that of Buddhism and Hinduism. Both Jainism and Sikhism were, like Buddhism, reform movements within the fold of Hinduism directed against the domination of the Brahmins, the priests of Hinduism, and the rigidity and artificiality of their ceremonials. Sikhism is also said to have been an attempt to bridge the gulf between Islam and Hinduism.

Very early in the history of India, Hinduism emerged as the dominant way of life for the majority of the Indian people. The term "Hinduism" as used here means the same as "Brahmanism," the word sometimes used to describe the dominant religion of India prior to the eighth century A.D.

Historical Buddhism was born later than Hinduism, in the sixth century B.C. It was both the child and the opponent of Hinduism. Hinduism and Buddhism were both concerned with the continuous process of change which appeared to be characteristic of the universe. Hinduism, however, held that beneath this change there was a permanent reality which gave unity and permanence to the world. Buddhism, on the other hand, taught that change was really the nature of things and that there was nothing permanent in the universe. All things were transitory and impermanent. Hinduism taught that man had a soul. Buddhism denied the existence of an individual soul. Hinduism bestowed many gods on man, while Buddhism denied the existence of all supernatural beings.

After its founding in the sixth century B.C., Buddhism spread rapidly. During the reign of Emperor Asoka, a devout Buddhist who ascended the throne in 273 B.C., and who was the grandson of the founder of the Maurya Dynasty (322-185 B.C.), Buddhism flourished in India and expanded abroad. Evidence of Asoka's vigorous proselytizing can still be seen in India in the form of stupas and tall sandstone pillars. The stupas are round-domed structures of brick and stone which house Buddhist relics and serve as memorials. The pillars, which stand as high as forty or fifty feet, are surmounted by capitals which are usually decorated with symbolic Buddhist representations. Asoka, imbued with a missionary zeal, sent Buddhist missionaries to Burma, Ceylon, and as far as Egypt. Buddhism gradually penetrated most of Asia and became the religion of untold millions of people in China, Korea, Japan, Burma, Thailand, Cambodia, Laos, Viet-Nam, and Tibet. It became one of the world's great religions and continues to hold the allegiance of millions in Asia today.

In India, however, Hinduism slowly made Buddhism a part of itself through absorption and assimilation. What was not incorporated into Hinduism was abolished by the proselytizing zeal of the Muslims who saw in the superstitions and magical practices of a corrupt Buddhism the devil of idolatry. Thus Buddhism died in the country of its birth. Hinduism, the dominant thought of India for thousands of years, has, with the aid of Buddhism and minor religions, remained an ideological framework within which the people of India live and work.

CHAPTER 8

HINDUISM

Reality is one; sages speak of it in different ways.
—RIGVEDA I, 164

Hinduism attempts to be all things to all men. It tries to satisfy myriad needs and aspirations. It is a tolerant, accommodative religion, with a niche for every man and every god. Hinduism offers the scholar and mystic an opportunity for speculative thought on the most abstract level and for the most rarefied mystical experiences, at the same time providing the more literal-minded and worldly with a wealth of ritual, magnificent temples, and a god for every occasion. The detached and selfless seer is given identification with an Ultimate Absolute Reality as his final goal, while the less selfless has a personal God who loves and protects him on earth and finally rewards him with a place in heaven. Hinduism understands that individuals vary in their spiritual and intellectual capacities and that provision must be made for people on every level if all are to be satisfied.

Hinduism draws its inspiration and doctrines from a large body of ancient writings known as scriptures. These are divided into two parts—the Vedas, which are the primary and revealed source of Hinduism, and secondary scriptures which are authoritative elaborations upon the Vedas.

Much of the material in the Vedas was handed down for centuries by word of mouth. Finally put into written form during a long period of time extending approximately from 2000 to 500 B.C., they are known to the Hindu as *Sruti*, or "that which is heard." The Indian sages heard the eternal truths from the Godhead and recorded them for future generations. There are four Vedas—the *Rigveda*, the *Samaveda*, the *Yajurveda*, and the *Atharvaveda*. Each is divided into three parts which generally follow a chronological order—the *Mantras*, which are the basic hymns and verses and the core of the Vedas; the *Brahamas*, which are ritualistic and interpretative explanations of the *Mantras*; and the *Upanishads*, which are profound mystical and philosophic extensions of the truths revealed in the basic *Mantras*. The *Mantras* are sometimes called the Vedas because they are the heart of the revealed truths and the basis for the later elaborations. The *Brahamas* are largely the work of priests and deal with ritual worship. The word *Upanishads* has the literal meaning of "sitting near," which conveys the idea of knowledge acquired while seated around a teacher. Teaching based upon the *Upanishads* is called Vedanta, which signifies not only the end of the Vedas, but also the peak of Vedic knowledge.

The secondary scriptures are known as *Smriti*, or "that which is remembered." These writings are not revealed but are authoritative and include digests of earlier writings, manuals of philosophy, commentaries, rituals, codes of law and conduct such as the law of Manu, sacred stories like the *Puranas*, and epics illustrated by the *Ramayana* and the *Mahabharata*. The *Mahabharata* is the longest poem in the world, and its most famous part, the *Bhagavad-Gita*, is one of the finest gems in world literature.

UNITY IN DIVERSITY

The attempt to meet the needs of mankind at every level makes Hinduism a way of life that is bewilderingly diverse. The presence of 33,000 gods—33,000 gods is an Indian way of saying "countless gods"—and innumerable religious practices which apparently have no relation to one another, confuses the untutored. The multiplicity of sects and subsects, cults and philosophies, commentaries, and commentaries on the commentaries, creates the first impression that the body of Hindu belief and practice is highly disorganized and incoherent. This incoherence, however, is merely on the surface. Beneath this diversity there is a certain common core of doctrine which gives Hinduism a basic unity of thought and belief. An example of this unity in diversity is found in the Hindu conception of their many gods as really many manifestations of One Absolute Reality.

ONE ULTIMATE REALITY

Hinduism teaches that the thousands of gods revered and worshipped by the faithful merely symbolize and represent aspects of One Ultimate Reality that transcends the measure of form, name, and personality. The gods contained within the Hindu pantheon are limited portrayals of that which is unlimited. Hinduism senses that for most men the formless and nameless must be made concrete. Only a select few have reached that level where the Absolute can be grasped as it is and not garbed in some particular body. Three main gods represent the Hindu trinity; they possess their own heavens, wives, children, and servants. Representing three functions of the Ultimate Reality, they are Brahma, the Creator; Vishnu, the Preserver; and Siva, the Destroyer. Worship of these gods resulted in the birth of separate sects and cults dedicated to Vishnu and Siva and many forms of these two gods, but always there was the deep realization that belief in these gods as discrete personalities was a concession to the sense organs, a surrender to the demands of the human heart which required some material expression of a reality that transcends human imagination.

Gods are not the only manifestations of an Ultimate Reality; all things in the universe, including man, are but so many representatives of it. The Ultimate or Supreme Reality is the whole animate and inanimate universe. The cosmic character of Hinduism can be seen in this relationship between man, the universe, and the Ultimate Reality, for neither man nor any material object, living or nonliving, can be viewed as standing apart from anything else.

In every man there is an essential self that is called *Atman*. It is divine and transcendent, beyond the mind, the body, and the senses, and one with the Ultimate Reality, or *Brahman*. Although no name can describe this Ultimate Reality, the Hindus generally refer to it as *Brahman*. Atman and Brahman are two names for the same thing—Atman is the Ultimate Reality viewed subjectively, while Brahman is the Ultimate Reality viewed objectively. Thus man is one with all things in the universe because he is another manifestation of the Supreme Reality. The *Upanishads* exclaim: "The essential self or the vital essence in man is the same as that in an ant, the same as that in a gnat, the same as that in an elephant, the same as that in these three worlds, indeed the same as that in the whole universe."

LIBERATION FROM THE FINITE

Everything is really and essentially one; the multiplicity of material objects apprehended by the senses obscures and hides the true reality that pervades all things. In this illusory but tangible world,

Hinduism teaches that the many gods, the variety of rituals and creeds, and the other human accommodative institutions are not ends in themselves, but are means provided to aid man in reaching his ultimate goal of liberation from a particular body.

The essential self of man is imprisoned in an individual body, mind, and understanding, which is finite, ignorant, and egotistical. The body is finite because it is limited to the world of the senses, ignorant because it views the world as so many separate objects distinct from each other, and egotistical because it thinks of itself as a particular individual reveling in its uniqueness. Hinduism teaches that the final goal of human life is *moksha,* or liberation from finite human consciousness to a high and divine consciousness of the Ultimate Reality or that of which everything is a part. Man's destiny is not happiness on earth or in heaven, nor is he destined for suffering on earth or in hell, but rather his ultimate goal is a realization that he is one with a Supreme Reality which encompasses both man and the universe.

Man must rise above this body which obscures and conceals a self that is infinite and one with all things. He must liberate himself from the concept of individuality and separateness from all other things and struggle to realize the true nature of himself and the universe. When he has realized that he is one with the Ultimate Reality, he is no longer subject to the limitations and restrictions of the body; he then becomes identified with Brahman, that is, pure existence, pure consciousness, and pure bliss. As one Indian has remarked, "We believe that the worst of all evils is the ego, the 'I am.' The more we can squash it, the better." The goal of every Hindu is to escape from the bondage of individual existence. This is not easy; for most people it is a long and complicated process necessitating a number of separate and varied existences before liberation is attained.

REBIRTH

The Hindus believe in rebirth or the transmigration of self. The essential self of man is really one with the Ultimate Reality; it has no beginning and can have no end. The self of a newborn infant is old beyond the conception of time; its body is merely a new form for an eternal spirit. Since the self is one with the entire universe, it is not restricted in the form it may assume. Like water, it may fit itself to any type of container. In succeeding generations, the self may reign as a god, destroy as a demon, bloom as a flower, crawl as a snake, wander as a tiger, or silently meditate as a Hindu seer.

The entire universe is a collection of temporary living quarters for selves struggling toward liberation and final release from their wanderings. Life is like a journey over a bridge, across which man must travel to reach his destination but upon which he does not build permanently. It is a lower stage of experience necessary before passing to the higher level of identification with a Supreme Reality. For the Hindu, each individual existence becomes his primary burden, for it is a prison enslaving an essential self which should be free. There is always hope, however, for he knows that each prison is merely temporary, and, if he uses his time well, it may be his last temporary residence in the world of matter and multiplicity. Sir Edwin Arnold in *The Light of Asia* poetically catches this idea:

> *Only, while turns the wheel invisible,*
> *No pause, no peace, nor staying place can be;*
> *Who mounts may fall, who fall will mount; the spokes*
> *Go round unceasingly.*

KARMA

The sequence of rebirths is determined by the law of *karma*. *Karma* literally means "action" and particularly action done in the past which determines the individual's present condition of existence. Karma operates like a moral law of causation whereby the present acts of an individual produce concrete results at some future time or existence. No deed is lost. No act is without result. Morally good acts produce good results; morally bad acts produce bad results. In one sense man's present life is determined because it is the result of the sum total of all his previous acts. In another sense the present condition of the individual is self-created. "Each is his own destroyer or preserver, as he follows evil or good." In each current existence man is fashioning his future life. Karma works with certainty and inevitability for the *Mahabharata* states: "As among a thousand cows a calf will find its mother, so the deed previously done will find and follow its doer." The *Mahabharata* describes karma as the unseen which shadows man everywhere.

> *Yes, all the deeds that men have done,*
> *In light of day, before the sun,*
> *Or veiled beneath the gloom of night,*
> *The good, the bad, the wrong, the right—*
> *These, though forgotten, reappear,*
> *And travel, silent, in their rear.*

A man's position in society and all the inequalities and sufferings of life are the results of the inexorable law of karma.

SPIRITUAL PROGRESSION

Implicit in the concepts of rebirth and karma, or moral causation, is a certain spiritual progression, which reaches its culmination in the liberation of man from the endless torment of the wheel of birth and rebirth. A man is closer to the Ultimate Reality than an animal, an animal is closer than a plant, and a plant is closer than a lifeless object. So a good man is closer to liberation than a bad man, and justice and mercy are valued more highly than injustice and cruelty. Spiritual values such as beauty, love, and righteousness are of more importance than intellectual values such as logic, keenness, clarity, and other skills. Below the spiritual and intellectual skills come biological values such as health and vitality and finally material values such as wealth and the like. Hinduism uses a spiritual and moral yardstick to judge and order the actions of man and society. This attitude is revealed in the caste structure, by which Indian society is organized, and in the institution of the stages of life called *asramas,* by which each Hindu is supposed to order his life. The belief that specific duties exist for each of the four castes and each of the four orders or stages of man dominates Hindu social thought and practice.

CASTE

A caste is a social group whose membership is determined by birth. The caste system developed early in Indian history. It is believed by some that the system had its origin in the division between the fair Aryans who invaded India many centuries ago and the dark-skinned non-Aryans whom they conquered. Scholars who accept the economic origin of the system maintain that the fourfold caste division of society is really based on a practical division of labor. The Brahmin caste was concerned with priestly and intellectual duties; the Kshatriya caste undertook the conduct of wars and government; the Vaisaya caste was occupied with commercial and agricultural pursuits; and the Sudra caste performed the more menial and servile work of the community. There were many subcastes, but generally speaking, all Indians could be placed within these four groups. Finally, there were the outcastes, sometimes called the depressed or scheduled castes, who were the lowest of the low in India and who were deprived even of those few benefits that those in the lowest castes possessed. Even these groups were called castes, because they too divided themselves into groups with special rules that regulated their lives.

Each caste is usually governed by an elaborate code of conduct which regulates most aspects of the lives of its members, such as drinking, eating, social intercourse with other castes, and like matters. Generally, the members follow the same occupation, marry within the caste, and confine their social activities to each other. All within the caste are brethren and are supposed to aid each other in time of need.

The caste system conforms to the law of spiritual progression because the most spiritual caste, the Brahmins, occupy the top position in the system, while the least spiritual, the outcastes, occupy the lowest position. Caste is regarded by most as determined by the law of karma. Thus, the good deeds performed by a man in his present existence might merit for him a higher caste position in a future existence. Theoretically, this caste system, as ordered through the method of spiritual progression, is supposed to result in a harmonious Indian society arranged like a co-operative hierarchy. Each caste is supposed to carry out those special duties, whether intellectual and ruling functions or more servile tasks, which are commensurate with their spiritual capacities. Like most theoretical arrangements, this one represents a considerable departure from actual practice.

The caste system will be treated more fully when the social life of India is discussed.

STAGES OF LIFE

The concept of spiritual progression is manifested not only in caste divisions but also in the division of the life of the individual into four successive stages called the *asramas*. Each stage of life is a progression from the baser to the more spiritual levels. These stages are: the student, the householder, the anchorite, and the *sannyasin*. The first stage is one of preparation and probation, in which the student lives an austere life and devotes himself to study and discipline. The second stage is one in which the individual carries out his responsibilities to society by raising and supporting a family and by taking an active part in the affairs of the community and the state. After this active period, the individual withdraws from the bustle of life and enters the anchorite and third stage, where he engages in meditation and study for the second time. Finally, he enters the fourth stage of the *sannyasin*, wherein he completely renounces all possessions and attachments. At such a stage the individual is often found leading the life of a wandering ascetic. Since Hinduism holds renunciation and nonattachment to material objects as the highest of values, the *sannyasin* is believed to have reached the apex of spiritual life on earth, and for this reason he is revered by the Indians above all men.

DHARMA: A GUIDE FOR THE LIVING

The practical and accommodative quality of Hinduism is strikingly illustrated in the provision of a rule or guide for man in his journey over the bridge of life. This rule is called *dharma*. The word *dharma* is translated in many ways and means different things at different times. It has been used to indicate duty, law, morality, conduct; it has sometimes embraced the conception of the entire rule of Hindu life and the whole duty of man. It has been used to refer to the individual duty of a king or warrior, or the group duties of a particular caste; it has denoted both sacred and civil law. But no matter what the context or the particular meaning of the moment, dharma fundamentally acts as a guidebook directing man how to behave in this world of matter and the senses, while, at the same time, furthering his spiritual progress toward his final liberation. Of course, the dharma for each man in this existence is determined by his previous karma.

Hinduism realizes that, besides his final goal of liberation from the bondage of the body, man has certain material ends which arise from the needs and desires of this same body he seeks to escape. There are certain natural desires, instincts, and appetites of the flesh which man must satisfy. The Hindu accepts this natural world in which he must work out his salvation. Although he seeks to escape from it, he does not fight against it. He does not seek to control nature so much as he tries to conform to it; he works with the natural processes rather than against them. Since nature is basically one with himself, to struggle against nature is to struggle against oneself. The true Hindu is close to nature and he reveals his closeness in his practices of bathing and eating and in honoring streams and mountains. There are also social demands, such as the maintenance of a family, aid to dependents and the needy, and other obligations that man must meet in this temporal world. Dharma regulates the expression of these natural desires and this search for material welfare in such a manner that both work toward the final goal of man—liberation. It advises man to satisfy his appetite in a moderate and temperate fashion. It directs his method of gathering wealth for the support of his family so that this act is not a mere material action but is one infused with spirituality. In this way dharma attempts to bring spirit and matter together and to bridge the gap between the eternal and the temporal by making every act further both spiritual and material progress simultaneously.

Dharma, the Hindu guide to right conduct, is not only vitally interested in man's material and spiritual ends, his caste, and the four stages of life; it also directs his actions in other aspects of his life. For instance, Hinduism emphasizes the virtues of truth, nonviolence, sacrifice, purity, and renunciation or detachment. Truth is one of the most important virtues an individual may possess. It is a criterion by which the character of an individual may be judged. Nonviolence stems from the belief that essentially all things are images of one's own self and consequently should be respected. In modern times, Mahatma Gandhi advocated nonviolence not only for the individual but also as an ideal for international life. Gandhi thought of Hinduism as the search for truth through nonviolence. Sacrifices are necessary if the world is to function properly. Purity is both ceremonial and moral, for all the purificatory practices prescribed by the Hindu scriptures were designed to bring about the *moral* purity of the individual. Perhaps, however, the greatest virtue a Hindu might practice is renunciation or detachment from all ties to this material world. This includes detachment from the good as well as the evil things of the world.

Hinduism synthesizes the spiritual and material ways of life by advising man to renounce the passion and attachment which accompany action, but not action itself. It believes that the renunciation of all earthly matters, along with an exclusive preoccupation with the contemplation of spiritual matters, can be reconciled with the individual's responsibility to participate in the affairs of his community and society. The Hindu ideal is to be in the world, yet not of the world; to act in the world, yet not be attached to these acts, or their results. When one works without attachment, no new karma is created. Thus, the Hindu will further the progress of his society and the liberation of himself at the same time.

CHAPTER 9

BUDDHISM

> *No village law, no law of market town,*
> *No law of a single house is this—*
> *Of all the world and all the worlds of gods*
> *This only is the law, that all things are impermanent.*

Buddhism, unlike Hinduism, traces its origin to a definite historical period and a single founder. Historical Buddhism was founded in the sixth century B.C. by Gautama Buddha, who is often simply called the Buddha or the "Enlightened One." The Pali spelling *Gotama* is frequently substituted for the Sanskrit spelling *Gautama*. Since the Buddha was a prince of the Sakya tribe, he is sometimes referred to as *Buddha Sakyamuni*, i.e., "Buddha Sage of the Sakya Tribe." Much of his life is veiled by the myths that have gradually accumulated over the centuries, but certain aspects of his life are accepted as fact.

Gautama Buddha was the son of a chieftain of the Sakya tribe who ruled an area in the foothills of the Himalayan Mountains which was located within the boundaries of the modern kingdom of Nepal. Trained from childhood in those arts befitting his high station, especially war, he enjoyed all the advantages that power and wealth could procure at that time. He married, and when he reached the age of twenty-nine, his wife had a son called Rahula. The same year Gautama Buddha left his home and family, his wealth and power, and started on a quest that resulted in the founding of a new religion.

Tradition tells us that chance meetings in quick succession with an old man, a sick man, a dead man, and a religious beggar caused Gautama Buddha to realize for the first time the staggering truth

---

Eugene W. Burlingame (trans.), *Buddhist Parables* (New York: Yale University Press, 1922). Used with permission.

that life is filled with misery and decay. The impact of these meetings was all the greater because, up to this time, Gautama's father had sheltered him from the harsh realities of the world. After this sudden awakening, he had no peace of mind but saw himself old while still young, poor while still rich, sick while healthy, and dead while living. This quick fading of happiness and pleasure into old age, suffering, and death troubled him deeply.

Haunted by the universality of suffering, the inevitability of decay, the passing of pleasure, and the brevity of life, he left his home and sought answers from scholars who tutored him in the Vedas and the *Upanishads*, the source of Hindu truths. Unsatisfied, he left them and tried to find answers in the practice of asceticism. Since this life of austerity merely ravaged his body and brought him nothing but a closer view of death and suffering, he rejected asceticism as sterile and unprofitable and began to follow a middle way between the two extremes of pampering and punishing the body. Then, one day, six years after he had begun his search, while sitting in meditation under a tree, he was suddenly enlightened as to the cause of man's suffering and the cure for these sorrows. With this inner illumination, he became the Buddha, or the "Enlightened One." From that time until his death about forty-five years later, he devoted himself to a life of service to his fellow man. He taught others the way he had discovered to escape from a sorrowful existence that had plagued the world for ages beyond count. This way is Buddhism.

BUDDHIST LITERATURE

The teachings of Buddhism are to be found in an extensive literature which was written after Gautama Buddha's death in both the Sanskrit and Pali languages. This literature was supplemented by later writings, largely in Chinese, Tibetan, and Japanese. These are the languages of the people who, together with the people of South and Southeast Asia, responded most enthusiastically to the teachings and practices of Buddhism.

Buddhist literature is grouped around two major schools of Buddhism—*Hinayana* and *Mahayana*. Hinayana, literally "Lesser Vehicle," is sometimes referred to as Southern Buddhism because it is stressed in Ceylon, Burma, and Thailand. Southern Buddhists prefer to use the term *Theravada* instead of Hinayana when referring to the kind of Buddhism they follow. Hinayana or Theravada is more concerned with the literal teaching of Gautama Buddha and demands more of the individual. Mahayana, "Greater Vehicle," is sometimes called Northern Buddhism because it is emphasized in China, Tibet, Japan, and Korea in northern Asia. It appears to be more compassionate and demands less of the individual. Mahayana is concerned more with the example and heart of Gautama Buddha than with his teaching.

The Hinayana canon, written in Pali around 80 B.C., is supposed to be a reliable presentation of Gautama Buddha's original teaching. This canon is known as the *Tripitaka*, or "Three Baskets." The *Basket of Discipline* contains the rules and precepts for members of the Buddhist order. The *Basket of Discourses* consists of discourses given by either Gautama Buddha or one of his disciples and includes the *Dhammapada*, a well-known anthology of Buddhist sayings. The *Basket of Higher Doctrine* contains seven works discussing principles and special doctrines. The Mahayana scriptures, a later development of Buddhist thought, were generally written in Sanskrit. The important works in this school include *Saddharmapundariks*, or "The Lotus of the True Doctrine," and *Sukhavativyuha* or "A Complete Description of the Blessed Land" of Buddha Amitabha. Amitabha Buddha is the compassionate lord of the Western Heaven to whom millions of Buddhists direct their prayers for mercy. *Prajna-paramitas*, "Perfection of Wisdom," is a collection of *sutras* teaching the doctrine of "Emptiness," *Sunyata*. These include *Vajracchediks*, or "Diamond Sutra."

IMPERMANENCE AND CHANGE

Buddhist writings teach that everything is impermanent and constantly changing. All things, animate and inanimate, human and divine, are transitory, momentary phenomena in the universe, mere passing scenes in the moving pictures of life. Gautama Buddha expressed this thought by saying "Whatsoever is an arising thing, all that is a ceasing thing." Not only are all things short-lived, but during their life-span a constant process of change accentuates the fleeting character of their existence. Nothing remains as it is, for every moment witnesses the changing character of all things. The Buddhist refers to this change as the process of becoming. The young men of this generation become the older men of the next generation; the fresh plant of the morning becomes the withered plant of the afternoon; the soaring mountain of this age becomes the lowly hill of a future age. This is the nature of all things. All things are bound to the wheel of change and decay.

MAN IS SOULLESS

Since they consider all things impermanent, the Buddhists logically hold that the individual has no permanent self or soul. He is a creature made up of five *skandhas,* or components. These five components are: (1) the physical body, (2) sensations or feelings, (3) perception, (4) volition or predisposition, (5) consciousness. Man is merely the embodied collection of five components and owes his existence to them. When these components fall apart, the individual dies. The death of the physical body signifies the final dissolution of that particular embodiment of skandhas, and no permanent self or soul lingers on.

Although Gautama Buddha did not believe that a permanent soul or self remained after death, he did teach that something continued, for he believed, like the Hindus, in rebirth or continued existence. It was, in fact, the purpose of the Buddha to free man from the bondage of continued existence. Because he was vague on this point, this part of his doctrine has been explained in various ways. One theory is that man's *karma* continues after death. *Karma* is that moral law of causation by which all the acts of man have their good or bad effects in some future period, generally in another existence.

After the death of an individual, his karma, or the sum of all the good and bad results of his previous acts, enters into another five skandhas which together with the karma will live on as another individual. Karma is the result of actions and operates through skandhas just as electricity operates through metal and air. There are always skandhas being formed to receive karma. The individual lives on because his acts formed the karma which in turn united with five skandhas to create another individual. The present individual is identified with the individual of a former existence through the karma, but not through a soul or self. Viewed in this light, karma is the cause of the continued existence of man, and it will continue to be embodied until enlightenment is attained. The sum total of a man's actions in each existence keeps the wheel of life spinning through each successive existence.

THE FOUR NOBLE TRUTHS

Two major statements were made by the Buddha immediately after he was enlightened under the tree. These are expressed by the Buddhist as the Four Noble Truths and the Noble Eightfold Path. The Four Noble Truths are: (1) suffering is universal; (2) the cause of suffering is desire; (3) the elimination of desire is the cure for suffering; (4) the Noble Eightfold Path is a practical technique of action designed to help man eliminate desire.

The great overwhelming fact of suffering is every man's fate. Pain, sickness, and death are constant reminders of the endless sorrows of the world's people. Even the few pleasures that man sometimes experiences are a cause of suffering, for the realization that all pleasures are transient brings sorrow. Man is condemned to be frustrated until he overcomes ignorance, for every pleasure, impermanent by nature, is merely the beginning of some sorrow. All things are doomed to death and decay, and to oppose this inevitable fate is to suffer inevitable sorrow. These sufferings are multiplied by continued existences, since suffering and existence go hand in hand. Only the termination of this continued existence by means of enlightenment can bring relief from continued suffering.

Desire is the cause of suffering. Desire also causes rebirths into other existences and hence continued suffering. The human heart craves all manner of things, riches and power, health and long life, things existing and things nonexistent. Craving for these things is the cause of suffering because such craving is founded on the hope of permanent satisfaction, either on earth or hereafter, and such permanent satisfaction can never be obtained on earth because change is man's fate, nor in heaven because the gods are subject to the same law of impermanence and change as are men. Besides, the individual has no self or soul which continues after death. The only way to avoid suffering and continued existence is to crush all desires and sever all earthly attachments. The man who has suppressed all his desires for permanent satisfaction, for existence, for individuality, will become an Enlightened One—a Buddha. When a man is enlightened, when he realizes that impermanence, change, and suffering are the rule of individual existence, he understands that there is no self and that man must learn to dispel this illusion of self if he is to be free. When he comprehends fully the permanence of impermanence and change, he is ready to enter into that indescribable state of "Thusness" by which the Buddhists describe *Nirvana*.

To reach Nirvana is the goal of all men. Nirvana has been described as a state of desirelessness and impersonal ultimate reality, but actually it is a state or condition that only those who have reached Buddhahood can completely comprehend. Literally, the term *Nirvana* means "extinction." One who has attained Nirvana has no desire of the senses, no craving for life, but an enlightened understanding of the nature of man and the universe.

Like the Hindus of his day, Gautama Buddha believed that salvation meant escaping to Nirvana. The flame blown out by the wind no longer exists; nor does the person exist who has been liberated from name and body. He is then beyond the Wheel of Life and is superior to any god who is still tied to continued existences. The destruction of desires breaks the karma-chain of continued existences, and to sever the karma-chain is to discontinue the existences of the individual and his suffering. The mind approaching Nirvana has attained to extinction of all desires.

THE NOBLE EIGHTFOLD PATH

Gautama Buddha was a practical man. He gave man certain ethical guides and commandments to help him destroy all desires, escape the tragedy of life, and reach his final goal of Nirvana. Desire is suppressed by following the Noble Eightfold Path of ethical conduct and mental discipline. These precepts consist of (1) right knowledge, or a knowledge of suffering, its cause and elimination, and the absence of superstition or delusion; (2) right aspirations, or high and worthy intentions; (3) right speech, characterized by kindness, frankness, and truthfulness; (4) right conduct, which is peace-loving, pure, and honest behavior; (5) right livelihood, or practicing an occupation that does not injure any living thing; (6) right effort, or making an effort in self-training; (7) right mindfulness, or having an active, alert mind; and (8) right meditation.

Gautama Buddha did not teach a Godhead or even a real future life for the individual. Gods and heavens were subject to the same laws as all the universe, and therefore could provide little satisfaction for man. They could not help man, for they too were impermanent and subject to change. Buddha was greater than any god. In fact, Buddha considered any speculations about the Godhead and the nature of God as a waste of time. His doctrine compelled man to walk alone in working out his salvation; it denied him all help from any supposed God or gods as well as a future heaven.

THE SPREAD OF BUDDHISM

Buddhism spread rapidly after the Buddha's death. Asoka (296-237 B.C.), a famous Indian emperor who was converted to Buddhism, devoted a great part of his life to the propagation of Buddhist doctrines. He sent missionaries to many parts of the world. Gradually, all India and the neighboring island of Ceylon were converted. Then Buddhism spread eastward and southeastward to the present lands of Burma, Thailand, Laos, Cambodia, Vietnam, and Indonesia. It entered China during the first century of the Christian era and became an integral part of Chinese life. During the seventh century A.D., Buddhism entrenched itself in Japan with the conversion of Prince Shotoku Taishi. During the eighth century, Buddhist missionaries introduced Buddhism into Tibet where it took a mixed form called *Tantrism*.

Buddhism still plays a prominent religious role in Asia, except in Pakistan, Indonesia, Malaya, India, and the Philippines. Pakistan, Indonesia, and Malaya are mostly Muslim today, Hinduism in India gradually absorbed Buddhism, and the majority of the Filipinos are Christians. In China, Buddhism is but one of several religions that the Chinese have harmonized. The Chinese are Buddhists, Taoists, and Confucianists at the same time. In Japan, Buddhism shares her religious role with Shinto, an indigenous religion.

In both China and Japan, Buddhism is divided into various sects which give different interpretations of Buddhist doctrine. Many of these sects had their origin in China and were later carried over to Japan. There is no question, however, that Buddhism has greatly influenced the ethical and artistic development of all the areas it has penetrated.

CHAPTER 10

SOCIAL LIFE IN INDIA

A surging river of new ideas and new practices is threatening the traditional social life of India. National and international events are impinging upon the daily lives of the people with increasing regularity and demanding change. But the people are resisting, for attitudes and customs buttressed by thousands of years of tradition are not easily overturned. Consciously or unconsciously, willingly or unwillingly, the Indian people today are in the process of meeting a challenge to their traditional social life, a challenge which they can neither completely accept nor completely reject. They are trying to adapt and absorb it in much the same manner in which they accommodated other alien challenges over the many centuries of India's past.

Change is evident in India—particularly in the cities—but the old social ways are still cherished and the new has not yet usurped the place of the old. Many of the traditional social institutions and customs endure with their vigor undiminished and their hold upon the people unbroken. To ignore their customary social life is to ignore and misunderstand the Indian people. To be unappreciative of the Indians' longing to preserve what has been held dear for many centuries is to be insensitive to the wellsprings of the Indian heart. The modern may be necessary and rational, but for many Indian people the old is necessary and sacred.

Change may not be wanted, but it is often necessary if a people are to move forward rapidly in their social, economic, and political development. Although the traditional caste system into which most of the Indian people are gathered is regarded as basic to Hindu society, and its perpetuation held a sacred duty, many Indian leaders believe it to be one of the greatest obstacles to the unification of the nation. Caste, with its rigid segregation of groups, tends to keep people apart rather than bring them together. One of the primary goals of the modern leaders of India is to unify the nation, because they realize that any substantial and rapid progress is contingent upon the united efforts of all, and they are patiently—sometimes impatiently—trying to moderate the divisive tendencies of communal groupings and harmonize their differences. Gandhi gave a spiritual and moral encouragement to this harmony when he bestowed upon the Untouchables—the outcastes of India—the name "Children of God" and pleaded that they be treated with more tolerance and respect by the more fortunate castes. Some leveling of the high barriers of caste will undoubtedly quicken India's progress toward the goal of a completely united people.

The family is also a basic social institution of India, and it is cherished and protected by laws, written and unwritten, customs, attitudes, and religion, which all combine to uphold its sanctity and integrity. Formerly in India its importance was vivified by the custom of estimating the population of an area in numbers of families rather than in numbers of individuals. Traditionally it was a large household, rooted deeply in the soil, and requiring many hands to wrest a living from the land. It was a *joint family,* for members joined together in eating, in worshipping, and in holding property. Today a great many Indians still live and die within the secure embrace of such families, but a growing number do not. The exodus of people from the farming communities to the city, the absorption of many villagers into factories and plants, the advancement of education and the movement of the educated young into professions and skilled occupations, are taking large numbers from the traditional families and causing them to form new and smaller families that are more suitable to their physical environment and economic condition. The traditional family is still the pattern for large areas of India, but other family patterns are evolving in response to the changing times.

Greater opportunities and new national and international demands are broadening the scope of the traditional role of women in India. Obedience, sacrifice, and service still characterize the role of women in India, but many now render service to the community, the nation, and the world, not merely to their own home and family. Indian women are reaping the benefits of their country's new emphasis on education, and their horizons are no longer limited to home and village. It is true that the vast majority of Indian women are still devoting their whole efforts to the family and the home, but the number working in broader domains is increasing daily.

The traditional social life of the people has not been radically changed for most Indians, but all have been affected by the new forces to some degree. The absorptive talent of the Indians is at work, and when the process of adaptation is finished, if it ever is, the result will also be something new, and something Indian.

CHAPTER 11

CASTE IN INDIA

It is better to do one's duty badly than another's well.
—MANU X, 97

Caste is a word used to describe the system of social groupings into which most of the people of India are gathered. The Indian community is composed of a large number of distinct social groups, or castes. Basic to Hindu society, the caste system is the result of the association of many different types of people and numerous social and occupational groups within a common territory and cultural system.

It developed over a long period and in various ways. When the fair-skinned Aryans conquered North India around 1500 B.C., they introduced into Indian society a class division based on physical differences. The fair Aryans became the superior class; the darker-skinned aborigines were reduced to an inferior position in society. In the course of time other people entered India and took over a higher or lower place in the social system depending upon their power. Groups were also distinguished by their occupations and professions. Since people tend to associate largely with members of their occupation, early in Indian history classes were differentiated on the basis of function and work. From these occupational groupings there developed group customs, group attitudes, and a keen feeling of group solidarity which set the members of each occupation apart from other members of the Indian community.

Castes grew out of religious differences. Some were formed by breaking off from other castes, while others were formed by outcastes who had lost their own caste status for one reason or another. Primitive tribes responded to the more sophisticated economic and social system developing around them in India by holding themselves aloof and further emphasizing their own peculiar taboos and customs. At times some of these tribes became low-caste Hindus, entering the caste system as a body.

A complicated social system arose out of the associations of these physical, political, occupational, religious, and tribal separations. The Indian community divided into many distinct sections now referred to as castes. During the long course of India's history these castes grew and multiplied, as a continuous flow of new physical types, occupations, and other foreign elements had to be allocated a place somewhere within the community. Castes died out and new castes formed, but always the caste system remained the basis of the social order.

SOCIAL HIERARCHY

Castes are arranged on a social scale rising from the Untouchables at the bottom to the Brahmins at the top. It is not always easy to fix the exact place of each caste on the scale, but Hindu society can be viewed broadly as a grouping of castes in different layers of the social strata. Three great caste groupings may be distinguished— the twice-born group, the once-born group, and the Untouchables.

The twice-born include the Brahmin, or priestly caste; the *Rajputs* and those who claim descent from the *Kshatriya*, or military caste; and the *Vaisya*, or mercantile and agricultural caste. These are the elite castes of India. The Brahmin caste traditionally ranks first among this group and its members are generally regarded with honor. This group is called twice-born because its members have two births, a physical birth when they are born into the world and a spiritual birth when they are initiated into the mysteries of religion and given the sacred thread to wear. The sacred thread is a kind of string which is looped over and hangs from the left shoulder. The Brahmin's thread should be made of cotton, a Kshatriya's of hemp, and a Vaisya's of wool.

The once-born, or those who lack the second spiritual birth, are those castes who claim to be the modern representatives of the *Sudras*. Traditionally, the Sudras were supposed to serve the twice-born, but today this function is no longer descriptive. The members of this group are engaged in all kinds of skilled and unskilled work which has no connotation of service to the twice-born. This group includes people ranging from farmers, artisans, landlords, and moneylenders, to those engaged in all types of unskilled labor.

Untouchables constitute the lowest social layer of the Indian community. They were formerly known as the Depressed Classes, and are now officially called the Scheduled Castes. Gandhi called them *Harijans,* or the "Children of God." The Untouchable, as the name indicates, cannot touch anything without contaminating it. Belief in the contaminating power of an Untouchable is so great that, in South India, a scale of distances was worked out within which different groups of Untouchables may not approach a Brahmin. For example, one kind of Untouchable may not come within eight yards of a Brahmin, another twelve yards, and still another sixteen yards. The members of this group perform those jobs which the Hindus consider most degrading. Caring for and touching the dead, removing filth, sweeping, and working with leather.

Within each of these broad groups of twice-born, once-born, and Untouchables there is also an inner hierarchy. The Brahmin is the highest caste of the twice-born group and therefore at the apex of all the castes of India. The Rajputs and the present-day representatives of the Kshatriyas rank second, and the Vaisyas and their representatives rank third. The caste rank of the once-born is often determined by the relationship of a particular caste within this group to the twice-born. Generally speaking, the closer the relationship to the twice-born, the higher the rank of the caste within the once-born group. Thus, caste rank might be specifically indicated by the twice-born's acceptance or refusal of water and food from a particular caste member of the once-born group. Whether or not a member of a caste within the once-born group can touch one of the twice-born is also a criterion for judging the rank of that caste. The Untouchables are divided into a bewildering number of castes organized on a graduated social scale. The gap between the lower and higher castes of the Untouchable group is regarded by the members of this group as being as great as that between the Untouchables and the Brahmins.

The various castes are further divided into smaller divisions called subcastes. The members of these subcastes generally follow the same pattern of social life and use the same food and drink as the main caste. However, the subcastes are essentially exclusive social groups. Sometimes they are so exclusive that they consider themselves as separate castes. Subcastes are often further divided into smaller groups which have their own special rules and regulations. The factionalizing of Indian society has sometimes been carried to unbelievable extremes.

Membership in a subcaste or smaller subdivision may determine an individual's position in the main caste, but it is the main caste which determines his position in the Indian society. The subcaste conditions a member's relations with those who belong to the main caste, but it has little influence upon his relations with other main castes in the Indian community.

PRINCIPAL CHARACTERISTICS OF CASTE

The principal characteristics of the caste system are: (1) members marry within the caste; (2) caste members eat and drink with each other and not with members of an inferior caste; (3) members practice a common occupation which is generally hereditary. Exceptions to all these characteristics can be found in India, especially with regard to the practice of a common occupation.

Marriage within the caste is the regulation most rigorously enforced today. Should a man or woman marry outside the caste, he or she may be expelled from the caste and become an outcaste, a most terrible fate for an Indian. He is generally ostracized by his clan members and often by his own family. He has less security than the members of the lowest caste, and he is often shunned and insulted by other Indians. The marriage of a woman to a member of a caste inferior to her own is considered an unnatural act, and even her parents are liable to be reduced to the inferior caste into which their daughter has married. A girl can marry a man of equal rank or a man of superior caste. The latter practice is known as "marrying up," or *hypergamy*. A high caste man may sometimes marry down, but the female may marry only with her equals or superiors. Because of this restriction, it is often difficult to find suitable husbands for daughters, and parents are often forced to expend great sums of money on dowries in order to obtain suitable matches.

Hindu law permits concubinage, especially when the wife is barren. Concubines may be taken from outside the caste, provided the castes they come from are clean. High-caste males may also take mistresses, provided these women are members of castes from which they may accept water and that these mistresses do not cook their food or eat with them. It should be noted that these practices are frowned upon by Indian leaders today.

Many of the young educated Indians today have no personal objection to marrying outside their castes, but the social pressure on their own and the girl's families are so great that they hesitate to do so. They resolve the conflict by marrying someone chosen by their parents who has also met their own approval. Intellectually, they reject the convention that forces such a marriage arrangement, but they conform because it is the practical thing to do under the circumstances.

Marriage outside the subcaste is much more common today than formerly. Although such a practice is generally frowned upon, it does not bear the same stigma as marriage outside the main caste. The furor over a marriage outside the subcaste often dies down after a short period of time, but the social ostracism that results from a marriage outside the main caste is permanent.

There is some change taking place in India. Some modern Indians are marrying outside their castes. It is not uncommon to see newspaper advertisements, inserted by Indians who are looking for mates, frankly stating that caste is no obstacle to marriage. A typical advertisement of this kind will read:

Matrimonial

Good match for handsome, highly qualified Brahmin,
27. Class I officer. Monthly income over rupees two
thousand. *Caste no bar*. Girl main consideration.

In studies made among college students it was found that one-half of the Brahmins and four-fifths of the non-Brahmins approved of marriage outside of caste. It must be remembered that these were college students and, as such, represent a very small minority of the Indian population.

EATING AND DRINKING

As a general rule, orthodox Hindus are required to dine with members of their caste only. The eating and drinking of the orthodox Hindu is carefully governed by regulations which apply to the food itself, the persons who cook the food, the hands which serve the food, and the company with whom the food may be eaten.

The kind of food that the Hindu is permitted to eat varies with locality and caste. The Brahmin does not eat animal food or drink alcoholic beverages. Other castes frequently eat the meat of animals, especially mutton and goat's flesh. Most of the low castes in India are vegetarians, but this is a matter of necessity and not of choice. Most of them are too poor to buy meat.

The great majority of the Hindus will not eat the meat of the cow or peacock because they consider these animals sacred. The monkey is also honored and protected in many parts of India. The cow is revered by the Indians, and they commonly and lovingly refer to her as their "Mother." It is impossible for a Hindu to eat the flesh of a being he regards with such veneration and love. "May you eat beef!" is the worse curse one Hindu can fling at another.

Kachchi—Hedged with Regulations. Most of the restrictions with regard to the preparation of food and the company with whom the food may be eaten apply to the food known as *kachchi*. Kachchi is food, such as boiled rice, peas, beans, and wheat cakes, which is cooked in water. These items make up the daily food of the orthodox Hindu.

When preparing kachchi food, great care must be taken lest even the shadow of an Untouchable fall upon the food and defile it. If this should happen, the food is immediately thrown away. Should it be touched by an unclean caste, a European for instance, it is also thrown away. Foreigners in India have had the embarrassing experience of having even the lowest castes refuse to accept food from their impure hands. No orthodox Hindu will accept food from a European, or from a Muslim for that matter. The orthodox Hindu will eat with no one who is not a member of his caste or subcaste. If he cannot cook his own kachchi food, he must find a member of his own caste or subcaste or a Brahmin, who will prepare it for him. Brahmins are regarded as sanctified people and they do not defile the food. In fact, to have a Brahmin serve a caste is a sign of that caste's respectability. For this reason Brahmins are much in demand as cooks. It is common to find Brahmin cooks in the various prisons of India because only a Brahmin cook is satisfactory to all the prisoners.

Before he eats, the orthodox Hindu bathes his feet and hands carefully. Some eat with their waist bared; others eat completely stripped with the exception of a loincloth. Stories are told of orthodox Hindus who, even in the coldest weather, took off their clothes, bathed, and ate half-naked, exposed to the raw forces of nature.

Pakki—Less Regulated. There is another kind of food called *pakki* which is less susceptible to contamination. Pakki is food which is cooked in *ghee,* or clarified butter—butter that has been liquefied by boiling—and not boiled in water. It includes such foods as parched grains, curds, fruits, and sweets. This type of food can be eaten without much fear of contamination because it has been purified by being cooked with ghee, a product of Mother Cow. It can be eaten even after it has been touched by members of a caste regarded as clean but not, of course, after being touched by unclean castes. This is the kind of food which the orthodox Hundu traveler eats. It is jokingly said that Hinduism has one kind of food for the traveler and another kind for the Hindu who stays at home.

Other Ways of Pollution. Sea voyages pollute the orthodox Hindu because they make pure water unavailable. The orthodox will accept water only from those castes whose touch does not pollute it. The only type of water so holy that it cannot be polluted by any hands is water from the sacred river Ganges. Few can carry enough of the Ganges water to suffice for the entire ocean trip, and consequently many Hindus are polluted and lose caste by going abroad. When an orthodox Hindu returns from abroad, the caste may require that he perform purification ceremonies.

A Hindu can be polluted by having something unclean come in contact with his mouth. For this reason the Hindu will not lick gum or postage stamps, use toothbrushes made of pig's bristles, or smoke the water pipe of one who is not of his caste. The *hookah,* or water pipe, is a symbol of caste intimacy. Indians refer to the state of an outcaste as the condition of being cut off from smoking and drinking with caste members.

EATING AND DRINKING TODAY

Industrialization and education have done much to relax the attitudes of orthodox Hindus with regard to eating and drinking.

Industrialization has created conditions which make the observance of food regulations extremely difficult. The building of factories which employ all kinds of castes and throw them helter-skelter together is one of these conditions. Industrialization is bringing increasing urbanization to India, and it is difficult to continue these elaborate ceremonial practices while away from home and living in a large urban area. The necessity of living in hotels and eating in public restaurants has accelerated the relaxation of Hindu eating habits. It is also difficult to avoid breaking caste rules when traveling on trains, ships, or planes. It is generally recognized that anyone who goes to a hospital for treatment must use hospital equipment. Spoons, glasses, instruments, which naturally have been used by other patients, do not defile the orthodox Hindu who has been hospitalized.

In a sample study of college students four out of five indicated that they would be willing to dine with anybody regardless of caste or religion. Again, it must be remembered that the views of college students are more liberal and rational than those of the majority.

OCCUPATIONS

Throughout the long history of India there has generally been some degree of craft-exclusiveness between castes. It is not uncommon even today to have an Indian give his occupation when asked to what caste he belongs.

In the self-contained and self-supporting villages of India, certain occupations are recognized as inherited caste callings. It is expected that at least one son of the family belonging to such a functional caste will follow in his father's footsteps and take up the caste trade. Such occupational groups include, among others, blacksmiths, barbers, potters, and washermen.

But caste is no longer a definite indication of a person's occupation. Rarely is a person's work equated with a certain caste. Any Hindu engaged in priestly duties is most likely a Brahmin, and any Indian found washing clothes, at least in North India, is most probably a *Dhobi*. However, modern Brahmins are to be found today working in a great variety of occupations ranging from soldiering, police work, mail carrying, and work as messengers, to cooking and farming. Thus, although a man may be a Brahmin, he is not necessarily engaged in priestly work.

The increase in India's population and industrialization has led many Indians to desert the occupation of their forefathers. Over a long period of time too many people became occupied with making one product, with the result that the supply soon outstripped the demand, and the occupation would no longer support the number of people engaged in making the product. Also, the increasing number of cheap, machine-made products flooding India's markets has forced many of the native products off the market and abolished many trades and crafts. This process has forced many Indian artisans and craftsmen to seek other occupations.

Education and the ambition of lower castes to rise higher on the caste hierarchy have also affected occupational patterns in India. Many of the lower castes can elevate their status only by changing the character of their occupations. Any caste which deals with leather goods, sweeps the streets, or takes care of the dead must change its occupation to something else, say agriculture, if it wants to escape the low esteem in which it is held. Many castes have altered their standing in this manner, and this is another reason why castes and subcastes are continually forming and changing in India. Education is opening up more areas of work for the young Indian of today. India needs engineers, technicians, teachers, doctors, nurses, chemists, physicists, and a host of skilled workmen to man the modern state. The leaders of India are encouraging young men and women to embark upon these new careers and thus leading the younger generations even further from the traditional paths of their fathers.

Although there are still a number of functional castes in India which have hereditary tradition, many of the members of these castes no longer take up hereditary occupations. There is no obligation to do so at the present time. Modern Indians are entering those occupations which promise them rewards, not merely those formerly practiced by their fathers.

CASTE GOVERNMENT

The caste governs itself. It is an autonomous unit within Indian society which makes its own laws—many of them unwritten—and enforces them. The caste decides who will be members and who will not. It is the caste which expels members for one reason or another, and it is the caste which decides whether or not these members will be reaccepted into caste membership. The caste judges and condemns and the caste fixes the penalty for each offense.

The caste is commonly governed by a council composed of caste elders, prominent members, and a headman. Although the headman is sometimes elected, the office is more often hereditary. This governing body is called a *panchayat*. The number of members of this council is not fixed but varies from caste to caste. Generally there are as many councils as there are subcastes. The number of caste councils is determined by such factors as the amount of interdining and intermarriage, the size of the area, the availability of transportation, and the number of caste members. For instance, there may be several caste councils where the members are numerous and located over a large area.

Although the caste council performs executive and legislative functions, it is mainly concerned with judicial duties, and most of its time is spent in hearing cases. It sits as a tribunal with the headman presiding as judge and the directorate acting as a jury. Most of the cases brought before it are concerned with marriage, eating and drinking, improper performance of ceremonial requirements, smoking with men of another caste, and breaking one or more of the caste's innumerable social and religious regulations. Penalties fixed run from the very harsh to the very mild. The harshest penalty is expulsion from the caste. If the expulsion is permanent, the unfortunate man is condemned to a life of isolation and misery on earth. On his death he may be deprived of the spiritual ministrations of the Brahmin priest which ensure him against wandering for ages as a disembodied spirit hereafter. If his expulsion is temporary, he may be restored by performing certain purification ceremonies. Fines are sometimes imposed, as are painful ordeals like begging for food, being beaten with sticks, walking with heavy stones around the neck, and being exposed to ridicule.

The caste councils maintain strict discipline and watch their members carefully. Because of the close relationship that necessarily exists among the various members of the caste, it is comparatively easy to find out even minor infractions of caste regulations. The life of caste members is somewhat analogous to the glass-house existence of people living in small towns. Lower castes are much stricter in the enforcement of caste regulations than higher castes and much better organized in the government and regulation of caste affairs.

THE FUTURE OF CASTE IN INDIA

During lengthy periods of chaos and disorganization, the caste system gave India a stability and continuity essential to the survival of its civilization. No matter under what alien king or conqueror the Indian was forced to live, he maintained his loyalty and devotion to the caste and in this way preserved Indian culture.

Caste has also given meaning and direction to the lives of the Indian people. Hindu writers often view caste as a co-operative rather than a competitive institution. For each man there is a special place in the community and a special function to perform. The acts performed by a man in a previous existence have determined his special place and duties, and caste provides a framework within which these particular duties can be carried out conveniently and co-operatively.

Nationalism has influenced modern Indian attitudes toward caste structure. It is urging people to stop thinking of themselves as belonging exclusively to a caste or subcaste and to think of themselves instead as primarily citizens of the Indian nation. Rabindranath Tagore wrote as follows:

> Nationalists say, for example, look at Switzerland, where, in spite of race differences, the peoples have solidified into a nation. Yet, remember that in Switzerland the races can mingle, they can intermarry, because they are of the same blood. In India there is no common birth-right. And when we talk of Western Nationality we forget that the nations there do not have that physical repulsion, one for the other, that we have between different castes. Have we an instance in the whole world where a people who are not allowed to mingle their blood, shed their blood for one another except by coercion or for mercenary purposes? And can we ever hope that these moral barriers against our race amalgamation will not stand in the way of our political unity?

Virtues such as loyalty, obedience, and devotion to the caste, which in the past helped to preserve India's cultural values and institutions, are now considered an obstacle in the path of India's unification. It is difficult to create a united nation while Indian society is divided. Therefore, Indian leaders argue, caste must go because it is delaying the growth of India into a modern nation-state. Modern India is dedicated to social progress. As long as millions of Indians are condemned to a lifetime of inferiority and hopeless degradation, declare the Indian leaders, there can be no real social progress in India. No society can make great social advances while millions of its members are segregated. These are the major reasons why many Indians think of caste as now being detrimental to the nation and society of India. The new constitution of India forbids discrimination because of caste.

The caste system of India is a living institution. Caste is not a rigid, unchanging system; it is a flexible system. It has survived because it has shown the ability to adapt to changing circumstances. The caste system is undergoing a radical change today in response to the shifting environment of the present time. Its religious or metaphysical rationalization cannot endure unchanged in an industrial, scientific age. Modern times demand new forms of social organization. Caste will remain at the basis of social life of India for a long time to come, but it will be a changed and changing system.

CHAPTER 12

THE FAMILY IN INDIA

With their teeth half-shown in causeless laughter,
And their efforts at talking so sweetly uncertain,
When children ask to sit on his lap
A man is blessed, even by the dirt of their bodies.
—KALIDASA

The Indian family is part of the larger caste group. The family is basic to the caste, serving as the mechanism for enforcing the numerous caste regulations. In the family, caste members first learn their caste duties and are imbued with the caste spirit. It is the family which watches carefully over the actions of the members and warns and exerts various pressures when the individuals of the family tend to stray beyond the caste limits.

THE JOINT FAMILY

The family in India generally consists of parents, their married sons with their wives and children, all unmarried children, and sometimes other dependents such as aged parents, uncles, cousins, nephews, and brothers. This kind of family is commonly called a *joint family* because the family members join together in eating, in worshipping, and in holding property.

The average number of persons living in an Indian family is about six or seven, though in any given family there may be as many as fifty or more members and as few as two.

Common Property and Worship. Ancestral, and generally immovable, property is held in common. Family members are supposed to pool their resources and income, thus creating a common fund out

Poem by Kalidasa reprinted from A. L. Basham, *The Wonder That Was India,* copyright 1954 by Sidgwick and Jackson, Ltd., London. Reprinted by permission of Sidgwick and Jackson and Hawthorn Books, Inc., 70 Fifth Avenue, New York.

of which each is given what is required for living purposes. The head of the family, generally the oldest male, is responsible for the supervision of the common property and finances. He does receive advice as to the disposition of the common property from other family members, especially the adult males. Though extremely powerful, he is restrained by sacred law and custom from making any use of the common property that might impoverish his descendants or the present individuals in the family.

From the earliest times provision has been made for the division of the common family property. In such close association of several families, quarrels, jealousies, suspicions, and envious comparisons are bound to arise, which may eventually culminate in demands to divide the family property among the members. When such divisions occur, the families split into individual units and become the creators of new joint families.

Individuals within the family may sometimes own property in their own right. Gifts, personal earnings, and jewelry may belong exclusively to the individual and not be included in the common fund. The jewelry that a bride has received from her parents and others customarily remains her personal property and cannot be taken from her.

Males of the joint family worship together. Sons, grandsons, great-grandsons, and others join together in commemorating their ancestors in a religious ceremony called *Sraddha*. This ceremony is extremely old and is similar to Chinese ancestor worship in that it links the living and the dead. Sraddha is another method of determining membership in a family group. Those entitled to participate in this ceremony by offering rice-balls are regarded as genuine members of the family.

Headship and Responsibility. When the oldest male is too old or handicapped to remain as head, his eldest son assumes his position. If the grandmother is still alive, she often exerts tremendous influence, holding more authority than her eldest son and his wife, though technically and formally the headship descends in the male line.

Although the head of an Indian family carries great authority, he also bears great responsibility. From early childhood the individual has found his whole being and purpose revolving around family life. He has been indoctrinated with the necessity of preserving and

continuing the family line. He finds it almost impossible to with-
stand the dictates of family duty even when this duty conflicts absolutely with his own ambitions. There are several instances of young
Indians who gave up promising careers in order to take up family
responsibilities. A brilliant young student had a magnificent future
in psychology, but he was forced to give it up in order to ensure
the future of his family. As the new head of a family he was compelled to undertake a career in business so that the family might
have more income. Sacrificing his own future, he thus provided
more opportunities for the other members of the family. Another
promising young Indian retained his position as a clerk rather than
jeopardize his family's financial state by taking time off for future
studies.

MARRIAGE AND FAMILY

Attitudes and customs with regard to marriage also indicate the
importance of the family and the subordination of individual interests to its interests.

Marriage is thought of primarily in terms of protecting and preserving the basic family unit. It is not considered a private affair
of romantic passion between two individuals but a family matter
in which the individual has little, if any, choice. Traditionally, the
bride and bridegroom do not see each other until the marriage ceremony itself. In India, unlike Europe and America, love is supposed
to follow rather than precede marriage.

Because marriage is so essential to the preservation of the family, it is looked upon as a serious duty. Hindu parents have an obligation to find suitable mates for their children. Even though the
head of the family is not a parent of the unmarried members, he
still bears the responsibility of finding spouses for them.

The force of this obligation is so great that a Hindu family will
often go into heavy debt in order to marry off a daughter. The expensive wedding of a high-caste Hindu is borne almost entirely by
the bride's family. The social status of the bride's family generally
determines the amount of her dowry, and a high-caste son-in-law is
a high-priced item. He is expensive because there is no real necessity for him to marry early, whereas Indian girls are generally married off at an early age. In the past it was not uncommon for boys
of ten to thirteen years of age to marry girls two or three

years younger, though of course there were times when they married older girls. In 1929 the Child Marriage Act was passed making it a criminal offense to arrange the marriage of a girl before she was fourteen or a boy before he was eighteen. In 1949 the Child Marriage Restraint Act raised the girls' marriage age from fourteen to fifteen. Many Indians circumvent these marriage laws by betrothing their daughters at an early age. Betrothal is tantamount to marriage. Since unmarried daughters are a continuous drain on the family resources that offers no hope of a return, Indian families are especially eager to marry them off early. The author has conversed with many Asian fathers and prospective fathers on the economic disadvantages of a daughter. A typical conversation with an expectant father might run something like this:

Prospective father: I hope it is a boy.
Author: Why not a girl?
Prospective father: It is better to have a boy. A girl is of little future value to the house. I must feed her, clothe her, take care of her, and then marry her off to another family. Her marriage costs me money too because I must give her a trousseau and make a feast. What do I get in return for all this money I have spent on her! Nothing. She may even come back and ask for more things if the husband's family is poor or stingy. No, I want a boy. He will stay home and work and, when I am old, care for me.

Many modern educated Indians have emphasized the necessity of decreasing the amount of money that is spent for wedding ceremonies, especially among high-caste Indians. The fact that certain wealthy men have agreed to keep the wedding expenses within one year's income of the bride's father gives some indication of the vast amounts that are expended in marriage ceremonies and practices. Among some of the lower castes this situation is reversed, and the bridegroom must pay a dowry to the bride's father.

Since the customs and ceremonies relating to marriage arrangements and weddings are regarded as important to the security of the basic family unit in India, the community demands their continuance, even though these customs place a tremendous financial burden on some families. This is another revealing instance of the importance of the family institution in India. No sacrifice is too great to maintain it.

Marriages in India are usually arranged between families with the help of a middle-man. In India, as in China, these middle-men help families find suitable mates for their children and carry on all the many financial, religious, social, and other negotiations which are necessary to bring the marriage to a successful conclusion. The rise of cities has complicated the task of finding spouses, but the problem is partially met by the newspapers, which carry daily columns of matrimonial advertisements.

Generally speaking, whether the young man or woman is found by means of a middle-man or a newspaper, certain conditions must be met. There is the all-important question of caste. Does the prospective mate belong to a caste into which the boy or girl can marry? What kind of family does the individual come from? Is it respectable? What is its economic condition? A family too rich or too poor can present complications for the future. Does the family live nearby? Indians, especially those in villages, prefer the in-laws to live somewhere in the neighborhood. Since the passage of the new laws regarding age, the age of the prospective mates is also an important consideration. All-important is the matter of comparing horoscopes. When a Hindu child is born, the position of the stars is plotted and a horoscope drawn up by an astrologer. Prior to the final decision the horoscopes of the boy and girl are compared by a Brahmin teacher or learned man. If the two horoscopes favor a union between the two young people, the marriage can take place without fear of dire consequences. Finally, financial arrangements must be fixed, including arrangements regarding time and form of payment.

It is only after all these questions have been settled that a marriage can be held. Throughout the negotiations the individuals to be married have usually not been consulted. This is not their affair; this is a family affair. The heads of the two families, with the advice of their wives and other adult members, carry on the negotiations and make the final decision.

Many young modern Indians are following the Western custom of choosing their own wives. However, their number is still small, and the great majority of Indian marriages are being arranged as in the past.

Marriage among Hindus is a tie not easily broken, especially if they belong to the middle or high castes. The high-caste Hindu will do everything possible to prevent the dissolution of a marriage. Such an attitude was especially characteristic of traditional India. Even in the case of a woman caught in adultery, the old Hindus thought it better to punish her severely than to divorce her. The stability and permanence of the family is still valued too highly by the majority of Indians to have it broken by divorce.

Nevertheless, the number of divorces is increasing. Separation by divorce was legalized under certain conditions by the Bombay Divorce Act of 1947. The new proposed Hindu Code Bill allows for divorce proceedings, but divorce remains rare.

CHILDREN AND THE FAMILY

The child is living evidence of the successful continuation of the family. He is the important result of a duty well done. The families who arranged the marriage, the couple who participated in the marriage, have accomplished their aim—the extension of the family by the procreation of children. The child represents a link with the future as well as the past. In the faces of their children the family sees the creators of other families and a long, long line of other generations stretching endlessly into the future. The child is the happiness of the family.

A child is primarily a member of a family and only secondarily the specific offspring of a specific couple. He is responsible to a group, not merely to one or two individuals. For this reason relationships within the family are often quite blurred for the child. If his father has more than one wife, the child might refer to all the wives as mother. He uses the same word for both brothers and paternal cousins. The child might be as close to his aunt as to his real mother, and he looks upon all females as having the same functions in the family. He finds happiness and security within the wide embrace of the large Indian family. Loved and cherished by the entire family, wrapped in great protective layers of affection, he develops a sense of security which never leaves him throughout life. The male child is especially cherished and favored by the Indian family.

At this time the child imbibes a sense of responsibility and obligation toward the family which never really leaves him. It is not uncommon in India, or elsewhere in Asia, to see children of five or six taking care of even younger children. The teaching of the individual's duties with regard to the family starts early, and fundamental to all these duties is the preservation, stability, and continuation of the Indian family.

CHAPTER 13

THE WOMAN OF INDIA

> As a general rule the horizon of the Indian woman is bound by the four walls of her courtyard. She is taught the truth that the highest ideal of life is service, but to her so often that means only service to her husband and her family.
>
> —G. S. DUTT

The Indian woman leads a life of obedience, sacrifice, and service. She is taught from early childhood that she must sacrifice herself for the happiness of others. She thinks little of her own desires, but gives her attention, almost exclusively, to the needs and wants of her parents, her husband, her children, and her community.

The woman of India has both traditional and modern models of ideal womanhood which she is taught to emulate.

TRADITIONAL MODELS: SITA AND SAVITRI

The foremost traditional model of Indian womanhood is Sita, the heroine of India's famous epic the *Ramayana*. "God bless you and may you be another Sita" is the lovely blessing that Indian girls often receive from older women. Sita gave up a comfortable life and followed her husband, Rama, into a jungle exile. She successfully resisted the seductive enticements of the demon-king of Ceylon who had kidnapped her, and after her rescue threw herself on a great fire to prove to Rama her innocence and constancy. Even after her innocence was proved when the fire rejected her, she suffered banishment and social ostracism. It would have been natural for her to have rebelled against her husband for his unjust treatment, but Sita remained a submissive, obedient wife and in all things bowed to the will of her husband. "She did as Rama told" is the crowning compliment paid her by the Indian community.

G. S. Dutt, *A Woman of Bengal, Being the Life of Saroj Nalini* (London: The Hogarth Press, 1929).

Another well-known model of the ideal Indian woman is Savitri. She also gave up high station and wealth and shared a life of exile in the jungle with her husband, Prince Satyavan.

When she married him, she was told that one year from that date he would die. Savitri, a courageous, persistent woman, prayed and fasted during that first year of marriage that the gods might spare her husband's life. She still refused to accept the decree of destiny even after the Lord of Death, Yama, came and separated Satyavan's soul from his body, bound it with a cord, and led it away. Savitri followed Lord Yama, pleaded and argued with him, and refused to stop her stubborn pursuit. Struck by the magnitude of her love and devotion, Lord Yama released the soul of Prince Satyavan and permitted him to return to the world of the living. To this day an Indian bride may be called upon to be another Savitri.

MODERN MODELS: RAMABAI RANADE AND
SAROJ NALINI

Ramabai Ranade, the wife of a prominent Indian official, is a modern model of Indian womanhood whose autobiography reveals a gifted and devoted life. Besides performing her many household tasks, she spent long hours educating herself, primarily to increase and improve her service to her husband. Ramabai sums up her philosophy of life in these words: "A wife's truest obligation is to protect her beloved husband from suffering of any kind at any time. This is her desire throughout her life, and to this she bends every effort in things great or small. This is her blessed privilege and her religious duty." [1]

Saroj Nalini, another modern ideal for the woman of India, made herself into a well-educated woman in order to be of greater service to her husband and to society. She was a devoted wife and mother and loved her husband with self-sacrificing passion. She wrote of him, "I only want your love while I live on earth, and your feet to lay my head on when I pass away."

Saroj Nalini not only provides a model for Indian women to follow in serving their immediate relatives, but also exemplifies for them the new woman who serves the greater community of the na-

---

[1] Ramabai Ranade, *Himself, An Autobiography of a Hindu Lady*, translated by Katherine Gates (New York: David McKay Company, 1938). Used with permission.

tion and the world. Rabindranath Tagore, the great philosopher-
poet of India, stated that the modern ideal is no longer that of the
woman who is merely a housewife and nothing else, "but the
woman who works for the weal of the home and community alike."
He believed that this ideal was realized in Saroj Nalini's life.

SERVICE IN THE HOME

Although increasing numbers of Indian women are giving more
time and effort in the service of their nation, the vast majority of
them still spend most of their energies within the home. It is only a
few highly educated professional women that serve the community
exclusively. Most Indians, especially villagers, still consider marriage
the only respectable career for an Indian woman, and most Indian
girls are taught to look forward to a life of married service. The
1951 census revealed that 61.2 per cent of all females were married
or widows. Between the ages of thirty-five and forty-four only 0.1
per cent of the women remained unmarried.

Even the formal education of Indian girls is designed to prepare
them for marriage. In this transitional period, the husband sometimes wants a bride who can be a companion as well as a manager
of the household and a mother of his children. Consequently, education is often stressed because it helps procure husbands for the
girls. The schools generally reinforce the ideas of obedience, sacrifice, and service with which the girls are first indoctrinated in the
home.

The girl of India is generally well prepared to assume the duties
required of a good wife. She has been well trained in the art of cooking and in the care of the home. Even in homes where there are
servants, wives take great delight in preparing dishes for their husbands and children. Village girls are taught a variety of duties associated with the farming home. One of the first tasks the village
girls are introduced to is the preparation of cow-dung for cooking.
Straw is mixed with dung, stuck against a wall to dry, and
then heaped in piles. Dung makes a good fire and burns with an
intense, smokeless flame. The girls are also taught to husk rice, grind
grains, and help with the harvesting and planting of the fields. Most
girls learn these tasks early, and what they do not learn the mothers-
in-law soon teach them.

The Indian bride must be a virgin. From puberty on she is taught to maintain a certain reserve and distance from all men with the exception of her closest relatives. In traditional India care was taken that the boy and girl did not meet before their marriage, and the girl rarely, if ever, saw her husband prior to the wedding night.

Traditionally, the Indian girl has little choice in picking her husband. It is the duty of the parents to choose a husband; it is the duty of the girl to serve well the husband selected.

Certain changes are evident in modern India. Occasionally, love matches take place but these are the exceptions rather than the rule. Wherever such cases occur, there is often conflict between the young couple and their two families because of the radical break with customary ways. In present-day India, the engaged individuals are shown photos of each other, and sometimes they see each other in person before the marriage night. In the cities, and particularly among the young educated set, betrothed couples go out together, but this practice is still frowned upon. Even after the marriage has taken place, the woman is supposed to maintain a modest demeanor in the presence of men.

THE WOMEN IN THE FAMILY

The position of the woman in the family varies from stage to stage of her existence in the household. Each passing stage of life in the family brings new duties, new responsibilities, and new authority.

When she arrives in the family as a new bride, she is quiet, unobtrusive, and self-effacing. She is expected to show deep respect to the parents of her husband and to observe strict propriety toward her brothers-in-law. She must observe numerous restrictions and regulations. She should not cook or serve rice to the older members of the family. She should not prepare the offerings for ritual worship. Neither she nor her husband should manifest any affection for each other in public. No matter how great the provocation, she must always obey her husband and mother-in-law.

When she becomes a mother, her status changes. She is given a greater amount of freedom and is treated with much more respect. Children are a mark of success. Now she is prized more by the entire family because she has fulfilled her duty as a woman and a wife. Motherhood is revered in India. Gandhi expressed this reverence when he said: "Today the Gita is not only my Bible or my Koran; it is more than that—it is my mother. When a woman becomes a mother, she becomes a goddess. For woman is the eternal field in which the self is born." A woman is proud to be a wife and a mother. She lavishes tender care and devotion on her child, her husband, and her family. The child never forgets the love and care he received from his mother, and the most cherished memories of Indian men revolve around their mothers. There are innumerable examples of self-effacing love of the wife for her husband, and a gentle solicitude for his health and welfare is a quality that suffuses the women of India.

As she grows older in the household, she wins more and more freedom until she may eventually rule the domestic matters of the house. She may assume the position of mother-in-law and have daughters-in-law of her own to rule and teach. She finally attains the fullness of dignity and respect when she becomes the ruling matriarch of the family, and her influence continues to increase with age and experience.

When a woman becomes a widow, she enters a period of sorrow that often endures until her death. Social custom forbids Indian widows to remarry. This custom, formerly applicable to high-caste women, has gradually grown to include all widows, no matter what their caste. Usually this custom does not cause undue hardship to a widow whose children are grown, because she can continue to live, relatively happy, in her own household, surrounded by her children and grandchildren. If, however, she has no children of her own and is still young, she is often unhappy. India has many widows; in 1951 there were about 25 million. An Indian commentator, S. Chandrasekhar, has written: "The paucity of females keeps up the custom of early marriage for girls. Early marriages customarily involve considerable disparity in age between husbands and wives. This difference in age increases widowhood. Since widows cannot remarry, widowhood increases the shortage of eligible brides, which accentuates the paucity of females. Thus the vicious wheel whirls on." [1] The young widow is expected to live a life of severe simplicity. She should wear a white *sari* without a border and never adorn her body with jewelry. She must eat only one meal a day, which is cooked by her alone. This meal should contain no meat, fish, honey, wine, or salt. Perfumes are forbidden, and many

---

[1] S. Chandrasekhar, "The Family in India," *Marriage and Family Living,* Vol. 16, November, 1954, pp. 336-342. Used with permission.

widows cut their hair very short. A widow is expected to spend her time in prayer and meditation and religious exercises. She should not attend the Indian festivals which the Indians enjoy very much, nor should she manifest gaiety or joy. A widow is believed to bring bad luck, and consequently is seldom welcomed by others at their gatherings. She is condemned to a life of austerity, unhappiness, and frustration.

Remarriage of widows has been legalized in India, but the pressure of public opinion operates to prevent such a practice. Virgin widows do occasionally remarry. Marital advertisements appear from time to time in the newspapers stating that virgin widows are acceptable. Some effort is being made in modern India to train young widows to take up constructive work that will benefit the nation and the community.

SUBORDINATION OF WOMEN

It is customary to speak of the subordination of the women to the men of India. An old Indian saying states, "As a girl she was under the tutelage of her parents, as an adult, of her husband, and as a widow, of her sons." Even the Buddhist nun, advanced in age and sanctity, is regarded as subordinate to the youngest male novice of the order. The Law of Manu, the canon law of India, stresses this subordination in harsh, unyielding language, stating that "She should do nothing independently even in her own house."

The Indian woman must accept the authority over her, whether from her parents, her husband, or her elders. She must find satisfaction and pleasure in her dependent role of service and in being needed, loved, and approved by those close to her. Most Indian women do not regard themselves as inferior to any man, but as having a different function to perform in life. Most do not desire to take over male functions, but do desire recognition that their role in life is also important. They consider that it is not a question of equality of rights, but a question of different functions which carry their own unique duties and rights. When each individual performs his assigned duties, a harmony of social life results. The duty of the woman of India is to transmit the cultural heritage and create new families.

Moreover, it is not entirely true to say that all decisions are made by the husband. Here, as in many instances, there is a gap between theory and practice. The wife has a great deal to say about the up-bringing of the children, their work and play, and their future employment and marriage, and she exerts a strong influence in the management of the house. It is the women of India who transmit to the children the old traditions and legends of India and give the children their religious instruction.

It is the Indian women of the villages who often block modern progress because of their conservatism and reluctance to change traditional ways of life. Reformers have found time and time again that reform was only possible after they had convinced the women of the benefits of change. Women have died rather than leave the seclusion of the *purdah,* and women still remain the bulwark of Indian traditional values.

Ultimate decisions are formally announced by men. The women, however, exercise great influence in the making of these decisions and often exercise a veto power after they have been made.

TRADITIONAL INDIA: CONFLICT AND CHANGE

Many traditional attitudes in India with regard to women are now being modified. The forces of conservatism and progress are in conflict. Generally speaking, it is the city people and the educated classes—these two groups are usually synonymous—that favor the progressive changes. Great Indian leaders like Gandhi, Nehru, and Ram Mohan Roy are exponents of this progressive, educated Indian class. They even permitted their children to marry outside the caste. Opposed to this educated class are the great mass of Indians living in the villages, especially the womenfolk of these villages. However, even the educated classes do not favor a quick, radical change, but a slow, orderly modification of social customs.

The problems created by the current campaign to educate Indian girls highlight the conflict between these two forces. The goal of compulsory education for all conflicts with the work requirements of the poorer villagers who need the girls to help in the farm and household work; every hand is needed to keep the spectre of hunger from the family. Moreover, the villagers feel that they do a better job of training the girl for marriage than could a formal school. Many of the schools are becoming co-educational, a practice contrary to the customs of the Indian people who strive to keep the girls separated from the boys, especially from the time of puberty onward. Education takes girls from the home and makes them independent. Many modern girls are starting to work toward a career which requires long years of preparation unhindered and undistracted by the duties of marriage. Marriage is delayed, and many boys will not marry girls who are extremely well educated. Villagers view a single woman over twenty with suspicion and her family with disfavor.

These problems engender conflict within the girl's family and within herself. She has been indoctrinated from early childhood with the conviction that marriage is her primary duty in life, and she knows that by refusing to accept this duty she is rejecting her purpose in life as conceived by the Indian community. But the desire for education is irresistible. Even women in *purdah* learn to read and write. A male teacher in India solved the problem of teaching one group of women secluded by *purdah* by putting up a cloth curtain between them and himself and then teaching them blindfolded. In the cities it is now normal for girls to go to school. In the villages the rate of literacy among the girls is rising rapidly.

The combination of education and increasing industrialization has created a situation in which conflict is inevitable. Girls are taught not to compete with boys, but to co-operate with them by concentrating on specific duties assigned to them as females. Emphasis is placed upon distinction of function, co-operation, and harmony. On the other hand, increasing education brings them into competition with men. New careers are opening up for them in fields formerly dominated exclusively by men. Thus, changing circumstances are bringing a new emphasis upon independence, competition, and individual initiative, as opposed to submissiveness, co-operation, and group harmony.

Expansion of the communication system in India has introduced other new elements into the life of the Indian woman. It is practically impossible for her to keep at a distance from men while traveling in crowded buses, trains, and airplanes. More and more girls are traveling by themselves on bicycles, in cars, and in public vehicles. This was rarely done in traditional India.

Changes are occurring within the family circle. Formerly, men and women did not eat together. Today it is not uncommon. Although most Indian men and women do not address each other by their first names, this practice is beginning to creep into the conversation of educated Indians.

The father is assuming more responsibility for the care of the child. Although some of the more conservative women grumble at this usurpation of their traditional functions, the father's participation in caring for the child was not unknown in ancient India. The Maina Canon speaks of fathers holding the children in their arms and staggering around like weak camels under their squalling sons. The Canon went on to say that fathers got up in the middle of the night to put their child to sleep and scrubbed their baby's dirty garments. There is no doubt that many Indian fathers today are staggering around in the middle of the night trying to put their howling children to sleep.

Some Indian women responded to the call for independence from Britain with the same single-minded devotion that they formerly reserved to the service of the family. Some went to jail, marched in the streets, participated in civic disobedience programs, and rallied all classes behind the independence movement. The numbers of such women are destined to increase. India's rapid industrialization, broadening education, and political crises—all the social and economic requirements of a great emerging nation—are slowly modifying traditional attitudes. The social life of the Indian people is changing, and the Indian woman is changing too.

One characteristic of the Indian woman has not changed. She is still dedicated to a life of service. But this aim is now expanding beyond the home to embrace the nation and the world.

CHAPTER 14

POLITICS IN INDIA

> *A king should not attempt*
> *to gain the earth unrighteously,*
> *for who reveres the king*
> *who wins unrighteous victory?*
> *Unrighteous conquest is impermanent,*
> *and does not lead to heaven.*
> —MAHABHARATA

Political thought in India today uniquely combines ideas and institutions imported from the West and attitudes and concepts inherited from classical times. This marriage of classical India and the modern liberal West has resulted in a political product which is both old and new.

Because of the strong and lengthy influence exerted by the British upon India, the political philosophy and institutions of the Republic of India bear a close resemblance to those of Great Britain. Many provisions of the Indian Constitution of 1950 reflect the principles upon which British, American, and other liberal democracies base their political institutions. The preamble to this Constitution declares that the purpose of the Republic of India is ". . . to secure to all its citizens: Justice, social, economic, political; Liberty of thought, expression, belief, faith and worship; Equality of status and opportunity; and to promote among them all Fraternity assuring the dignity of the individual and the unity of the Nation."

Despite these Western expressions the leaders of modern India are steeped in the wisdom and spirit of classical India. Mahatma Gandhi, the father of India, exemplified intense spirituality, an

---

Excerpt from the *Mahabharata* reprinted from A. L. Bashan, *The Wonder That Was India*, copyright 1954 by Sidgwick and Jackson, Ltd., London. Reprinted by permission of Sidgwick and Jackson and Hawthorn Books, Inc., 70 Fifth Avenue, New York.

ascetic attitude toward life, and adherence to a code of conduct peculiarly Indian in form and content. Since the past has played an important role in shaping their attitudes and opinions, and since India's present problem stems from ancient roots, there can be no real grasp and appreciation of her contemporary political life until something is also known about her past political life.

INDIA'S PAST

Archeological discoveries show that there were civilized people living in India as early as 3000 to 4000 B.C. Due to the lack of written historical records, we know very little about them. It is theorized, however, that the creators of this early culture were people called Dravidians, who entered the country from central Asia, intermarried with the aborigines, and eventually spread all over India. Today the main centers of Dravidian influence are in South India.

Around 2000 B.C. this ancient civilization was destroyed. It is from this time, beginning with the Aryan invasion of India, that the classic Indo-Aryan civilization is traced. The period from 2000 B.C. to about 500 B.C. is known as the Vedic period of Indian history. It was during this long interval that the *Brahmanas* and early *Upanishads* were written and the foundations of Indo-Aryan culture were laid. The Aryans were originally a pastoral people, divided into many tribes, who came into India from the west and northwest —the historical invasion routes into India—gradually penetrated all of North India, settling on the plains of the Ganges and Jumna rivers, and drove the Dravidians to the east and south of the country. Thus began a conflict between the Aryan invaders and the Dravidians which even now has not been entirely settled.

South India has resisted the unifying efforts of Indian Aryan rulers from the time of classical India down to the modern period. The people of this region are guarding their rights as jealously today as in the past.

Development of Kingship. The Aryans slowly pushed over northern India and organized themselves into broader political groupings as families, villages, and tribes joined to form well-defined territorial units. Some of these territorial units evolved into kingdoms; others became oligarchies and republics. Thus, early in India's history, North India served as a breeding ground for the development of the country's political thought and culture. Throughout India's long history, it has been the center of India's political life, and it is not strange that the capital of the Republic of India, New Delhi, is located there now.

Kingship became the characteristic political institution of the Aryans. North India divided into a number of territorial units which were almost continually at war among themselves and with others. Disunity and disorganization, fear and unrest, were the rule rather than the exception, and the people needed the unity and power that result from working together under one leader in order to protect themselves from the conditions of anarchy that then prevailed. Kingship was necessary in order to counteract the "law of fishes," which is the metaphorical way the Sanskrit language describes a state of anarchy, in which the larger fish swallow the smaller without hindrance. Only the legally established coercive power of the king could prevent the chaos that existed under the "law of the fishes." This concept is still fundamental in the political thought of the Indian people.

The idea that kingly power is a trust is one of the basic principles of Hindu political thought. Since kingship arose in India to satisfy certain needs of the people, the king was judged in terms of his performance in meeting these needs. He retained his office if he efficiently carried out the duties assigned him; he was deposed if he failed. If a king did not carry out his duties, he was regarded as unrighteous and would eventually perish from the earth. Some Indian political theorists even held that an unrighteous king could be assassinated. The conviction that political leaders may be removed from office if they do no fulfill the functions assigned to them is still a cardinal principle of the Indian political system.

Assemblies of the People—Samiti and Sabha. Early Vedic kings were checked by two powerful institutions known as the *samiti* and the *sabha.* The *samiti* was an assemblage of all the people; it had the power of electing or appointing a king, and deposing him. The *sabha* was a council of influential men to whose advice the king was bound to listen. Generally Brahmins, or priests, and the elders of the community, they advised the king on political and other matters.

From around 1000 B.C. to about 600 B.C. the influence of the *samiti* and the *sabha* slowly decreased. Continual wars plaguing North India during this period led to a consolidation of the king's authority. Kingship became hereditary, and the two assemblies were superseded by a council of ministers appointed by the king. The *samiti* disappeared as a political institution, and the *sabha* was transformed into a royal agency entirely dependent upon the king's will and exclusively devoted to carrying out his commands. The king became the central authority in the state and the people looked to him rather than the assemblies for their protection.

THE VILLAGE IN POLITICS

The village has given a certain degree of continuity and stability to the political life of India. It was the basis of the *samiti,* or general assembly, and it enjoyed a great deal of autonomy during the Vedic Period. Whenever a strong central government administered India, as during the Maurya Dynasty, 321-185 B.C., and while Great Britain ruled India in recent times, the independence of the village was somewhat curtailed, but village self-government has been fundamental in Indian political life from the Vedic Period to the modern era.

Usually, the village had a council, known as the *panchayat,* which governed it. It functioned inside the village no matter what government was in power. Traditionally, the *panchayat* consisted of five of the most respected people of the village, and a headman who frequently represented the central government. In some localities, the village was governed by committees chosen by lot or operated under a form of constitutional government; in others, all householders actively participated in the decision-making process.

In all periods of India's history, the village community worked together on public projects such as irrigation, roads, temples, collecting taxes, or caring for community land. The Republic of India is now trying to encourage the villagers, who make up the vast majority of the population, to work on the national level with the same enthusiasm and spirit that sparked other work on the local level. As one method, it is trying to revitalize the *panchayat* councils.

REPUBLICAN INSTITUTIONS

Republican institutions started to develop around the eighth century B.C. and survived in some areas, especially the western part of India, into the fifth century A.D. These republican institutions developed at the same time as political power was being consolidated in the person of the king. The Sakyas, the tribe to which Gautama Buddha belonged, had a republican form of government. Gautama Buddha himself preferred the republican type of political organization and based the organization of the Buddhist clergy on a constitution borrowed from some Indian republic, perhaps his own.

The character of these republics varied from place to place. Some republics held large assemblies where all the important political decisions were made. It is reported that, in one instance, there were 5,000 councillors in a parliament. In another republic, political power was limited to less than 800 families, while the total population was over a million and a half. In some republics, political participation was hereditary; in others it was not. Some republics had a house of elders, and in another the leadership of the army was vested in an elected chief.

No systematic theory of republicanism developed in ancient India, and the Guptas, who rose to power in North India in the fourth century A.D., finally succeeded in destroying both republics and republicanism in India. Rule by king and royal authority continued to dominate the political history of India down to modern times, when the idea of republicanism was revived by the entrance of Western nations, particularly Britain.

DIVISION AND UNITY

Divided and disorganized throughout most of her history, India has been the battleground of many warring kingdoms. From the time the Aryans arrived in India to the time of the Muslim invasions, which began in the eleventh century, during this period of over two thousand years, there were only three relatively short periods of unified government in North India.

In the fourth century B.C. Chandragupta Maurya unified India under one ruler for the first time in its history. Asoka, the grandson of Chandragupta, brought the Maurya Dynasty to the apex of power and prestige. He combined in his person the powers of a monarch with the duties of a Buddhist monk. His great goals of life were the propagation of the teaching of the Buddha, the consolidation of royal power, and the renunciation of warfare as a means of conquest and Indian expansion.

The substitution of royal ministers for the people's assemblies, and the invasions from Central Asia and elsewhere, pointed up the need for a unified front under one leader. The new religions of Buddhism and Jainism also supported and increased Asoka's authority because they needed his help against the Brahmins, advocates of the established religion. Finally, Asoka himself undertook to increase his own authority by fostering the spirit of nationalism among the people of India. One of the means he used was to set up pillars all over India on which he wrote ethical precepts in one language, Pali.

Asoka's renunciation of war at the height of his fame has had an enduring influence upon the political thought of the Indians, an influence which was dramatically evident during the latter part of Gandhi's life when he and his followers stressed the concept of nonviolence as a means of obtaining political ends. The dramatic picture of thousands upon thousands of Indians sitting passively under the blows of British policemen, as they followed Gandhi in a campaign of civil disobedience, was striking evidence of the power of the idea of nonviolence. It worked. This ideal is still basic to Indian political thought, although India supports an army, navy, and air force and has sometimes used them to achieve a political goal.

Asoka also established a policy of toleration. He published an Edict of Toleration which stated in part:

> King Priyadarse (Asoka) honors men of all faiths, members of religious orders and laymen alike, with gifts and various marks of esteem. Yet he does not value either gifts or honors as much as growth in the qualities essential to religion in men of all faiths.
>
> This growth may take many forms, but its root is in guarding one's own speech to avoid extolling one's own faith and disparaging the faith of others improperly or when the occasion is appropriate, immoderately.
>
> The faiths of others all deserve to be honored for one reason or another. By honoring them, one exalts one's own faith and at the same time performs a service to the faith of others. By acting otherwise, one injures one's own faith and also does disservice to that of others.[1]

The Indian people have preserved this heritage of toleration. One of the most attractive features of Hinduism is its tolerant acceptance of other religions and other beliefs. It is fundamental to the teaching of Hinduism that there are numerous roads to the libera-

---

[1] Quoted from *The Edicts of Asoka*, ed. and trans. by N. A. Nikam & Richard McKeon, University of Chicago Press. Copyright 1958, University of Chicago.

tion of the spirit. Within its wide embrace there is room for all, no matter what their spiritual needs or beliefs. Toleration was bequeathed by Asoka to the Indian people, and this heritage still retains great vitality and commands respect in India.

Asoka is so highly regarded that the new Republic of India has adopted the capital of an Asokan column for the device of its state seal. The emblem on the national flag is the Buddhist wheel which stands for the law and which was copied from one of the Asokan pillars.

Cultural Unity and War. The Maurya Dynasty left behind it the ideal of a universal emperor, but it also left behind a number of kings who thought they were destined to become that universal emperor. Consequently, it became customary for kings to assume such titles as "Great King of Kings" and "Supreme Lord." Even unimportant princes called themselves by sonorous titles. It was a world of many states competing with each other, but acknowledging a common culture and way of life. This condition is not very different from that of the Western world which generally admits to a common culture but is politically divided.

Conflict and intrigue characterized the relations between the various kingdoms in this political climate. Although Asoka renounced war as an instrument of policy, the martial tradition grew, and war became the chief occupation of statesmen and kings. In fact, it was regarded as part of the warrior's duty, or *dharma*, and good in itself. Such ideas helped to keep India a jungle and prevented the unification of the nation under one emperor.

The Doctrine of Circles. The basic concept which underlay the relations of one kingdom with another during this period might be termed the "doctrine of circles." Briefly, this doctrine taught that neighboring contiguous kingdoms were natural enemies, while kingdoms beyond these neighbors were natural allies. Thus, it was common practice for the Indian king to ally himself with the kingdom beyond his neighbor for the purpose of encircling and destroying the kingdom between them. Of course, its destruction made the allies neighbors of each other, and the process started all over again with the former allies now enemies and targets for each other. Under these circumstances, all alliances were temporary, and all friendships impermanent.

The accepted Indian political structure was that of a dominant political unit in the midst of a circle of kingdoms. When the highly centralized Maurya Dynasty fell, this was the type of system that prevailed in India. A large kingdom directly administered a central core of territory, while around it were grouped a circle of vassals who acknowledged this overlordship of the central kingdom. Kingdoms became vassals by conquest and to acquire more vassals became the king's principal ambition. Of course, these surrounding vassals were a constant source of trouble and real threat to the overlord, for any ruler who wanted to keep his dominant position had to be careful lest he in turn become the vassal of a former vassal or a neighboring kingdom.

The Gupta Dynasty—the Second Unity. Beginning with Chandragupta in 320 A.D. most of India was once again united under one rule, the Gupta Dynasty. This dynasty reached its peak under Chandragupta II (375-415 A.D.) and coincided with the most glorious period of classical Indian civilization. During this period Indian art and literature reached full maturity. Indian sculpture of this time rivals the finest in the world. Colleges and universities were filled with students, and Nalanda University enrolled students from all over Asia. A Chinese visitor, Fa-Hsien, commented on the atmosphere of peace prevalent everywhere, the lack of crime, and the fact that there was little, if any, oppression of the people.

By 550 A.D. continued invasions from the northwest finally overcame the Gupta rulers, and the dynasty disintegrated into the familiar pattern of many kingdoms that made war on each other for supremacy. With the exception of the period when King Harsha became emperor in 606 A.D. and ruled for forty-one years, not until the modern era was India to realize again the ideal of a unified country under one beneficent ruler. To the turmoil and dissensions that already plagued India was now added the additional troubles of sustained Muslim invasions.

FOLLOWERS OF ISLAM

From the beginning of the Muslim invasions of India from the northwest in the eighth century until the establishment of the Mughal Empire in the sixteenth century, India was torn apart by the quarrels of kingdoms and warring princes seeking to grasp a throne. Muslim Turks, Muslim Persians, Muslim Afghans, and Muslim Mongols in successive waves stormed into India looting, killing, and seizing territory. It is true that some Arab Muslims came to India by way of the sea and peacefully for trade, but these Muslims were never politically powerful.

For over five hundred years the Muslims could not establish a stable regime under one leader. Rule over the city of Delhi and the surrounding lands was the prize sought by all, but the authority of the Delhi throne was slight and its occupants in continual danger. Both the rulers and the frontiers of the Delhi kingdom were perpetually changing. More often than not, the governors of the various provinces, nominally subordinate to the Delhi throne, actually ruled as independent sovereigns in their own right.

This scene of disunity began to change when Babur, a descendant of the famous Turkish conqueror Tamerlaine, brought great parts of North India under his control. His grandson, Akbar, conquered more of India and established the Mughal Empire upon a firm base. Akbar became emperor in the middle of the sixteenth century and his reign coincided roughly with the rule of Queen Elizabeth of England and Philip II of Spain.

Akbar, an energetic and capable ruler, brought to much of India the first peace and unity that the people had known for a thousand years. The Mughal Empire maintained itself firmly in power until the middle of the eighteenth century when anarchy, chaos, and disorder once again became widespread in India.

Although the Muslim rulers were in many ways tolerant and understanding, they usually regarded the native Hindu civilization with a measure of contempt. Hitherto, the Indians, though continually weakened by factional quarrels which left them an easy prey for invaders, were usually able to absorb their conquerors eventually and thus win final victory. They failed with the Muslims. Probably because of the character of their religion, the Muslims firmly resisted assimilation. But not entirely, for they did acquire some Indian characteristics which had their source in Hinduism.

This resistance to assimilation, together with the heritage of struggle, kept high the barrier between the Hindus and the Muslims. The division between the two cultures was preserved when, in 1947, the territory of old India was split between the new Muslim-dominated state of Pakistan and the Hindu-oriented Republic of India. These two new nations reflect also the impact of Western nationalism.

WESTERN NATIONS IN INDIA

The first Western nation in the modern period to reach India was Portugal, whose sailors landed on Indian soil in the latter part of the fifteenth century. Portuguese, Dutch, French, and British entered India in greater and greater numbers, and by the middle of the nineteenth century all India, including the nominally independent princes, was subject to Great Britain. British rule in India lasted until 1947 when India and Pakistan were established as free and independent nations with dominion status within the British Commonwealth of Nations. India became a Republic in 1950; Pakistan, in 1956. Prior to independence, the British were the primary source of Western thought and attitudes in India.

Hindu Reaction. Indian Hindus reacted to the coming of the West to India in three ways.

(1) A small group of well-educated Indians almost completely abandoned their former way of life and thinking for that of the West. In the beginning this group was very influential, but gradually, as nationalism grew in India, their influence over policy-making waned. There are still many Indians, living mostly in large urban areas, who are little affected by the classical tradition of their ancestors, but their influence is negligible.

(2) The Brahmo Samaj group attempted to create a synthesis of the best in Hinduism and Christianity. Ram Mohan Roy, sometimes called the father of the Indian renaissance of the nineteenth century, was the leader of this group. He started his career after witnessing his sister burn to death on the pyre of her dead husband. This practice, called *suttee*, has now been abolished in the new India. Roy's followers were influential in the nineteenth century, but in the twentieth century they also declined in prestige and influence.

(3) Another group reacted in an actively hostile manner to this infiltration of Western ways of thinking and acting. Fearing that this alien culture would eventually destroy India's classical tradition and civilization, members of this group became the leaders in reviving Hindu culture and in calling attention to the glories of the past. Their vehement rejection of foreign concepts and renewed loyalty to the classical Indian tradition became one of the bases of

modern militant Indian nationalism, which swept over India and finally culminated in the sovereign Republic of India.

Nationalism. One of the most significant results of the impact of the West on India was the growth of nationalism. Indians for centuries have recognized their cultural unity, but it was only after the British established their rule over India that they learned to consider themselves as members of a common nation as well. There were many reasons for this growth of nationalism. British common law and administration brought to different Indian factions and groups a sense of unity because all were forced to follow similar behavior. The British established an educational system in India which stressed Western culture, history, attitudes, and beliefs. Eventually Western-trained Indians aspired to live by Western ideals of freedom and liberty. British rule in India was an obvious contradiction to British teaching. Then, too, the British were giving the Indians a knowledge of the West at a time when Western nationalism was flourishing.

They also gave India a common language. Formerly, India's multiplicity of languages and dialects prevented even educated Indians from communicating with one another and constituted one of the most serious obstacles to national unity. The problem persists, but the imposition of English as the common language proved to be a partial solution. It facilitated the creation of the Indian press which provided the Indians with a medium for molding public opinion, an outlet for their grievances, and an excellent means of propaganda. Thus, by establishing political unity and educating the Indians in their way of life, the British also fostered national feeling and helped to develop the intense patriotism which motivates many Indians today.

REPRESENTATIVE GOVERNMENT

The British example of parliamentary government has resulted in the establishment of a representative government in India. Since the British ruled India for such a long period of time, it was natural for Indians to think of democracy in terms of British political institutions. As does Great Britain, the Indians have a cabinet which performs the executive tasks of government and is responsible to a legislative body made up of two houses which are collectively known as parliament. This parliament is elected by the people. The members of the cabinet must also be members of parliament.

Instead of a queen or king, as in England, India has a president who presides as titular head of the state. The president of India, however, like the president of France, has little actual political power. In India, as in Great Britain and France, the Prime Minister is the functioning head of the government. As in England, he is head of the largest political party in the country or the party which holds a majority in the lower house of parliament. At the present time Jawaharlal Nehru is the Prime Minister and also heads the Congress Party which holds an overwhelming majority of the *lok sabha,* the lower house of the Indian parliament.

The British brought to India the idea of rule by law to replace the concept that the king was the sole giver and interpreter of the law, with no appeal from his ruling except by rebellion and force. Rule by law, one of Great Britain's most cherished political ideals, was passed on to India along with other teachings on personal rights. The new Constitution of India contains many provisions guaranteeing those freedoms and rights of the individual which are cherished and preserved as the basic foundation of Indian life. At the same time, the Indians understand and appreciate the democratic aspects of the British political heritage. In the amalgamation of these two futures lies democracy's best hope for a peaceful and progressive orient.

The interaction of old and new forces is resulting in a synthesis of classical Indian culture with that of the West.

This synthesis has expressed itself in many ways. For instance, the scientific spirit has been rekindled in modern India. Indian scientists, like all modern scholars, now emphasize the necessity for an attitude of rationality and for scientific analysis based upon empirical evidence. Yet Indian philosophers and thinkers have preserved their aptitudes for exploring the soaring reaches of man's thought, explorations which demand intuition and imagination of the highest order. The negative aspects of India's classical tradition which bound some of her finest minds in the chains of rigid customs and traditions have been swept away, and a new vitality and resurgence of an awakened people permeates all India.

CHAPTER 15

PAKISTAN

The founder of Pakistan, Quid-i-Azam Mohammad Ali Jinnah, expressing the will of the people, declared that Pakistan would be a democratic State based on Islamic principles of Social Justice.

—PREAMBLE TO THE CONSTITUTION
OF PAKISTAN (1962)

Pakistan is the geographic expression of a Muslim fear of Hindu oppression. When Great Britain prepared to give independence to the people she had long dominated, the Muslims became greatly fearful of Hindu dominance and absorption because the Hindus represented the overwhelming majority of the inhabitants. To escape this prospect, the Muslims urged a division of the former united territory based upon religious affiliation. This was done. The borders of Pakistan follow rather closely the Muslim concentrations on the subcontinent of India, but not all Muslims were included within Pakistan borders nor all Hindus excluded. About 86 per cent of the country is Muslim, 13 per cent is Hindu, and the remainder is composed of Christians, Parsis, Buddhists, and others.

Although Muslims are to be found scattered throughout the area of South Asia, they are concentrated in two widely separated parts, namely in the western and eastern extremities of the Indo-Pakistan subcontinent. Accordingly, when the new state was created by the partition of former British India on August 14, 1947, both of these separated Muslim communities were placed within the one state of Pakistan. As a result, Pakistan is composed of two distinct land units —one in the east, known as East Pakistan, and the other in the west, known as West Pakistan—which are separated from each other by over a thousand miles of Republic of India territory. Pakistan was born physically divided.

The roots of the force that created Pakistan go back to the entrance of the Muslims into India in the eighth century A.D. Gradually, under the leadership of a succession of dynamic and able generals and statesmen, most of India was brought under the control of the followers of Islam. Their successes culminated in the establishment of the Mughal Empire which brought to India an administrative unity it had not possessed for centuries.

The invaders of India who preceded the Muslims had no culture or belief comparable with the Indian's in distinctiveness and appeal and therefore were usually absorbed into the cultural and religious life of India. The Muslims were different. They possessed a religion which had spread over much of the civilized world and a culture of Middle East and Persian origin which was the equal of the Indian's and in some ways superior. Under the sponsorship of the Muslims, this Persian culture eventually pervaded the middle and higher levels of Indian society so that Persian language and literature, Persian art and architecture, became an integral part of the cultural life of India. The Muslims were imbued with a deep pride in their religion and regarded the Hindu and Buddhist religions as inferior to their own. Moreover, millions of Indians embraced Islam. They believed that it offered them more hope, freedom, and tolerance than the Buddhism and Hinduism with which they were familiar, and they were drawn by its social teachings. It appealed to the women because Islam demanded that wives be given fair treatment and maintained in a reasonable state; daughters could inherit property, and women could divorce their husbands if necessary. All were drawn by the Muslim's conceptions of racial equality and the brotherhood of man, for many Indians found the caste system of India a heavy burden to bear, and Islam had no castes. Within Islam, the race, social status, or economic condition of a man is immaterial; all men are equal before God.

Some Indians, of course, became Muslims to enhance their chances of advancement under Muslim rule, but their numbers were relatively few. It was not essential to become a Muslim to attain power; many Hindus have held positions of high authority under Muslim rulers. The famous Muslim emperor Akbar bestowed power upon numerous non-Muslims during his reign in India. Nor is it correct to say that Islam converted by the sword in India. Although some incidents of this nature might be cited, they remain the exception rather than the rule. The vast majority of Indians who were converted to Islam saw in Muslim beliefs and practices something that appealed to them.

Thus the Muslims brought to India a new faith and system of practices which were embraced by a quarter of the entire Indian population at the time of partition in 1947. During the centuries they lived together in India, both Hindus and Muslims influenced each other's thought and practices, but Islam and Hinduism retained their distinctive religious features, and their followers remained separated by distinctive ways of life.

With the fall of the Mughal Empire in the eighteenth century, the Muslims declined in power and wealth. Their empire had sustained them for many centuries, and when it was lost to them, they were forced to renew the basic sources of their faith and to turn to other means for the preservation of their heritage and communal feeling. They re-emphasized the values that undergirded Islam and the unique characteristics which differentiated it from Hinduism. They proceeded to co-operate more with the British, who had succeeded to the Mughal Empire, in an effort to counteract the greater numerical strength of the Hindus. Many of them felt that the Congress Party, which was founded in 1885, was a threat to their independence of thought and action because it was dominated by a Hindu majority. In 1906 they established the Muslim League, which eventually became their primary political instrument in advancing their cause. Muhammad Iqbal, a great Muslim poet who died in 1938, proclaimed the idea of a homeland for the Muslims in India where they could practice and renew their faith without hindrance. He even gave it a name, *Pakistan,* "Land of the Pure." Then Mohammad Ali Jinnah, the father of Pakistan, led the modern movement which culminated in the creation of the state of Pakistan.

The Hindu leaders of the Congress Party underestimated the deep emotional appeal a separate Islamic homeland would have for all Muslims and the tenacity and organizational ability of Jinnah. They appeared to forget the history of Muslim and Hindu separateness and the lengths the Muslims were willing to go to establish their own nation where there would be no danger of absorption and no possibility of domination by others. The Hindu-dominated Congress refused to part with any of its power, and so an impasse was reached which even British diplomacy could not solve short of the partition of India. The Muslim League, under the leadership of Jinnah, held the same power over Muslim India as the Congress Party did over Hindu India, and it was adamant in its demand for a separate state. Finally, on August 14, 1947, the British Parliament gave dominion status to both India and Pakistan, and the Muslims of India had their homeland.

A few months after the birth of Pakistan, Mohammad Ali Jinnah summed up the motivating force that sustained him and his Muslim followers during the arduous and often tense months and years prior to independence. "The creation of a State of our own was a means to an end and not an end in itself. The idea was that we should have a state in which we could live and breathe as free men and which we could develop according to our own way of life and culture, and wherein the principles of Islamic social justice could find free play."

The principles of Islam are basic to the Republic of Pakistan. The preamble to Pakistan's Constitution, as published in 1962, begins:

> In the name of Allah, the Beneficent, the Merciful; Whereas sovereignty over the entire Universe belongs to Almighty Allah alone, and the authority exercisable by the people is a sacred trust. . . .

> And whereas it is the will of the people of Pakistan that . . . the principles of democracy, freedom, equality, tolerance and social justice, as enunciated by Islam, should be fully observed in Pakistan. . . .

> The Muslims of Pakistan should be enabled, individually and collectively, to order their lives in accordance with the teachings and requirements of Islam. . . .

This is not to say that Pakistan discriminates against other religious groups or minorities, because the Constitution of Pakistan provides for religious and personal freedom, and the first president of Pakistan, General Iskander Mirza, stated that "As long as I am Head of State, I will regard the honor of my Hindu Pakistani brethren as my own and I shall be personally responsible for their well-being and safety." However, there is no doubt that every official act of Pakistan is infused with the spirit of Islam.

Islam is an important ideology to millions of Asian people besides the Pakistanis. The followers of Islam are found in Indonesia,

Malaya, China, the Philippines, and other Asian areas. The Republic of India has a population of Muslims estimated at between 30 and 40 million. It is important that an ideology that has created nations and is still influencing the thought and activities of so many Asians be understood and appreciated.

CHAPTER 16

ISLAM

God is most great!
God is most great!
I testify that there is no god but Allah.
I testify that Muhammed is the prophet of Allah.
Arise and pray; arise and pray.
God is great;
There is no god but Allah!
—THE CALL OF THE MUEZZIN TO PRAYER

Islam is a complete way of life. It embraces the social, political, economic, and cultural life of its followers as well as their belief in God and His commandments. Islam is concerned with the total man, and all his acts receive their justification and direction from the teaching that is ultimately embodied in the Koran, the holy book of the Muslims, which contains the final and complete revelation of God's truth to man. The Koran is filled with laws which should govern the daily practical affairs of man, for Islam is vitally interested in how men should live together and in their individual material welfare. Islam deals explicitly and in detail with the treatment of women, the conduct of war, race relations, the equality of man, marriage, interest rates, health, and a host of other matters which are included in the whole life of man. Islam seeks to bring the total life of man into harmony with God.

MISCONCEPTIONS ABOUT ISLAM

Islam is a much misunderstood and misrepresented religion. Over the centuries it has been portrayed by many Western writers and speakers as an anti-Jewish and anti-Christian religion, while in fact Islam teaches religious tolerance. In his charter to the city of Medina, Muhammed, the prophet through whom God revealed the truths of Islam, said: "The Jews who attach themselves to our commonwealth shall be protected from all insults and vexations;

125

they shall have an equal right with our own people to our assistance and good offices." He also stated that both Jews and Christians shall be permitted to practice their religion as freely as the Muslims. The Islamic Republic of Pakistan has given concrete expression to this creed of toleration by guaranteeing religious freedom in its Constitution.

Islam recognizes the truth that is contained in the doctrines of Judaism and Christianity and confirms Abraham, Moses, Isaiah, Jesus, and others as true prophets of God who preceded Muhammed. Muhammed was the last and final prophet and therefore is called "the Seal of the Prophets." Islam holds that the Old Testament of the Jews and the New Testament of the Christians were revelations from God, and those who believe in them are called "People of the Book." But these revelations are incomplete, and thus the necessity for the Koran, which embodies the complete and uncorrupted revelation from God. Although Abraham correctly revealed the oneness of God, the Jews who came after him forgot this revelation and took to themselves golden idols. Jesus was chosen by God to reveal this and other truths, but his followers made him a god, thus dehumanizing him and humanizing God. Jesus, like Muhammed, was a true prophet and a man, not a god.

Western novels and serious historical and religious works have often indicated that the sword was the primary instrument of conversion for Muslims. They allege that it was the practice of the Muslims to give the nonbeliever two choices—conversion or death. There have been incidents when Muslims, caught up in the fury of war or lacking knowledge of the basic tenets of Islam, have used force to convert others to their faith, but the history of many religions is strewn with zealots who have utilized torture and force for this purpose. The followers of Islam have probably sinned less in this regard than the disciples of other religions. Muslims, as a rule, adhere closely to the injunction of the Koran: "If it had been thy Lord's will, they would all have believed,—all who are on earth! Wilt thou then compel mankind, against their will, to believe!" (Surah X, 99) And in the Koran it is also stated: "Let there be no compulsion in religion." (Surah II, 256) And "Unto you be your religion, and unto me mine." (Surah CIX, 6)

A conception of Muslims as addicts of war has also grown up in Western minds. Islam does permit its followers to resist evil, and those who injure others wrongly may be punished to the full extent of the injury. The Muslims also believe in the concept of a *jihad,* or "holy war," in which those who die become martyrs and go immediately to heaven. But this holy war must be a defensive one or waged to right some wrong. The Koran states: "Defend yourself against your enemies; but attack them not first: for God does not love transgressors." (Surah II, 190) Even when they are engaged in a righteous war, Muhammed required his followers to spare the women and children, sacred objects, and fields of grain and orchards, and to refrain from mutilating the wounded and the dead. Maddened by the passion of war, many forgot the precepts of Muhammed, but these are the basic teachings of Islam on the conduct of war.

Islam has been repeatedly slandered as a degrader of women and a refuge for lascivious men whose libidinous desires may be fully and legitimately satisfied under the protective cloak of religion. Numerous historical romances, past and present, employ this stereotype of Islam to inject sex and spicy incidents into the story. Thus an image of Islam as basically carnal is passed on from generation to generation of Westerners. The only feature of Islam known by many Westerners is that it permits polygamy. Such an image does not present a complete and true picture of Islam's teaching and practice with regard to women. At the time Islam was born in Arabia in the seventh century, women were in a most degraded state. They were at the complete mercy of their husbands and fathers to do with as they liked; they had no inheritance rights; infant daughters were unwanted and frequently killed; and marriage was often conditional and temporary with no recourse for the woman should her husband divorce her, as husbands frequently did. Women were looked upon as mere playthings or work animals to be discarded when their usefulness was over. Muhammed did much to mitigate this evil. He prohibited the killing of daughters and demanded that they have the right of inheritance of the family property. His enlightened laws gave to the women of his day and later a status much higher than formerly and prepared the way for the astounding progress that the modern Muslim women are making today toward full equality with men.

Islam views marriage very seriously. A woman must give her full consent before she can be married to any man even if he is a king.

Although divorce is permitted in Islam, it is not regarded as a routine solution but as an exceptional one. Before most Muslim marriages, the prospective husband is required to set aside for his future wife a certain sum of money which might be termed a dowry.
She may take this dowry at the time of marriage, but it is hers to
claim whenever she desires it. Should they be divorced, she may
take possession of this dowry, if she has not already received it at
the time of the marriage or thereafter, and the former husband must
support her until she remarries. The Koran states: "For divorced
women maintenance should be provided on a reasonable scale.
This is a duty for the righteous." (Surah II, 241) Wives are also
permitted to initiate divorce proceedings themselves. Islam has elevated the status of women from its previous deplorable depths and
given them a certain degree of social, legal, and economic security.
But what about polygamy?

The Koran does state: "You may marry two, three, or four wives,
but not more." (Surah IV, 3) But Islam lays down a hard condition
for those who desire more than one wife, for the Koran also states
that if a man cannot deal equitably and justly with more than one
wife, he shall marry only one. (Surah IV, 3) This means that a man
cannot have more than one wife if he cannot give them all the same
material benefits, the same love, the same respect, and the same
treatment. Since this is an almost impossible condition for the
ordinary man, the true follower of Islam cannot generally practice polygamy. This hard qualification has oriented most Muslims
toward monogamy, and today there are relatively few Muslims
who have more than one wife.

MUHAMMED: THE PROPHET OF ALLAH

Muhammed was the man through whom Allah (God) transmitted the teachings of Islam to His people. Though a prophet only,
he was not an ordinary prophet, for to him God gave the special
task of revealing His truth and His divine law in its *most complete
form*. There were other prophets before him—Abraham and Jesus
were two—but he was the last and final member of this chosen few.
He was "the Seal of the Prophets."

Muhammed was born in Mecca, a city located within the present
boundaries of Saudi Arabia, about 571 A.D. His father, mother, and
grandfather all died before he reached the age of nine. He was

then brought up by a kindly uncle for whom he worked as a shepherd. Although he grew up in an atmosphere of lawlessness, sensuality, treachery, and war, he managed to remain aloof and unscarred by the atrocious practices of his time. He is described as a youth of mild and kindly disposition whose charity and helpfulness made him beloved by all who knew him.

When he was twenty-five, Muhammed was employed by a rich widow named Khadija. They grew to esteem each other's qualities and finally married, even though Khadija was fifteen years older than Muhammed. Muhammed was married to her for twenty-six years and took no other wife until after her death. He always spoke of her with endearment, and to all Muslims she is the epitome of the faithful and devoted wife. A man who, in a social environment which favored polygamy and temporary marriages, remained married to one wife for so many years cannot be said to have been overly inclined toward polygamy. Although Muhammed did take other wives after the death of Khadija and in the last years of his life, there is no evidence that he was motivated by sensuality. His later wives were, for the most part, widows of his followers who had died in the cause of Islam, and he married them primarily to provide them with economic security and to prevent them from falling into evil hands. He married an African woman in order to teach his followers that Islam believes in racial equality. Islam is not color-conscious, and the spectacular successes it has had in Asia and Africa attest to the efficacy of its teaching on racial equality. It is reported that Muhammed treated all his wives with the same consideration and respect.

HISTORY OF ISLAM

From one point of view the history of Islam starts with God. God was the real founder of Islam, and the truth that was revealed through Muhammed is a truth that always was and always will be. Much of this divine truth had already been revealed to man through such prophets as Abraham, Moses, Isaiah, and Jesus, but Islam was its confirmation and culmination. The Koran states: "This Koran is not such as can be produced by other than God; on the contrary, it is a confirmation of revelations that went before it and a fuller explanation . . . wherein there is no doubt—from the Lord of the Worlds." (Surah X, 37)

Muhammed traced the ancestry of the Arab people back to Adam through Abraham. Abraham had two sons, Isaac by his wife Sarah, and Ishmael by his other wife Hagar. Sarah forced Abraham to banish Ishmael and his mother from the tribe, and they went to Mecca. Thus Ishmael became the progenitor of the Arabs, while the descendants of Isaac are the Jews.

From an external or historical point of view the history of Islam began in the seventh century of the Western calendar, when God revealed his truths to Muhammed. Muhammed was upset and puzzled by the barbarism and savagery which characterized the world into which he was born. Why must these conditions exist? What could be done to mitigate and modify the evil and folly of man? He sought answers everywhere to these troubling and perplexing questions, but mostly he sought within himself. He found a lonely desert cave outside of Mecca, and there he meditated for long periods of time on the vexing problems of life. There must be a reason and a solution for these evils which afflict mankind, for they were largely man-created.

Muhammed found the answer to his questions but not in himself; he found the answer in God. As he thought and fasted in his quiet cave, sometimes for nights and days without pause, the reality of God became more and more the content of his contemplation. God soon became the silent and unseen companion of his vigils; and then one night He spoke to him through one of His angels. "Proclaim!" He said. Muhammed was startled, and replied. "I know not how to proclaim." "Proclaim!" He repeated the second time. Muhammed was now thoroughly frightened, and again answered, "I know not how to proclaim." "Proclaim!" the voice demanded a third time. Muhammed could resist no longer, and timidly he asked, "What shall I proclaim?" The answer came quickly:

> *Proclaim—in the name of your God*
>   *The Creator,*
> *Who created man from a clot*
>   *Of congealed blood.*
> *Proclaim! Your God*
>   *Is most generous,*
> *He who has taught man*
>   *By the pen*
> *Things they knew not.*
> —Surah XCVI, 1-5

From that moment on Muhammed knew no rest or peace on earth, for he was destined to cry out to all men, both present and future, the hope and glory and truth of Allah. He was committed to the divine purpose of bringing Allah to man, and man to Allah, and he could not pause while even one man did not know the revelation of Allah. The voice that was heard by Muhammed in the stillness of his desert cave so many years ago is still heard around the world today when the *muezzin* cries out, "I testify that there is no god but Allah. I testify that Muhammed is the prophet of Allah."

The citizens of Mecca did not find the new mission of Muhammed to their liking. His revelations of Allah demanded too much of the individual, threatened the established customs of their society, and, more important, might impede the flow of pilgrims into Mecca and wealth into their coffers. Pilgrims came to Mecca because of many gods, and if one God superseded them in Mecca, the number of pilgrims would certainly dwindle, for many gods have a greater pulling power than merely one. The pilgrims journeyed to Mecca to pay homage to their gods at the sacred shrine of Kaaba. Originally, the Kaaba was built by Abraham and Ishmael and dedicated as a place of worship to the one God, but over the years the original meaning of the Kaaba was obscured, and it became a shrine of many gods. After the citizens of Mecca accepted Islam, Muhammed rededicated the Kaaba to Allah, and it became Islam's most sacred shrine. Today pilgrims pour into Mecca from every part of the earth in numbers far exceeding those who came prior to the teachings of Islam. The concentrated and infinite power of the one God was a far greater attraction to pilgrims than the diffuse and finite power of many gods.

But Muhammed's fellow-citizens did not know this at the time, and they savagely persecuted him and his followers, who were beaten, starved, imprisoned, and finally driven from the city. The cruelties and tortures inflicted upon the early Muslims rival some of the sufferings of the early Christians. Thus in 622 A.D. Muhammed and his followers were forced to flee secretly from Mecca to Medina where he was welcomed and honored. This migration is known as the *Hijra,* and the Muslims date their calendar from this year, using the symbols A.H., "After Hijra." This migration was the beginning of the amazing spread of Islam, and when Muhammed died in 632 A.D., or 10 A.H., all Arabia belonged to Islam. A century after his death the people of Armenia, Persia, Syria, Palestine, Iraq, Egypt, and Spain were ruled by the followers of Islam. They even crossed into France where their advance was checked by Charles Martel at the Battle of Tours in 732 A.D. But although frustrated in Europe, Islam continued to expand in Asia and Africa. Today there are about 500 million Muslims throughout the world, but the greatest concentrations of them are found in Asia, Africa, and the Middle East. Islam is a dynamic, living ideology which continues to attract millions of men and women.

THE KORAN

According to the teachings of Islam, Muhammed was the last of the prophets through whom God's message was transmitted to mankind. He was not God but the instrument God used to convey His truth to man, and although Muhammed is revered and honored by all Muslims as Allah's prophet, he is not worshipped. God's revelation as spoken through the voice of Muhammed was recorded in a holy book called the Koran (*Qu'ran*), which is the final authority in Islam, and for all Muslims the written word of God. The Koran has 114 chapters, or *surahs*, which range in length from 286 to 4 verses. Most Westerners find the Koran difficult reading, but to the Muslim it is an incomparable work. Many Muslims think that in the translation of the Koran from Arabic, the original language, to other languages much is lost of the symbolism, poetry, richness of imagery, and nuances of thought. Perhaps it is for this reason that so much time and effort is spent in teaching the followers of Islam to read the Koran in the original Arabic. God gave to man a complete revelation through Muhammed, and it is the sacred duty of Muslims to insure that it is known completely. Even after a quick reading of the Koran one is struck by the fact that Muhammed, who could neither read nor write, dictated a book which reveals an amazing knowledge of Jewish and Christian traditions and history, and a penetrating insight into the psychology and nature of man. The laws and ordinances that are promulgated throughout the Koran have withstood the vicissitudes of time and are still applicable to man. The social and ethical teachings of the Koran possess the stamp of permanency because they continue to meet the needs of the community and the yearning of the human heart. Of course, the good Muslim would not be amazed by the wisdom displayed in the Koran because it contains the words and knowledge of God, not Muhammed. The voice was the voice of Muhammed, but the thought and the words were of God. Nonetheless the voice had a magnificent tone and it reverberates through the pages of the Koran. For such a message, God chose a man whose voice could be heard through the ages.

Very early in the history of Islam problems in the interpretation of the Koran and in the adjustment of the Muslims to the requirements of Islam arose. As a result another authority developed, based upon tradition and anecdotes, which describes what Muhammed said, did, or tolerated among his followers. This authority is called the *Hadith* or *Sunna*. The *Hadith* supplements the Koran and is equally authoritative in matters which are not treated in the Koran.

BASIC BELIEFS OF ISLAM

Islam teaches that there is but one God, and his name is Allah. Belief in the oneness of God is fundamental to the Muslim religion, and the primary purpose of Islam is to remind man that He exists and should be worshipped and obeyed. The opening surah of the Koran reads:

> *In the name of Allah, the Beneficent, the Merciful.*
> *Praise be to Allah, the Cherisher and Sustainer,*
> *The Beneficent, the Merciful.*
> *Master of the Day of Judgment,*
> *Thee alone we worship; and Thine aid we seek.*
> *Show us the straight path,*
> *The path of those on whom Thou hast bestowed Thy grace,*
> *Those whose portion is not wrath,*
> *And who go not astray.*
>
> —SURAH I, 1-7

God is eternal. He created heaven and earth, and He is all-powerful, all-merciful, and all-just. He is unique. Having no equal, He should have no rivals. From the time of the Prophet himself, the Muslims have reserved their harshest criticism for those who worship so-called gods, for they veil the ultimate truth *of the one God.* In the early days of Islam, Muhammed and his followers were continually harassed by the worshippers of many gods who feared and detested the revelation that there was but one God. When the Muslims invaded India, the more extreme among them took every opportunity to destroy what they conceived to be the idols of Hinduism and

Buddhism, which they found in temples and public places. They scolded the Jews for forgetting the revelation of Abraham that there was but one God, and they reproved the Christians for deifying Christ, for they should know that he was but a prophet, although a great one. That there is but one God, is the eternal foundation of Islam.

Islam teaches that God created man and endowed him with an immortal soul. Each soul is an individual soul. Islam values the individual: it does not, as Hinduism, regard the individual as impermanent or transitory, but as having a permanence that is eternal. Every person is differentiated from every other person by the quality of uniqueness bestowed on him by God. Islam stresses the duty of each individual to work out his own destiny. Each is responsible for his actions. This is not to say that men should not help each other—Islam very emphatically commands its followers to provide others with all possible material and spiritual assistance in their efforts to reach God—but it is to say that, ultimately, it is the decision of each individual whether he follows the will of Allah or not. The Koran points out that "If anyone sins, he alone is responsible for his sin." (Surah IV, 111)

Islam teaches that there is a life after death for every person born on earth. Eventually, all must go to one of two places: heaven or hell. The Muslims believe that heaven is an abode of eternal delight where man may live forever together with God in rapturous peace and happiness. God does not dwell in hell, which is a place of eternal sorrow, torment, and despair. There are two paths which a man may walk in life—one is straight and leads to heaven and God, the other is crooked and leads to hell. It is for man to select, for the Koran says: "Whoever strays, he bears the full responsibility for his straying." (Surah X, 103) At the end, God will judge which of the two paths man has chosen to walk.

Islam seeks to guide man through life by encouraging him to undertake good deeds. Essentially, the good life for a Muslim is founded upon the five pillars of Islam.

THE FIVE PILLARS OF ISLAM

The first pillar is the creed, "There is no god but Allah, and Muhammed is His Prophet," which should be recited daily by the faithful. Generally, Muslims say this creed many times in the course of a day, but essentially it is only required to say it with faith and understanding once in a lifetime. The teachings of Islam are based on the fact of one God, and it is necessary for all Muslims to affirm this God with their tongue, at least once, but preferably every day and many times a day. The oneness of God must be indelibly engraved on the minds and hearts of every Muslim.

". . . and Muhammed is His Prophet." Muhammed was the man chosen by Allah to reveal His Word to man and has, therefore, a most honored place in Islam. By the frequent recitation of his name and title Muslims recall that it was under his leadership and direction that Islam was born in the hearts of men and that he merits their esteem and remembrance. But this recitation also recalls to them that he was a prophet only and must not be deified.

The second pillar of Islam is prayer. The Muslim should pray five times daily—before sunrise, at noontime, during the midafternoon, at sunset, and after sunset. Islam permits deviations from this schedule if, for example, adhering to it is likely to bring serious harm to the petitioner. One of the striking human qualities of Islam is the fact that it permits exceptions to many of its requirements under extenuating or abnormal circumstances.

A Muslim can pray anywhere. Although there are thousands of magnificent mosques scattered around the globe, it is not required of a Muslim to pray in a mosque. The whole world is a mosque for him, and he is urged to spread his prayer rug, and pray, wherever he finds himself at the scheduled hour of prayer.

Muslims should pray facing toward Mecca. This practice symbolizes the unity of Islam and is a respectful remembrance of Abraham. Before starting his prayer he should wash himself—his hands, his mouth, his face, behind his ears, his neck, his arms up to the elbows, and his feet up to the ankles. One should be as pure and as clean as possible before approaching his God in prayer. Here, as in other matters, Islam permits an exception, for if there is no water, and the Muslim of the desert might often find it impossible to obtain water, the Koran urges him to go to clean, high ground and rub his face and hands with its earth. The practice of compulsory washing five times a day instills in the Muslim the habit of cleanliness, and it is characteristic of Islam that, in this and other instances, it links together what is good for the body and what is good for the soul.

The Muslim stands with his thumbs touching the lobes of his ears, saying three times, *"Allahu akbar"* ("God is most great"). Still standing, but with hands clasped on his chest, he then recites the opening surah of the Koran, followed by a shorter surah of his own selection. An example of a short surah is the CII.

> *In the name of Allah, the Beneficent, the Merciful.*
> *Proclaim the Allah, the One!*
> *Allah, the Eternal, Absolute.*
> *He begetteth not, nor is He begotten;*
> *There is none that can compare to Him.*

He then bows placing his hands on his knees, saying, "Praise be to God, the Most Great." He stands again, praying, *"Allahu akbar."* ("God is most great"). He then kneels down, places his hands and face on the ground, saying, "Praise be to God, the Most Great." He also recites other prayers. He returns to a kneeling position, sits on his heels, and prays again. He repeats this ritual several times, always accompanied by prayer. He concludes by turning his head first to the right and then to the left, saying in each position, "May God watch over you and bless you."

The frequent prayers are designed to keep the Muslim ever mindful of his God and the duties required of him. The ritual is symbolic, but it also serves to keep him alert and conscious of the prayers he is reciting. When he turns his face to the right and to the left at the conclusion of his prayer, he is bestowing the peace of Allah upon his neighbors, whether there be anyone present or not, and thus he is reminded of the brotherhood that must exist within Islam.

Charity is the third pillar of Islam. Muhammed established a graduated tax of two and one-half per cent on the entire holdings of each person, a tax which adds up to one-fortieth of the entire wealth a Muslim possesses. Those who have must give; those who have not are excused. This is a high tax, and far exceeds the taxes which many modern states impose upon their citizens. In a real sense, Muhammed instituted a share-the-wealth plan which incorporates old-age pensions, social security, and other features of the welfare state. The money collected from this tax is used to succor the poor and the needy and to provide for the aged. The tax is also a kind of insurance because it is used to liberate debtors from their debts. In a sense Islam acts like a benevolent aid society, for the tax money is also used to assist wayfarers and to free captives from their bondage. Islam's teaching on charity helps to knit the family and the community more closely together, for it is the responsibility of Muslims to provide for their parents, impoverished kinsfolk, and neighbors. The funds collected are also utilized for religious purposes, such as the building and maintenance of mosques and the spread of Islam. In this use it resembles the tithing system of the Christians. Good Muslims, who faithfully and religiously observe the teachings of Islam on charity, do not find it easy to amass wealth.

Observing the month of Ramadan is the fourth pillar of Islam. The ninth month of the Arabic lunar calendar, Ramadan is important because during this month Muhammed received his revelation from God, as embodied in the Koran, and made his momentous *Hijra*, or migration from Mecca to Medina. In memory of these two most significant events, every Muslim, except those who are sick, involved in war, taking a journey, or excused by other exemptions, must fast from sunrise to sunset. No food, drink, smoke, or anything else should pass their lips during this period. After sunset it is permitted to take food and drink. Islam imposes this arduous fast upon man to teach him self-discipline and to remind him that he is in reality a weak creature who constantly requires the sustaining nourishment of his God. It also compels him to experience the searing and sickening pangs of hunger so that he will feel compassion for the hungry ones he meets, or who seek him out, and provide for them.

Pilgrimage to the holy shrine of the Kaaba in Mecca is the fifth pillar of Islam. Every Muslim who can, should visit Mecca and the Kaaba at least once in his lifetime, to renew his faith on the sacred ground which was blessed by Abraham when he erected the original Kaaba to the one God and where Muhammed was born and God first spoke to him. Here, the two sheet-like garments which all pilgrims must wear when approaching the Kaaba hide distinctions of status and wealth and publicly proclaim the equality of all before God. This same theme of equality and fraternity is evident when the Muslims pray within their mosques, as they usually do on a Friday. There is no reserved place in the mosque for the rich or the powerful. The possession of material goods or earthly power means nothing in the sight of God, and beggar and rich man, peasant and king, pray side by side, paying homage and adoration to their common God. The gathering of Muslims in Mecca from the far corners of the earth is a dramatic expression of the international brotherhood that links Muslim to Muslim within the shelter of Islam.

Because it affords an opportunity for Muslims from many different lands to meet and talk with one another, the pilgrimage to Mecca promotes international understanding within Islam. The unifying factor of one religion permits them to exchange ideas and information with less suspicion and antagonism than if there were no common ideology. Thus, the fifth pillar of Islam not only provides for the spiritual growth of man, but also furthers the concept of international brotherhood and understanding.

CONCLUSION

Islam is an accommodative ideology. It does not try to mold all men into one strict pattern of life, and it allows for individual and cultural differences, provided the basic teachings of Islam are preserved. It realizes that men live in different environments, and it adjusts itself to this diversity without sacrificing basic doctrines. Islam is a complete way of life for all who believe.

CHAPTER 17

EAST ASIA

East Asia is a term used to designate that part of Asia controlled by the political units of Communist China, North and South Korea, Japan, and Nationalist China based on Formosa. Communist China and Korea are mainland nations, while Japan and Formosa are island territories lying near the eastern and southern coasts of the mainland. The nations included in this area are close to one another geographically, and, generally speaking, the lives of the people reflect certain common physical and cultural characteristics.

CONGESTION ON "THE GOOD EARTH"

Since only a small portion of the total land is suitable for farming, most of East Asia's millions are confined within a small land space. China has a population of approximately 700 million, most of whom live in less than one-third of her land area. Japan, about the size of California, has over 90 million people, most of whom are concentrated in about 15 per cent of her land. The heavy pressure of tremendous numbers of people on a small portion of the land has led to an intensive cultivation of the soil, a great waste of human labor, and some of the highest food yields per acre in the world.

Farming is the main occupation of the people. The search for food is continuous, unending. Much is demanded of man and the land. The Asian farmer exhausts himself in a prodigal effort to gain a living from the soil; sometimes he even becomes a beast of burden, pulling the plough himself. Every little bit of land is coaxed into producing as much food as possible, not only once, but in some places two and three times a year, and often more effort and tender care is lavished on the good earth than is given to the children or wife of the farmer.

This concentration of great numbers of farmers in the same areas has resulted in the establishment of numerous villages. The villages in many rural areas are located so near each other that the result-

All but a small fraction of East Asia's land area belongs to China. As this map of the conflict areas in Asia illustrates, the Chinese Communists are attempting in every possible way to make their philosophy predominant (see pp. 282, 325).

ing scene resembles a rambling and loosely structured urban settle-ment, rather than a rural farming community. This congestion of villages is usually found in the rice-producing regions of East Asia, which are located south of the Ts'inling Mountains in China, gen-erally south of the island of Hokkaido in Japan, and wherever there is good soil and adequate water in Korea and Formosa.

Most of Korea's farmland is located in South Korea; North Korea, which has a Communist government, also has farming lands, but it is more noted for its industry and natural resources. The food-pro-ducing area of Formosa is located on its western shores facing the southern coast of mainland China. North of the Ts'inling Mountains in China, and in the Hokkaido part of Japan, where wheat is a more important crop, the farms are larger and the villages located farther apart.

In the Communist state known as the Mongolian People's Re-public, one million people occupy a land area of 604,000 square miles. The nation embraces the old homeland of the conquering Mongols, who by the thirteenth century ruled a vast territory reaching from China to Western Russia. As their power gradually declined, they became subjects of the Chinese; but after the estab-lishment of the Chinese Republic in 1911, they drove out the Chinese officials. In a treaty with Russia in 1945, the Chinese re-linquished their claim to Mongolia, and the Mongolians now rely on the might of Russia to protect them from the might of China. The people continue to cherish a nomadic way of life, herding their flocks and driving their horses over vast stretches of their land.

CHINA

China is the outstanding geographic, cultural, and political fact of East Asia. All but a small fraction of East Asia's land area belongs to China. The great rivers, the great mountains, the great plains, the great deserts, and the great plateaus of East Asia are all found within her borders. These borders contain 3,691,500 square miles and a population of 700 million that is increasing by 12 or 15 million a year. The civilization of East Asia is to a degree the civilization of traditional China. For centuries China possessed the most important civilization in East Asia. Highly original, it grew and matured largely independent of other cultures because barriers of mountain, ocean, desert, and jungle separated East Asia from the rest of the world. The geographic proximity of the countries of East Asia facilitated the spread of Chinese civilization to Japan and Korea.

Korea was visited early by Chinese immigrants who carried their language, culture, and customs with them. Gradually all of Korea came to be dominated by the culture of these settlers and their descendants. Korea is separated from Japan by only a few miles of water, and the Japanese were soon attracted by this culture. Korea thus served as a bridge over which the civilization of China traveled to Japan. The languages, the arts, the philosophy of Korea and Japan all reflect the cultural penetration of China into other areas of East Asia. The literature of Korea and Japan is written in ideographs which were borrowed from China. Confucianism, the dominant Chinese philosophy, was incorporated into the official ideology of Korea and Japan, and to this day it influences millions of Koreans and Japanese. There is a striking similarity between the art and architecture of China, Korea, and Japan. Even the clothes which the Japanese wear today, with the exception of Western dress, are thought to be copies of old Chinese costumes.

This dominant cultural position of China was strikingly shown in her contemptuous attitude toward her neighbors, whom she generally referred to as "barbarians." It was right and proper that these barbarians should come to China to learn about civilization, and thousands of students from Japan, Korea, and other neighboring lands went to China where they studied, among other things, philosophy, art, calligraphy, literature, and government. They took this learning back to their own countries where they became centers of Chinese learning which they spread among their fellows.

For many centuries China's neighbors also acknowledged her political dominance. Every year many countries, both far and near, indicated their subordination to the Empire of China by sending tribute to the court at Peking. China graciously acknowledged this tribute by sending back better gifts than were given her. The exchange of gifts served to stimulate trade and commerce between China and the other lands surrounding her, and in time there developed an economic interdependence in this area. For example, for more than fifty years Japan's prosperity was to a large extent based upon her economic relations with China, Korea, and Formosa.

It would be incorrect to say that the Chinese were not influenced by the thought and actions of other Asians and non-Asian people.

Probably the earliest and greatest impact made by India upon any people was the gift of Buddhism to China. Buddhism permeated the life of the Chinese and exercised an influence upon them that is immeasurable in its depth and breadth. Buddhism penetrated China during the first century of the Christian era and slowly became an integral part of Chinese religious life, finally blossoming into full flower during the T'ang Dynasty, one of the greatest periods in Chinese history. The Chinese interpreted and modified the Buddhism they had received and transmitted it to the Koreans and the Japanese who, in turn, molded it to fit their own special needs.

More recently, from the West has come the political thought of nationalism, democracy, and communism. Supreme authority during the two thousand years of imperial China was lodged in the emperor, who was ultimately the supreme law of the land. Under the leadership of Dr. Sun Yat-sen, the father of the Republic of China, the imperial system was abolished and a more modern government established based on his political ideas. From 1911 until approximately 1949 his "Three Principles of the People" were the political philosophy which guided the leaders of the Chinese people. Since the establishment of a Communist government on the mainland of China, the followers of Dr. Sun have carried on a government in Formosa based upon his political philosophy.

The present government on the Chinese mainland is based upon the principles of Communism as enunciated by Marx, Lenin, and Stalin and interpreted by Mao Tse-tung, the leader of the Chinese Communists. The Chinese Communists are attempting in every possible way to make their philosophy predominant in Asia. They have had some success in achieving this aim as evidenced in the Communist states of North Korea and North Vietnam and the occupied territory of Tibet.

In view of the long and strong influence that the Chinese have had, and have today, upon the thinking and actions of many Asians, it is important to examine the ideology, religion, social life, and politics of traditional and modern China.

CHAPTER 18

CHINESE IDEOLOGY

Confucianism, Taoism, and Legalism, the major schools of Chinese philosophy, can all be characterized as man-centered and thus world-centered. They are almost exclusively preoccupied in seeking to establish right principles of conduct which, if followed closely, must necessarily eventuate in a better human life on earth. In their optimism about the chances of achieving this better life, they differ significantly from Buddhism, an Indian import, which is deeply pessimistic about man's prospects for earthly happiness and looks to a nonearthly existence for an escape from suffering.

THE BACKGROUND OF CHINESE THOUGHT

A partial explanation for the singularly "practical" nature of the great Chinese philosophies may perhaps be found in the circumstance that all of them originated between the fifth and third centuries B.C. This was a troubled period for China, characterized by civil war and profound disturbances in economic, social, and political life. It was a transitional period when old institutions had seemingly lost their value but nothing new had yet taken their place. The people of China had two basic needs: to end the bloody wars between the states, and to establish a new social order. It was with these very real human problems that Chinese ideology was concerned.

To understand these ideologies it is essential to have some awareness of the historical circumstances which determined the character of Chinese society. After they had defeated the Shangs in the twelfth century B.C., the Chou kings established a feudal system in China in order to hold the conquered people in subjection. They placed vassal lords in charge of areas which varied in size and population and gave these lords rank generally commensurate with the size of the territory they governed. On condition of a strict obedience to the Chou king in matters affecting the kingdom, they were given full authority over their domains. The right to rule was, or soon became, hereditary. Political authority was retained by the descendants of the Chou kings and the ruling families within the feudal states assigned to them. The right of the old and noble families to rule derived from the belief that only they could invoke the supernatural aid required for the prosperity of the state in peace and war. They alone, according to popular belief, could make the sacrifices at the ancestral temples and at the altars of the land and the grain. If the rulers' sacrifices should cease, it was thought that the state would fall on evil times. The feudal order of society was thus secured by the partnership of the hereditary aristocrats and the spirits to whom they made sacrifices.

Gradually the foundations of the feudal order were whittled away. By the eighth century B.C. the royal authority was seriously diminished. During the period 772-481 B.C. the vassal lords acted more and more like state sovereigns. The basis of political authority became no longer spiritual sanction, but superior military force. By the time of Confucius in the fifth century B.C., the feudal kingdoms of the Chou Dynasty had been replaced by a group of independent states engaged in a struggle for political mastery of all China. The period from 481-221 B.C. in which this struggle took place is known as the Warring States Period. It ended with the triumph of the state of Ch'in over all other states and the unification of China under one emperor.

It can be seen that the fifth century B.C. was an age when the customary ways of living and thinking associated with feudalism had broken down and a new concept of society was desperately needed. Perceptive men of intellectual talent and humanitarian concern rose to the challenge of disorder. The great schools of Chinese philosophy were born.

Looking at the chaos around him, Confucius proposed a new politics and society which would retain many of the old rituals and diplomatic formalities but would be grounded in the moral responsibility of the ruler for the welfare of the governed. Viewing the same ruins, the Taoist concluded that the evils of the time were the inevitable consequences of any ordering of human life for social or political ends. They taught that man could be happy only in the absence of society. Under similar unhappy circumstances the Legalists decided that the solution lay in increasing the power of the ruler. They developed skill in the organization and supply of armies and the use of diplomacy in the interests of the state.

From the time of Confucius in the fifth century to the second century B.C. these three philosophies and a number of lesser schools of thought competed for supremacy, although none of them were accepted as orthodox. This era is known as the Period of the Philosophers. Around 100 B.C. Confucianism was adopted as the orthodox Chinese philosophy. The years between this date and the twentieth century are known as the Period of Classical Study because during this time the development of Chinese philosophy focused on the interpretation of Confucian, Taoist, and Buddhist writings rather than on the discovery of new institutions and ideas. China was now a unified nation with a single orthodox ideology based on a modified Confucianism.

BUDDHISM MET A NEED

Buddhism entered China around the beginning of the Christian era. At first it was frowned upon because it was thought that the concept of reincarnation was a fantasy and that the celibacy of monks was a disgraceful practice since it prevented a man from having descendants. Moreover, the authorities feared that the spread of this foreign religion would seriously threaten their power. It expanded rapidly, however, especially among the common people, and by 381 A.D. most of the people of northwest China were Buddhist. Winning converts also among the rulers and scholars, by the time of the T'ang Dynasty Buddhism was found everywhere in China.

There are a number of reasons why this religion found a home in China and attained such a prominent position in Chinese life.

From the second to the sixth century A.D. the people were beset with famine, wars, banditry, and political oppression, and Buddhism brought them hope. It taught that life was evil and death was only a pathway to a glorious heaven. It offered to rich and poor alike such compassionate deities as Amitabha Buddha and Kuan-Yin. Promising that justice would ultimately triumph, it taught that there was a rule of law throughout the universe and that everyone would be rewarded and punished according to strict justice.

Buddhist teaching dealt with fields of speculation which Confucianism and Taoism had generally left untouched, namely, the hereafter. Confucianists and Taoists did not regard this life as preliminary or probationary to another life in some hereafter. They were primarily interested in bettering human society and handling human problems. Interested in the dead only from the viewpoint of making them happy and obtaining blessings from them for themselves, they did not emphasize the question of death or give an answer to the problem of suffering.

Mahayana Buddhism, on the other hand, painted a graphic picture of the heaven and hell that awaited the good and bad people of the world. In this sense it possessed a more comprehensive doctrine than Taoism and a more spiritual character than the ethical code of Confucianism. Buddhism provided the Chinese of this period, from the second to the sixth century A.D., with a hope of material and spiritual benefits which attracted great numbers of them to the Buddhist faith.

CHAPTER 19

CONFUCIANISM

Do not do to others what you do not wish yourself.
—Confucius

Confucianism takes its name from Confucius, the Latinized name of its founder, Kung Fu-tzu. Confucius was born in 551 B.C. and died in 479 B.C. During his lifetime he attracted a number of disciples who, with later followers of his doctrines, are called Confucians.

From the time of Confucius until the second century B.C., the Confucians were engaged in a struggle to put their ideas into practice throughout China. The Legalists, the chief philosophical rivals of the Confucians, won a temporary victory when the state of Ch'in, 221-207 B.C., established a unified empire based on Legalist principles. Soon after the fall of the Ch'in Dynasty the Confucian philosophy was established as the official doctrine of the imperial government (early in the Han Dynasty, 200 B.C.-220 A.D.). Only with the destruction of the old educational system early in the twentieth century did the cult of Confucius become weakened. Confucianism lost its favored position with the institution of the Republic of China in 1911, when a mixture of Confucianism and Western liberal thought, as propounded by Sun Yat-sen, the father of modern China, became the official political theory of the state.

The content of Confucianism comes from many sources. Many ideas came from a period prior to the time of Confucius. For example, ancestor worship, sacrifices to the dead, spirits, and ceremonials, which are found today in the Confucian cult, were handed down from early Chinese times. Confucianism later drew on other schools of thought, including Legalism, Taoism, and Buddhism. Generally speaking, however, most of the fundamental doctrines are taken from speeches and writings attributed to Confucius and his important disciples, Mencius and Hsun Tzu. They are gathered together in a number of volumes collectively called the Confucian Canon. This canon consists of nine works which are divided into two groups known as the *Four Books* and the *Five Classics*. The *Four Books* consist of: (1) *The Analects*, or Sayings of Confucius, which contain the recorded teachings of Confucius himself; (2) *The Book of Mencius*, written by one of the greatest exponents of Confucian thought; (3) the *Great Learning*, a short treatise on Confucian ethics; and (4) the *Doctrine of the Mean*, which deals with universal harmony and ethics. The *Five Classics* were: (1) the *Book of History*, an unhistorical book edited in the interests of an ethical objective; (2) the *Book of Changes*, a treatise on fortune-telling based on sixty-four hexagrams; (3) the *Book of Poetry*, or *Book of Odes*, a collection of early folk poetry of the Chou period; (4) *Ch'un Ch'iu*, or *Spring and Autumn Annals*, a history of Confucius' native state of Lu; and (5) the *Li Chi*, or *Book of Rites*, which deals with ceremony and ritual.

Because of the great antiquity of these nine books there has been considerable debate as to their authorship and dates of origin. It is generally believed that Confucius edited the *Five Classics* in order to preserve the best of China's historical tradition. Some think that Confucius wrote the *Spring and Autumn Annals* himself. The content of the *Five Classics* is derived from pre-Confucian times. The *Four Books* are commonly held to be the writings of the disciples of Confucius and are dated later than the *Five Classics*. All the books, however, are generally accepted as containing valid Confucian doctrine.

SYMPATHY AND THE FIVE RELATIONSHIPS

Confucianism teaches that man is compelled by his nature to live in the company of other men, that is to say, in society. Only unnatural and abnormal people live outside the communities. This social way of life is the best way to live, because it is only in society that men reach their fullest development and realize their potentialities. The universal human quality which leads people to live in society is called by Confucians *jen*.

The Chinese character *jen* combines the symbol for *man* and the symbol for *two*, a combination which conveys the idea of a relationship between persons. The meaning of this word has been rendered in English as "benevolence," "human-heartedness," "man-to-man-ness," and "perfect virtue." All catch part of the meaning, but no single word conveys the whole meaning of *jen*. "Sympathy" is perhaps the one word that best expresses the idea. Sympathy expresses such a close relationship between persons that whatever affects one, similarly affects the other. Sympathy is the entering into and sharing of the feelings and interests of another; it is a mutual affection and understanding that arises from a common nature and temperament. The quality of *jen* has all these meanings and more. *Jen* to Confucians was and is the very root of society. *Jen* implies a shared humanity that can find expression only in human relationships.

Jen also includes the desire to help others. Since it is a universal quality possessed by all men, men have the ability to help one another. You merely look into yourself for the answers to the problems of others. In a sense you contain all men in yourself; self-understanding leads to an understanding of the fears and hopes of others. *Jen* involves a desire to aid others to achieve their ends. The Confucians taught that "The man of *jen* is one who, desiring to develop himself, develops others, and in desiring to sustain himself, sustains others. To be able from one's own self to draw a parallel for the treatment of others; that may be called the way to practice *jen*."

In its negative formulation the quality of *jen* is restated as a practical Confucian maxim. "Do not do to others what you do not wish yourself."

In both its positive and negative aspects *jen* points the way to action. When one's feelings are in harmony with those of others, to assist others one has only to examine himself. There is a beautiful example of this sympathetic feeling for others in a poem of Tu Fu, one of China's greatest poets, who lived in the T'ang Dynasty, 618-907 A.D. In a poem written to a relative he says:

> *Please allow your western neighbor to pluck the*
> *   dates from the trees before the hall;*
> *She is a woman, without children and with no*
> *   means of support.*
> *Were it not for dire poverty, she would hardly*
> *   have come for these fruits;*
>
> *And to save her from embarrassment, we have to*
> *   be especially kind.*

> *She is of course needlessly afraid of a stranger*
>   *from a distance;*
>
> *I recall her complaints of the taxation that has*
>   *made her poor to the bone;*
> *The burdens of war on such persons! It makes me*
>   *shed bitter tears.*[1]

It is apparent that the Confucians wanted *jen* to be expressed in action.

"Right action" is defined by Confucians in terms of the duties and obligations implicit in five basic social relationships. These five relationships are: ruler and subject, father and son, elder brother and younger brother, husband and wife, friend and friend. All of them except the last involve the authority of one person over another. The inferior owes loving obedience and loyalty to his superior, and the superior owes loving responsibility to the inferior. However, it is the duty of the inferior to advise the superior as to the right course of action. Confucius described right action in a positive manner when he said:

> In the way of the Superior Man there are four things, to none of which I have as yet attained—to serve my father as I would require my son to serve me; to serve my prince as I would require my minister to serve me; to serve my elder brother as I would require my younger brother to serve me; and to offer first to friends what one requires of them.[2]

Addressing himself to the idea expressed in the maxim "What you do not want done yourself, do not to others," Confucius wrote:

> What a man dislikes in his superiors, let him not display in the treatment of his inferiors; what he dislikes in inferiors, let him not display in the service of his superiors; what he hates in those who are before him, let him not therewith precede those who are behind him; what he hates in those who are behind him, let him not therewith follow those who are before him; what he hates to receive on the right, let him not bestow on the left; what he hates to receive on the left, let him not bestow on the right: This is what is called "The principle with which, as with a measuring square, to regulate one's conduct."[3]

---

[1] *Tu Fu, China's Greatest Poet*, translation and commentary by William Hung (Cambridge: Harvard University Press, 1952). Used with permission.
[2] B. S. Bonsall, *Confucianism and Taoism* (London: The Epworth Press, 1934). Used with permission.
[3] *Ibid.* Used with permission.

Confucianism insists that the names father, son, ruler, subject, elder brother, younger brother, husband, wife, and friend indicate a certain type of conduct. When a son is lovingly obedient to the father and the father dutifully responsible for the son, the Confucians say that the names father and son have been rectified. If a man does not act like a father, a husband, an elder brother, a friend, then he is not really one, because the reality does not conform to the meaning of the terms. This is true for all other human relationships. The continual process of individual adjustment to a well-defined traditional role is a distinctive feature of Chinese society. A perceptive author, Mr. Francis L. K. Hsu, in his book *Americans and Chinese* has observed that "The Chinese tends to mobilize his thought and action for the purpose of conforming to the reality, while the American tends to do so for the purpose of making the reality conform to him."

The "just action" in a particular situation is called *yi*. When it has been decided upon, it should be carried out because it is just, but the correct decision can be made only if the weighing of the facts has been inspired by *jen*, that is, combined with a feeling of humane concern. Confucian justice is not a cold intellectual principle, nor merely a written code like that of the Legalists, but a kind of compassionate wisdom. The Chinese have many codes of law, but above and beyond the written law is the quality of sympathy which must enter into each decision.

Confucianism is, in many ways, a rule by man rather than by law. The concept of an impersonal abstract law which is binding upon all persons at all times and in all situations is alien to Confucian thought. The maintenance of peace and harmonious relations within a community is more important than a notion of absolute human rights. Consequently, peacemakers and middle-men are continually mediating disputes and settling all sorts of conflicts everywhere in China in accordance with the prescriptions of established custom and tradition and the circumstances of the particular case. Justice was what local public opinion thought fair and reasonable to all concerned under the circumstances, and decisions were made only after arbitration and compromise. No one party was considered completely right or completely wrong.

CEREMONIAL AND RELIGIOUS ASPECTS

Li is the specific manner in which the just action should be performed. *Li* has several meanings and is translated into English as "etiquette," "ritual," "ceremony," and "sacrifice." Both Westerners and Taoists have sharply criticized this ceremonial aspect of Confucianism. The West has represented it as a tiresome routine of ritual and pedantry and described it as superstitious, meaningless, and mumbo-jumbo. The Taoists detest the Confucians for their rituals and ceremonies, charging that they distort man's feelings in the interests of social conformity.

It should be made clear, however, that, dear as ritual in social relations is to the Confucian, it is not considered important in itself. Ritual and forms are important as language is important. They furnish a standard vocabulary for the expression of feeling; and it is a rich vocabulary.

Their use implies the existence of a norm of human behavior. Confucians believe that it is normal and right that one should experience certain feelings of respect or solicitude or sorrow in certain situations. Whereas the Taoists deplore mourning for the dead as a useless ordeal performed out of ignorance, the Confucians believe that one ought to experience a sense of loss on the death of, say, a father or mother, and that rites and forms of mourning supply a medium for the sincere and dignified expression of sorrow. If for some reason one does not experience sorrow, then the rituals are worthless, and that person should look into himself for the reason for his indifference.

To the Confucians the regular reverential observance of *li* cultivates the reverential feeling that graces social relationships and the exercise of political authority. Thus, *li* has an educational importance. In the *Li Chi*, a Confucian classic which provides a rich source of ceremonial forms, Confucius is reported as saying, "The instructing and transforming power of ceremonies is subtle; they stop depravity before it has taken form, causing men daily to move towards what is good, and keep themselves farther apart from guilt, without being themselves conscious of it." In addition to expressing these feelings, the rituals and ceremonies provide a specific guide for normal behavior.

Confucius himself was not much concerned with religion as such.

He mentioned it only incidentally, and although he appeared to believe in heaven and ancestors, he spoke little about these beliefs. However, when Confucianism became the orthodox doctrine of the empire, religious functions were incorporated into it. Confucius, along with his ancestors and his famous followers, became objects of worship and veneration. Confucian temples were erected all over the empire, tablets to Confucius and his followers were placed within these temples, and sacrifices and rituals were performed before these tablets and elsewhere.

In the Confucian cult one of the most important duties of the emperor was to maintain the proper relationship between himself and heaven. Heaven is generally interpreted to be an impersonal force. With this interpretation of heaven a Confucian could be an agnostic, and even an atheist. Heaven was, however, regarded as the governing authority of the universe and the final judge of right and wrong. The universe was resolved into a trinity of heaven, earth, and man. Heaven directs, earth produces, and man co-operates. When man co-operates, he prospers. When man fails to co-operate, he destroys the harmonious arrangements of the universe and suffers the consequences in the form of national disasters and calamities such as floods, droughts, and famines.

The emperor was charged with a particular responsibility in this regard. If he fell away from the state of moral perfection, heaven would cause the world to suffer its displeasure. To prevent this, the emperor was obliged to undergo a tiresome round of ritual observance, performing ceremonies and sacrifices by the calendar throughout the year. When the emperor fulfilled his role, the officials and common people theirs, and served the emperor well, then the empire was a harmonious society in which all men were tied together by bonds of right feeling.

The Confucian cult differed much from other cults in Asia and in the West. It was very rational. Little was said about an after-life; there were few visible objects of worship, and there was no god to save or condemn, or to whom responsibility could be relinquished. The cult was mostly limited rather sharply to the scholar class, which was tied together by the bonds of a common education and culture. The cult did not demand an unflinching faith in some fixed creed, but permitted the individual great freedom of personal belief. So long as Confucius remained the model of the scholar class, and the ceremonies were performed reverently and regularly, little more was demanded of the Confucian scholar.

THE FAMILY AND THE STATE

Confucians, both traditionally and today, give an important place to the family as a moral community. It is in childhood that personality has its main development, and a family life is a kind of social school in which the child encounters the problems of responsibility and privilege that he will meet in other forms in the world at large. Since the Confucians believe that the state is an extension of the family, the same attitudes toward authority and obedience that are valued in the family are also valued in the state.

In the days of the empire, the emperor and all the officials under him were referred to as the parents of the people. Subjects owed the same loyalty to the political authorities that they owed to the seniors in the family. The emperor sacrificed for the whole people much as the head of the family sacrificed for his particular family. In the Confucian view, if one learned to accept and perform the standard roles in relation to members of his family, he could understand and honor the obligations and privileges of public office.

The Master (Confucius) said: "In their nature at birth men are nearly alike, in their habits they are vastly different." (*Analects,* 17:2) The Confucians, knowing that these habits were the results of experience, emphasized the importance of education in forming character and in cultivating a moral standard. Education was largely ethical, for family heads and the political officials were responsible for the moral state of the people under their authority.

Confucians aimed to turn people into good family men and good subjects of the emperor. The officials were to provide a good example for the people, and the emperor was to show the way for all to follow. If he failed in this, the state must fall into decay.

Confucius said nothing explicitly about social classes, but he did discuss the relationship between the ruler and the ruled. He believed that the wisest and most humane men should rule because only they could be relied upon to rule in the interest of all. The educated man was honored above all others in China. Teaching and government service, professions which required a great deal of education, were the most honored professions. True, there were always corrupt officials who met the formal Confucian tests of office in order to enrich themselves, without thought for the people they governed. But what Confucianism aimed at in government was a tradition of selfless service. Adherence to the tradition would administer the empire and guide the emperor himself. In the course of time, and perhaps inevitably, the scholar-officials, or *literati,* came to form a distinct social class. Inclusion in this class was not limited by heredity, but by learning as tested in examinations of the imperial civil service. Most Chinese, by reason of poverty, were unable to learn Confucian literature and were thereby denied admission to the ruling group. Thus Confucianism became the special concern of a social class as well as the official philosophy of an empire. The dogmatic development of Confucian ideas was given impetus when Confucians came into their own as administrators of the Han Dynasty, 202 B.C.-220 A.D. Complicated ritual and etiquette are a handy and not uncommon device to exclude outsiders from a social class or group. Many people today use such means to maintain the so-called purity of their group.

Confucianism is sometimes dismissed as a mere rationalization of political authority by an exploitative ruling class. Taking all things into account, however, this estimate of Confucianism fails to gauge the truth of its basic propositions or objectives in the light of common human experience.

In the days of the empire the practical object of Confucianism was to promote and conserve a happier and a better ordered society through government. The basis of good government was the virtue of the ruler. The good example expressed by the ruler was a positive force capable of transforming people and making them better. This rule by example and popular response was stated by Confucius in a short sentence: "As the wind blows, so bows the grass." The need for virtue and rule by example was not confined to the emperor but also applied to the ministers who aided him. In politics, Confucius was not concerned so much with techniques as with morality. The business of government was as much to reduce corruption by moral education and example and, when needed, by punishment as it was to keep up irrigation works and defend the empire.

A Confucian state exhibits some features that distinguish it sharply from the nation-state of the West. "State" in the Western sense of that term implies definite territorial limits and sovereignty. The Confucian state was a universal state. All men ought to give their allegiance to the emperor. Foreigners and Chinese alike owe all they have to the service of the emperor. Racial or ethnic origins are theoretically irrelevant. Yellow man, white man, black man, red man all started off alike. A man was not born a Chinese. He might learn to be one. Being Chinese was a matter of culture, of obedience to the emperor, not of nationality. Naturally, this involved full acceptance of the customary role of the Chinese subject. Such an official philosophy led to two results: a remarkable degree of homogeneity and a marked absence of racial prejudice. A common culture, not a common skin, made all men brothers within the political family of China.

Successful revolution was justified by the Confucians. It was called the "Mandate of Heaven." This drastically limited the sovereignty or ultimate authority of the state. There was in fact no absolute sovereign in the Chinese system unless it was heaven itself, before which the emperor must himself bow as its adopted son. In effect the emperor must always subordinate his authority to the principles embodied in the Confucian canon and the precedents in the historical records compiled by Confucian scholars. No Emperor could say, without violating the Confucian estimate of his position, "I am the state."

THE CONSERVATIVE NATURE OF CONFUCIANISM

The unity and permanence of Chinese civilization is in large measure due to the contribution of Confucianism. For the past two thousand years Confucianism has been the ideology of countless generations of scholar-officials. A good knowledge of Confucianism was the only path to fame and the most influential positions in Chinese society. Anyone could obtain this knowledge if he had the desire, the opportunity, and the will. Regardless of his racial origin or ethnic group, no matter what class of society he was born into, if a person successfully proved knowledge through tests, he took his place among the leaders of Chinese society.

The family, which gave permanence and stability to Chinese civilization, was emphasized in Confucian thought. Confucians considered it the most important moral unit, and the state merely an extension of it. They protected family unity by law and custom; they encouraged its growth through the grant of privileges; and they prevented its breakup by reserving the harshest sanctions and punishments for those who violated family regulations and traditions.

The privileged position of the Confucians led at times to conservatism and arrogance. Since it was Confucianism that kept the scholar-officials and the leaders of the community in power, these men were strongly impelled to oppose ideological changes. Furthermore, the Confucians sincerely believed that they were the only civilized community in the world, that all beyond the boundaries of their culture were barbarians who had nothing to give the Confucians, but to whom the Confucians had much to give. To hold such a belief is to become arrogant and contemptuous of other beliefs and other cultures. One of the reasons for China's reluctance to change her way of life when first exposed to Western culture and technology was the degree to which Confucianism had permeated Chinese life and thought.

TAOISM

The duck's legs are short, but if we try to lengthen them, the duck will feel pain. The crane's legs are long, but if we try to shorten them, the crane will feel grief. Therefore we are not to cut off what is by nature long, nor to lengthen what is by nature short.

—CHUANG TZU

The philosophy of Taoism takes its name from the Chinese word *Tao* meaning "The Way." It is the first word of the Taoist book *Tao Te Ching*, "The Classic of the Way and Its Power." The three principal teachers of this Chinese philosophy were Lao Tzu, Tang Chu, and Chuang Tzu. Traditionally, Lao Tzu, "Old Master," was the founder of Taoism and the author of *Tao Te Ching*. Tang Chu lived about the fourth century B.C. Chuang Tzu lived approximately 369-286 B.C.; he is considered Lao Tzu's most distinguished disciple and is believed to be the author of the book of *Chuang Tzu*.

According to tradition, Lao Tzu was an older contemporary of Confucius, but modern scholars have questioned his very existence. They believe that the books attributed to Lao Tzu and Chuang Tzu were written after the period when Confucius lived by later members of the Taoist school.

THE NATURAL WAY

Taoism advised men that the best way to live is the natural way. He is happiest who lives in accordance with his nature. Man's fears, man's sufferings, man's problems, are the result of man's unnatural life. Man can be truly free only when he liberates himself from all artificial restraints. Taoism, which is also described as "The Way of the Uninhibited," stresses such words as "naturalness," "spontaneity," and "simplicity."

It is barely possible to suggest what the Tao is. The early Taoists

159

never directly defined it because they believed language incapable of adequately determining its precise meaning. "Those who know the Tao do not speak of it; those who speak of it do not know it." Chuang Tzu stated that he should not seek precision in trying to understand the Tao, for although he had journeyed across it, he still only knew where it began, and although he had wandered in its vastness, he did not know where it ended. The Tao lies beyond shape and feature like an uncarved block and is eternally nameless. Taoists spoke of it as "a shape without shape, a form without form." The Tao is the unseen power beneath the life and movement in nature. It is like the quiet unconscious processes of nature which flow without motive, without effort, and without end. Chuang Tzu states this idea poetically: "The sun and moon simply shine, and the four seasons pursue their courses. So it is with the regular phenomena of day and night, and with the movement of the clouds by which the rain is distributed." The Tao is like the stream of time, drifting along without goals and without purpose, and just as unexplainable. Certain of the Tao's properties are suggested by analogy with moving water. As water overcomes obstacles in its path by flowing around them, so the Tao overcomes by yielding; as rivers and oceans are great because they occupy the low places of the earth, so the Tao is great because it is lowly. The Tao, because it is the ultimate reality, is present everywhere in all things, in the fly, in the earth, in the wastes of body and kitchen. It is also infinite, for if you go back and back, you cannot discover its beginning, and if you go forward and forward, you will not find its end.

Flowing unceasingly and effortlessly in nature, the Tao is also the force that gives life and their particular nature to all beings. The nature of any particular being is found in the Tao's manner of producing and sustaining it. It is the nature of a fish that it cannot exist out of water. It is the nature of man that he must breathe air. Things differ in their natures and natural abilities. A duck is different from a crane, a horse is different from a man, and a dog is different from a cat. Although the Tao is continually changing the physical forms inhabiting the universe, the change is always in accordance with the individual nature of each form. To overrun this nature and act contrary to its commands is harmful because such actions interrupt the unconscious, natural, sustaining flow of the Tao. For instance, to subject horses to hunger and thirst, to force them to race and walk together in regular order, to place a bit in their mouths and lash them with a whip must harm them because all these things are contrary to the nature of a horse. Something is contrary to the nature of a being when it is artificial and man-made, external rather than internal. "What is of nature is internal. What is of man is external. . . . That oxen and horses should have four feet is what is of nature. That a halter should be put on a horse's head, or a string through an ox's nose, is what is of man." To try to shorten a crane's legs, or to try to lengthen a duck's legs, is contrary to the nature of these animals and therefore can only cause them pain.

Taoism affirms the right to spontaneous expression of one's individual nature and abhors social restraints. The fact that men live in society with conventional rules of behavior is contrary to the dictates of men's natures and therefore harmful. Social conventions are external to man and artificial and therefore must be considered unnatural. The early Taoists could not describe precisely the nature of man, or any animal for that matter, but they could teach what it was not. The wood of the living tree, unspoiled by alien hand, was the Taoist symbol of the natural state of men whose natures have not been inhibited by conventional values.

In its negative theoretical aspects, Taoism was a revolt against society by withdrawal from it. It did not preach a withdrawal from the physical presence of other men; rather it denied the validity of the social relationships established by them.

The Taoists, like other dissident groups in China, attributed their principles to a past golden age in order to make their philosophical innovation seem conservative and therefore more palatable to the people of their time. People once lived naturally, wearing clothes they had woven and eating food they had grown, and all creatures of earth and sky lived together in harmony. People wandered over the land like wild deer. Virtue was practiced unconsciously and knowledge was not valued. All things acted naturally without knowledge, without purpose, without unnatural desires, and without artificial restraints. All things were in harmony because all were unrestrained in the spontaneous expression of their natures. After the coming of the culture heroes—the inventors of conventions and morality and the seekers after knowledge—the perfect community became disrupted and was gradually lost to the memory of man. Then all submitted their natures to the harness of convention. The

world became confused because the Tao, the True Way, was obscured and hidden by the artificialities of man. The Taoists were in
revolt against society as an agent of the corruption of man which
separated him from his true nature.

The Taoists denied the validity of conventional notions of good
and evil. They saw conventional good and conventional evil as op-
posite sides of the same coin. The standards of value that society
invented created an evil for every good they defined.

The true good of all men was the free expression of their proper
natures, and if they should fail in this, nothing good could be said
concerning their condition. The conventional paragon and the
conventional thief were both of them pitiable distortions of their
natural selves.

THE TAOIST SAGE

Taoism asserts that another way by which men are led astray
from the paths of their true natures is by the improper use of the
senses. Improperly used, sense perception leads to the illusion that
things, which are merely manifestations of the Tao, have an existence independent of the viewer and other things. Thereupon two
forms of perversion become possible: (1) to desire things or fear
them, and (2) to have knowledge of them as things. The
Taoist sage, possessing all things because of his union with the Tao,
was not troubled by the illusion that they have a separate existence
and was therefore devoid of all fear, desire, and false knowledge.
This is not to say that the Taoists had no human feelings or lacked
the natural appetites of men. The sage rejoiced in the spontaneous
expression of man's nature and the satisfaction of his natural appetites. But the only true knowledge for the Taoists was the realization of oneness with the Tao that eliminated the distinction between knower and known.

Taoist philosophers contrasted the tranquil happiness of the
sage with the gnawing anxiety and fear endured by those whose
nature had been corrupted. One of the joys of sagehood, perhaps
the greatest of them, was the attainment of a sense of immortality.
The corrupted man, ignorant of the Tao, held fast to an illusory and
impermanent self. The everpresent threat of death intensified the
pain of his striving with the knowledge that he must someday lose
everything. It was quite otherwise with the sage. Since he felt him-

self to be one with the eternal Tao, he knew that his death was merely a change of form and had small significance. He awaited it without fear.

The practical consequence of the corruption of men by society and by errors arising from their senses is that they deliberately exert themselves for unnatural ends. They embroil themselves in politics and loud arguments, they fight with one another, and feel frustration in their search for fame. They arouse envy and constantly live in fear of death. The Taoist sage, on the other hand, never had the intention of seeking or doing anything, but did all things naturally and not for a purpose. Similarly the individual should act without the intention of acting, he should give without the intention of being generous, and smile without the intention of pleasing. In other words, every act should flow spontaneously from the individual's nature as the processes of nature flow in their inevitable course. The true Taoist's mind did not stop to pass judgment on itself. The thought should be as unthought-of by the thinker as the well-fit shoe is unthought-of by the foot that wears it.

One might reasonably suppose that the Taoist philosopher's impassioned rejection of society implied a corresponding rejection of politics. On the contrary, the Taoists developed a historically important theory of politics. Soon after Taoist philosophy was founded, Taoists yielded to the very human desire for political power. This power they based not in social virtues, or in ancestral spirits, but in the Tao. The Taoist sage, they believed, would of necessity be master of the world. Quiet, humble, and nonwilling, he would be one with the Tao and therefore in complete control of the myriad things of the universe. The sage-ruler would govern without appearing to govern. He would restore to the people the felicity of the golden age by filling their bellies and emptying their minds. This doctrine was eagerly taken up by the Legalists who found in it a theoretical basis for their totalitarian techniques.

POPULAR TAOISM

Taoism is an imaginative philosophy that has its best expression in the poetic system of the *Tao Te Ching* and the *Chuang Tzu*. The Taoist philosopher tried to liberate the minds of his hearers from conventional habits of thought that obscured the truth. In carrying out his mission of liberation the Taoist philosopher used startling paradoxes and vivid analogies, often in dialogue form, to excite the minds of his listeners. A typical paradox states: "The Tao in its regular course does nothing, and so there is nothing which it does not do." The Taoist delighted in speaking of the usefulness of the useless, the importance of the unimportant, the intelligence of the stupid, and the sight of the sightless. The analogies found throughout the early writings of Taoism show a feeling for life and movement in nature. Thus, the speaker in the book of *Chuang Tzu* illustrates a point by saying: "The tailorbird makes its nest in the deep forest, but only uses a single branch; the mole drinks from the Ho, but only takes what fills its belly."

Later Taoists gave a religious turn to the mystical aspects of the original doctrine. Many important Chinese gods, such as the gods of rain, fire, medicine, and agriculture and the kitchen gods, arose from the Taoist school. The impersonal and infinite force beneath nature became transformed into individual, finite human souls that, after death, became powerful spirits. The popular Taoism of later times increasingly filled the need for the magic that people often turn to when other resources fail them. The Chinese peasant sought the help of unseen powers because he lived on a narrow economic margin, and hard work and skill were not always enough for survival. As a consequence, the average man began to associate the Taoists with the world of spirits who must be placated and appeased. The Taoists were called upon more and more to select lucky days for weddings and funerals, to choose sites for housing, and in general to regulate those human activities peculiarly related to the world of spirits.

The debasement of Taoism in its popular form was clear in the Taoist practitioner's search for the elixir of immortality. He and his clients showed a fear of death that would have shamed such philosophical Taoists as Lao Tzu and Chuang Tzu. Further, Taoist alchemists profaned their philosophic heritage by attempting to transmute base metals into gold and silver.

Popular superstitions were not the only additions to Taoism. Ideas and practices of other schools also attached themselves to the Taoist tradition. Ritualistic practices, possibly of Indian origin, can be found in later Taoistic writings. Buddhism greatly influenced Taoism because of the mystical quality common to both schools of thought, and the Taoists in later days borrowed much of the external trappings of Buddhism, such as monasteries, statues, and the organization of priesthood.

Philosophic Taoism has remained through the ages of Chinese history a subject of study and meditation for the scholarly class of China. The Chinese scholar, like the Western scholar of Chinese thought, is intrigued and stimulated by the imaginative and acute criticisms that Taoism levels against many aspects of society and by its view of the nature of the universe. Taoism has also been reflected in Chinese poetry and painting. In their contemplative moods and in their love of nature the Chinese owe more to Taoism than to Confucianism.

CHAPTER 21

LEGALISM

> *When the guiding principles of the people become unsuited to the circumstances, their standards of value must change. As conditions in the world change, different principles are practiced.*
> —THE BOOK OF LORD SHANG

The Chinese called Legalism "the school of law" because it was a philosophy that stressed laws, imposed and interpreted by the ruling sovereign, as standards for the people's actions. Three works contain the main collection of Legalist writings: *The Book of Lord Shang*, traditionally attributed to Shang Yang (d. 338 B.C.), *Han Fei-Tzu*, compiled by Han Fei-tzu (d. 233 B.C.), the most famous of the Legalist writers, and *Kuan Tzu*, which was probably written by a number of Legalist writers.

Legalism was the first Chinese philosophy that became the official ideology of the nation. It provided the direction and philosophical foundation for China's first unified empire, the Ch'in Dynasty (221-207 B.C.).

TOTALITARIAN PHILOSOPHY IN CHINA

Legalism was a philosophy of expediency that had no place for permanent or absolute moral standards. The ruler should stand alone and be all-powerful. He was not subject to any higher authority. The ruler should lay down the standards by which the people of the state were to govern their lives. The Legalists believed that if the ruler based his actions upon absolute moral standards his authority would soon be lost and the state weakened.

The determining factor in all matters, the Legalists held, was the ruler's needs for the moment. These needs varied with time and circumstance; in each situation only those actions should be justified which helped to maintain or increase the ruler's power. The question of right and wrong in this context was determined by the individual ruler. The same act might be right for one ruler but wrong for the other. Schools of thought that sought in a real or imagined past for ways to solve the disorders of the Warring Period (481-221 B.C.) were rebuked by the Legalists who said that "There is more than one way to govern the world and there is no necessity to imitate antiquity, in order to take appropriate measures for the state."

The Legalists believed that society formed the man. As social conditions changed, so the people changed. Any solution for the problems of life must take into consideration this fact of a changing society. Because they believed that their teachings were based upon this fact, the Legalists thought of themselves as completely realistic.

They held that two problems not present in former ages complicated the social and political life of their time: the scarcity of material goods, and the increased value of state offices, especially that of the emperor. With regard to the first problem, the Legalists taught that material goods were abundant in former years, and because of the small population everybody had more than he needed. Therefore there was no disorder, for there was no need to compete with others. With the passage of time, as the population grew, the amount of material goods which could be shared by the people decreased. Competition, which then became the normal relationship between the people, grew so intense that it obscured the long-range goals of the general welfare and blinded the people to all things except their individual and immediate interests. Han Fei-tzu referred to the people as babies who were incapable of understanding why their heads were shaved or their boils lanced, who did not realize that these operations, though painful, were for their own good. The second great problem, according to the Legalists, was the struggle, then tearing the country apart, to obtain the office of emperor of China. They believed that in former times the office of emperor was not so lucrative as in their times, that formerly the emperor lived in a rough hut, ate the poorest foods, wore the clothes of a gatekeeper, and worked like a slave. In time, however, even the office of district magistrate provided enough to keep a family comfortable for generations. Of how much more value was the office of emperor. Consequently, the various independent states of China were engaged in continual warfare, each seeking the ultimate goal of hegemony over all the other states and each ruler seeking the position of emperor.

VIRTUE BY LEGISLATION

The Legalists thought that the solution to both problems lay in the establishment of a strong centralized government under the control of one ruler. Such a government would simultaneously increase the power of the state in relation to other states and in relation to its own citizens. The three important factors in the organization and maintenance of a strong centralized nation were: *fa,* or law; *shih,* or authority, position, power; and *shu,* or statecraft, methods or art of government.

The Legalists held that law was superior to virtue, morality, or ritual as an instrument for controlling the citizens of the state. *Jen,* or benevolence, did not enable a father to keep his children in order, much less could it enable a ruler to keep his subjects in order. Law, however, gave strength to a state: "No country is permanently strong. Nor is any country permanently weak. If conformers to law are strong, the country is strong; if conformers to law are weak, the country is weak." The laws promulgated by the legalists were intended to safeguard the power of the state; they were not instituted for the protection of individual rights or privileges. They were, in the last analysis, penal laws, instituted for the purpose of concentrating power more firmly in the hands of the ruler and enabling him to conquer other states.

Shih (power, position, authority) was another essential factor in the establishment and preservation of a strong centralized government. *Shih* represented dominance over others; the ability to influence and control man's actions. The office of ruler was the concrete manifestation of this power. No one could command the people's obedience until he had occupied the office of ruler. Thereupon he possessed the authority to rule the people through punishment or reward.

The Legalists thought that man was moved to action only through motives of self-interest, that is to say, through the hope of some reward or the fear of some punishment. Subjects obey their ruler, not because they love him, but because they fear him, and it was on this basis that the ruler must govern. In employing punishments no affection or extenuating circumstances must be taken into consideration. Even the smallest of infractions must be punished severely, and there were many instances of severe punishments for relatively small violations of the law, such as having a hand cut off for throwing ashes in the street or being cut in two for neglecting to denounce a culprit. The thought behind this attitude was that if small infractions were punished with severity, no one would dare commit grave infractions. Punishments and rewards, like the law, should be made known to the people clearly, simply, and in great detail. They should be definite, adequate, and inevitable so that there might be no ambiguity and confusion.

Shu (statecraft, methods or art of government) was the third essential factor in the creation and preservation of a strong centralized state under the dominance of one ruler. Since the ruler was the key individual in the state, the one who set the standards, gave directions, and kept the people in line by his application of rewards and punishments, the wisdom of his actions was the most important factor in the Legalist philosophy of expediency. In their books many pages are devoted to describing the manner in which he should rule and the relationship that should exist between him and his ministers. Well aware that the ruler needed men to govern the country, the Legalists advised him to delegate all his duties to them. He should do nothing but maintain the system of rewards and punishments and see to it that the ministers carried out the duties required by the offices they held. In fact, the ruler who truly understood the art of government could pass the time hunting and carousing, for his country would not suffer from his lack of attention to administrative details. This is the Legalist interpretation of the Taoist idea that the ruler rules by doing nothing, yet there is nothing that is not done. The ruler did not need to do anything after the methods for selecting and promoting personnel, and the duties of each office, had been spelled out in the law and backed up by a code of rewards and punishments that covered every situation. Certain other recommendations were stressed. The ruler should tell no one his wishes, not even his son, lest his ministers use this information for their own purposes. He must beware of corruption and bribery on the part of his ministers, especially with regard to his favorite concubines and mistresses, lest he be influenced while drunk or during some particularly tender interlude. He was cautioned against the attempt of ministers to advance their cause through his relatives and friends by gifts and palaces, trappings for his horses, or clothes for his wives.

MAN EXISTS FOR THE STATE

The Legalists contended that, in a world of competing states all striving for mastery, only two occupations should be encouraged by the central government—war and agriculture. The Legalist sage should mobilize the people to concentrate exclusively on agriculture at home and war abroad. Agriculture contributed directly to the strength of the state since food was essential for life, and war was the pathway to the control of all China. When the people were single-minded in these pursuits, the road to becoming emperor of all China was clear of all major obstructions.

The Legalists solved the difficult problem of recruiting people into these strenuous and sometimes dangerous occupations by resorting to their theory that man was actuated solely by self-interest. The ruler should make certain that profit came only from the soil, and fame solely through war. People, they believe, spend most of their lives scheming for profit and, when near death, are very desirous of a high reputation and fame. The ruler should bring about such harsh conditions at home that the people find life bitter when not tilling the land and dangerous when not fighting the country's battles. When this ideal condition was realized, the state would be strong and orderly at home, respected and victorious abroad. There should be no classes or occupations standing outside the law; only the ruler stood above it. Advancement should come only through proficiency in war and agriculture. Consequently, the Legalists attacked the aristocrats, artisans, hermits, innkeepers, merchants, soothsayers, scholars, and philanthropists. Artisans, who pander to the tastes of men through luxuries, were useless to the state, as were the hermits, who spend their days in foolish meditation. Innkeepers served only restless people who were probably plotting against the state; and merchants, scheming in their own interest, harmed the state through the creation of artificial scarcities.

The Legalists reserved some of their harshest criticisms for the Confucians, whom they termed the "good people." By "good" the Legalists meant those who would loyally protect friends and relatives who broke the law rather than denounce them to the state. This practice made the people stronger than the law and thus weakened the state; it was only when the law was stronger than the people that a state was strong.

Philanthropists were denounced as weakening the state by encouraging laziness and extravagance. It was wrong, said the Legalists, to tax the rich, who through thrift and hard work had won success, in order to feed and clothe those who through idleness and extravagance had become poor. The Legalists also opposed appeals to supernatural agents and insisted that private quarrels cease because the law alone determined guilt or innocence, reward or punishment. Everything must be subordinated to the good of the state, even the luxury of revenge.

THE LEGACY OF LEGALISM

In the Ch'in Dynasty, established in 221 B.C., Legalism saw its doctrines triumph. The state of Ch'in, by utilizing the methods advocated by the Legalists, conquered the other independent states of China and set up one nation headed by a ruler who significantly took the name of "The First Emperor." The country was divided into a number of administrative districts, laws and regulations were promulgated throughout the country, weights and measures were standardized, and all measures taken to unify the country under the control of one ruler.

After eleven years the emperor died, and by 207 B.C. the Ch'in Dynasty had lost control of the people. The Chinese did not take kindly to the rigorous punishments inflicted by the Ch'in rulers, and soon many of them revolted against this severe regime. Under the Han emperor Wu, who came to the throne in 140 B.C., Legalism, disguised by Confucian trappings, became again the dominant ideology of the state, but after Wu's death it passed away as an independent philosophy and exclusive ideological foundation for the government.

Legalist philosophy, however, left a legacy in codified laws, the unification of language, standardization of weights and measures, the destruction of the feudal domains, and the division of China into administrative districts headed by men of ability. It lived on in such concepts as individual land ownership, the taxing of the individual farmer by the state, and the development of irrigation projects which benefited the important occupation of agriculture. It also lived on in Chinese rulers who used their absolute power to oppress the people in order to advance themselves and the nation.

CHAPTER 22

BUDDHISM IN CHINA

Thou perfect master,
Who shinest upon all things and all men,
As gleaming moonlight plays upon a thousand
  waters at the same time!
Thy great compassion does not pass by a
  single creature.
Steadily and quietly sails the great ship
  of compassion across the sea of sorrow.
Thou are the Great Physician for a sick
  and impure world,
In pity giving the invitation to the Paradise
  of the West.
  —PRAYER FROM MASS FOR THE DEAD

When Buddhism passed from India to China, Korea, Tibet, and Japan, it changed from a religion demanding much of man to a religion of compassion promising much to man if he were faithful and devoted. This form of Buddhism is known as Mahayana Buddhism.

Mahayana Buddhism follows the example and heart of the Buddha more than his rigid teaching. It is concerned with the Buddha who, after his enlightenment, spent the remaining forty-five years of his life telling others about the path of freedom. His followers interpret this action as a social goal and ideal.

The story spread that, ages before, he had taken a vow to become enlightened in order to rescue suffering humanity. Before he was enlightened, he was a *Bodhisattva*, that is, one striving for enlightenment to fit himself to aid his fellow men. By heroic deeds in previous existences, he accumulated the merit which resulted in

From *Buddhism, A Religion of Infinite Compassion,* edited by Clarence H. Hamilton, copyright © 1952 by The Liberal Arts Press, Inc., reprinted by permission of the Liberal Arts Press Division of The Bobbs-Merrill Company, Inc.

his enlightenment in his final rebirth. A Buddha is not accessible to human beings once he has entered Nirvana, but there are those, Bodhisattvas, who defer entrance into Nirvana and remain behind on earth in order to help those who suffer. Buddhas and Bodhisattvas are both enlightened beings. The difference between them is that Buddhas are those who have entered into Nirvana, while Bodhisattvas continue their cycle of birth and rebirth in order to gain merit for others and guide them to enlightenment.

According to Mahayana Buddhism, the true follower of Buddha is one who follows the example of Buddha and becomes a Bodhisattva. Anyone who is moved by the suffering of others and seeks enlightenment for their benefit may become a Bodhisattva or Buddha. Buddhahood and Bodhisattva are stages open to all—merchant, banker, farmer, lawyer, or laborer. This spirit is caught in a poem[1]:

> O that I might become for all beings
> the soother of pain!
>
> O that I might be for all of them that
> ail the remedy, the physician, the nurse,
> until the disappearance of illness!
>
> O that by raining down food and drink I
> might soothe the pangs of hunger and
> thirst, and that in times of famine I
> might myself become drink and food!
>
> O that I might be for the poor an inexhaust-
> ible treasure!
>
> All my incarnations to come, all my goods, all my merits, past and
> present and future, I renounce with indifference, so that the end
> of all beings may be attained.

There are few great Bodhisattvas; and with the exception of Gautama Buddha who stayed on earth for many rebirths, Buddhas are beings in the heavens rather than on earth. The common people began to rely upon the merits of those whose compassion and pity were conceived to be infinite. Buddhas and Bodhisattvas became deities who were worshiped, adored, and prayed to. They were clothed in all the formal garments of an organized religion. Ex-

---

[1] René Grousset, *In the Footsteps of the Buddha* (London: Routledge & Kegan Paul, Ltd., 1932). Used with permission.

amples of these are: Kuan-yin (Japanese, Kwannon), the Goddess of Mercy; Wen-shu, the Lord of Wisdom; and Ti-ts'ang, who goes to hell (which the Chinese added to Buddhism) to save the suffering ones. These Bodhisattvas are found under other names in Japan, Korea, and Tibet.

AMITABHA: THE COMPASSIONATE BUDDHA

The greatest and most popular god is the Buddha Amitabha (O-mi-t'o in China, Amid in Japan). Ages before, he had taken a vow to save others, and through his good deeds done in countless ages, he created the "Pure Land" or "Western Paradise," a heaven where all will go who call upon his name. There, in the western part of the universe, he reigns with his faithful in perfect happiness.

It is called the Land of Supreme Happiness because all beings there do not suffer from any mental or physical pain and only enjoy pleasure and happiness of all kinds.

In this land of Supreme Happiness there are seven lakes, all adorned with gems. The lakes are filled with water which possesses the eight good qualities. . . . The bottoms of the lakes are strewn with golden sand. On the four sides of the lakes there are paths and steps of gold, silver, beryl, and crystal, white corals, red pearls, and diamonds. In the lakes the lotus flowers grow as big as wheels of chariots. . . .

In this land of Supreme Happiness the musical instruments of heaven are often played on grounds of gold. Three times a day and three times a night Mandarava flowers drop down like rain. . . .

Thus is described the Western Heaven which is ruled over by a Buddha of infinite compassion, Amitabha Buddha. All good Chinese Buddhists, those who call with faith and constancy upon the name of Amitabha Buddha, go to this magnificent place.

Another well-known compassionate being is Kuan-yin, the Goddess of Mercy, who also is ready and willing to succor the afflicted who seek her aid. Kuan-yin was originally a male deity known in India as Avalokitesvara, or "the Merciful One Who Surveys the World with Pity," but somewhere along the passage from India to China this divine being changed sex. Kuan-yin has sometimes been compared to the Madonna of the Christian faith. These two merciful beings are representatives of Mahayana Buddhism who captured the imagination and loyalty of the Chinese people in the past and who, along with the Western Heaven described above, continue to hold a favorite place in the hearts of millions of Chinese today.

All of the Buddhas and Bodhisattvas are the physical embodiments of Mahayana mercy and compassion. Mahayana Buddhism is a religion of compassion because it does not require man to rely solely upon himself for salvation. Prayer and worship, absent from the literal teaching of Gautama Buddha, are an integral part of Mahayana Buddhism. Prayers are said continually to the various Bodhisattvas requesting them to aid the petitioner in his efforts to obtain salvation. The verse addressed to Amitabha which heads this chapter is from the *Mass for the Dead* and vividly illustrates the deep faith of the people in his infinite mercy. The emotion, the hope, the humanity of Mahayana Buddhism were preferred by the Tibetans, Chinese, Koreans, and Japanese to the middle way and self-discipline of Hinayana Buddhism.

BUDDHISM BECOMES CHINESE

Buddhism in China played down its foreign elements and made itself as Chinese as possible. The abstract concept of Nirvana—the state or condition of desirelessness—was minimized, and a concrete place of happiness, like the Western Heaven of Amitabha Buddha, was given prominence.

It built on the foundations of the other ideologies popular during the early part of the Christian era. Since Taoism was popular among the commoners and intellectuals alike, Buddhists used Taoism as an instrument of conversion by taking over Taoist terms, writing commentaries on Taoist books, and identifying Buddhism with Taoist teaching and practice. The common elements in Taoist and Buddhist doctrine were deliberately stressed over and over again. At times, indeed, the truth was stretched in order to make Taoism and Buddhism agree. They honored Confucianism by speaking of a Bodhisattva as being an incarnation of Confucius, by naming a temple after Confucius, and by stressing the virtue of filial piety as an aspect of Buddhist teaching. Buddhist monks pointed out the similarities between Confucian and Buddhist morality, even going so far as to set up ancestral tablets in a special hall to honor the memory of their dead monks.

Buddhism attracted the scholar class because of its speculative nature and enticed the common people because of its ritual and ceremonial observances. Its appeal was reinforced by the literary labors of numerous Indian and Chinese Buddhist missionaries who made a determined effort to translate Buddhist literature into Chinese and to relate Buddhism to the observances and attitudes of the Chinese. Two Chinese Buddhist pilgrims famous for their travels between China and India are Fa-Hsien, who left China in 399 A.D. and spent fifteen years in India, and Hsuan-tsang, who left China in 629 A.D. and lived for sixteen years in India. Both of these famous travelers carried Buddhist books and manuscripts back to China with them. It is said that Hsuan-tsang and his pupils translated more than a thousand volumes into Chinese.

Buddhism showed its desire to co-exist peacefully with the rulers by not developing an administrative machinery in the monastic order and by not attempting to wrest the administrative machinery of the country from the Confucian scholars.

By showing itself not as an exclusive religion but as a complement to other Chinese beliefs, Buddhism penetrated and permeated Chinese life and became as Chinese as the native philosophies of Confucianism and Taoism. The Chinese were never thereafter at any particular period either Confucianist, Taoist, or Buddhist—they were all three simultaneously.

Buddhism was a tremendous intellectual force in China. It gave the Chinese a new look at the universe, at the individual, and at life. It provided the Chinese with a new literature and stimulated the production of new forms of music and religious art. It influenced Chinese painting and architecture, brought to China a message of justice and hope, and imbued the Chinese with a love and respect for all living things. It also served as a vehicle for carrying the culture of India and China to Korea and Japan.

CHAPTER 23

CHINESE SOCIAL LIFE

Patterns of social life are changing more rapidly in China than anywhere else in Asia. The old forms and social relationships are gradually being replaced by newer forms and relationships which are founded upon different values and ways of thinking. It is a time of social upheaval when generalizations previously used to describe many aspects of social life in China are no longer completely valid. Descriptions of such social institutions as the gentry, the family, the clan, marriage, and the status of women must be modified in the light of the swift changes that have taken place in China in recent years. However, the amount and pace of change vary with locality. Cities and urban areas have experienced greater and faster changes than the rural areas, for the peasant does not change quickly, and the ways and attitudes hallowed by the centuries press him to follow the traditional paths.

Traditional customs and mentality linger on in a changing, modern environment. The modern stress upon companionship and equality between men and women in Communist China has resulted in more mingling of sexes prior to marriage than was previously the case, and some couples now become engaged without their parents' approval. However, these same couples are extremely shy about showing their affection for each other in public, an attitude reminiscent of old Chinese social life. In negotiating marriage preliminaries, the tractor boss, or foreman, or member of their discussion group, may serve as the go-between for the two individuals. The go-between is traditional in China, but he usually negotiated between families rather than individuals. Instead of bowing before the elders of the family and the ancestral tablets during the marriage ceremony, many couples now bow before a picture of Mao Tse-tung and proclaim their intentions to serve the state instead of the family. In Nationalist China, now headquartered on Formosa, and among the Chinese living elsewhere in the world, there is also change. But it is more gradual, evolutionary rather than revolutionary, and more of the traditional practices are honored and retained.

The social life of the Chinese cannot be described as either traditional or modern. The old and new are reacting upon each other to form a composite of the alien and indigenous, the traditional and familiar.

CHAPTER 24

GENTRY AND PEASANT IN CHINA

Those who earn their living by labor are destined to be ruled.
—Mencius

The gentry and the peasantry were the two main classes of traditional Chinese society.

The gentry class, at the top of Chinese society, represented a way of life which all Chinese sought to attain. The hope of the various classes in China, especially the peasant class, was to become a member of the gentry class and follow gentry customs. Membership in the gentry class was open to the peasants, and a constant stream of peasants ascended into the gentry class during all periods of Chinese history. This may be one of the factors which helped to preserve the gentry as a vital class for so many centuries. One of the means by which members of the peasantry entered the gentry class was through education and government service. It was not uncommon for a bright peasant boy, educated through group effort, to pass the examinations and embark upon a government career. This achievement immediately placed him and his family in the gentry class. Other stepping stones were the acquisition of political power, military promotions, or wealth. The sons of these politically or economically powerful families would be educated, established in government careers, and thus introduced into the gentry class. Gentry families might also descend to peasant status. In almost every peasant family in China there are tales of some ancestors who were members of the government or prominent scholars in a particular field. Thus, a certain degree of mobility between gentry and peasantry was a striking feature of the social life of the Chinese people.

The gentry and peasant ways of life differed in many respects. The gentry led an easier existence, had more time to engage in social activities, and carried out the traditional ceremonies with greater pomp and on a more lavish scale. They were more concerned with political affairs and devoted much more time to cultural activities such as poetry, painting, essays, and the art of calligraphy or brush-writing. Other economic, social, and political characteristics distinguished the gentry from the peasantry.

ECONOMIC CHARACTERISTICS OF THE GENTRY

The gentry derived their income from land which they did not cultivate themselves or from other means that did not require physical labor. In imperial China one of their principal sources of income was a government position of one kind or another. This was also true of China under the Republic, but during this period industrial, commercial, and banking organizations also served as sources of income. Members of modern professional groups such as lawyers, doctors, engineers, and professors were considered members of the gentry class. Rents collected from their tenants varied with locality but were generally quite high, permitting the gentry to purchase such luxury items as paintings, musical instruments, porcelains, jewelry, and art objects of all kinds.

Great numbers of the gentry lived in towns. They moved there to increase their income, to be close to the political and cultural center of the community, and to lead a leisurely life with congenial companions.

Gentry families who stayed in the country and lived solely off the land soon became rather poor. These families, like all gentry families, grew fast, and eventually the family property was divided among the male heirs, creating a number of small landowners where there had been only one large one. By moving into the towns and supplementing their rentals with another source of steady income, the family could divide its property without radically impairing the economic status of its members.

Members of the gentry often supplemented their incomes by opening shops, frequently pawnshops and rice shops. Pawnshops were a common sight in Chinese towns. Because the Chinese were subject to periodic economic crises of one kind or another and frequently needed ready cash, the pawnshops were convenient sources of money and served as banks or lending agencies for the community. Their interest rates were high. Rice shops were also very profitable. Their owners bought rice cheaply immediately after the harvest and stored it until it was in short supply. Then they sold it at a high price or loaned it out at a high interest. Often twice the amount of rice was demanded in return, and if the loan was not repaid within a fixed period, the percentage of rice-interest was increased accordingly. This rice plus interest was generally payable at the next harvest, usually three or four months later. It was not uncommon for the original seller to have to buy or borrow the same rice he had grown.

Since the gentry were the source of scholar-officials who administered the government of imperial China and were the leaders and patrons of the intellectual and cultural life of the country, it was only natural that they should gravitate to the towns, which were centers of the administrative, political, and cultural life of the area. Towns also provided the opportunity and setting for living a gracious life of leisure. The gentry were a leisure class, abhorring physical labor. This aversion was one of the factors which for many years retarded the industrial development of China because the educated gentry youth refused to perform the physical labor so often demanded by the engineering and technical professions.

ECONOMIC CHARACTERISTICS OF THE PEASANTRY

The peasantry obtained their income mainly from the cultivation of the land and other physical work. It included owners of small pieces of land, tenants who cultivated the land for others, and farm laborers who received a salary.

The average Chinese peasant was a hard-working man. He spent most of his time working in order to produce enough food to feed his family. Often he was compelled to find ways to increase his income. Before the Chinese town and countryside were flooded with cheap machine-made products, the peasants supplemented their income by various types of handicraft work. They worked at night and in the slack season when the fields did not demand their attention; often the entire family participated in weaving, embroidering, working with silk, basket-making, or other skilled and semi-skilled tasks. They generally sold their home-made products in the nearby towns. Without this supplementary income many peasants would have sunk to an unbearable economic level. This was especially true of those peasants who had gone into debt and were attempting to pay off both the capital and the high interest on the loan. The supplementary income helped to keep them out of debt or, if they were compelled to borrow, permitted them to repay their loan without sacrificing their land. More often they used this additional revenue to buy the necessities of life. They seldom had enough to buy the nonessential items which the gentry purchased.

The constant and intensive work required to wrest a living from the land, and the necessity of augmenting his income by a handicraft of one kind or another, kept the peasant close to his home. He went to town merely to buy the few supplies he could not produce at home and to sell the few surplus things he produced. Otherwise, the town had little to offer him. The teahouses, the theaters, the restaurants, the house of pleasure, and the sing-song girls of the towns were not for him. He had little money and little time to spare. Such places of entertainment were primarily set up to provide amusement for the wealthy and the gentry. Occasionally, during festive occasions such as New Year's, theatrical companies would visit the villages or smaller market towns where the peasants came and watched the performance. Storytellers also roamed from village to village. Sometimes during the slack season the peasants would spend a little time in teahouses and in visiting neighbors. Funerals and festivals also provided an opportunity for feasting, gambling, and gossiping. However, in all these cases the entertainment was mostly confined to the rural areas.

Peasants looked at the towns with pleasure and displeasure. They liked the towns as concrete symbols of the way of life toward which they were striving. They dreamed of the day when they too could sit at leisure in a teahouse and enjoy the town pleasures. But they disliked the rents, the taxes, and the interest that flowed from them to the town gentry. From their point of view, towns were the living quarters of parasites, and they did not like to dwell on the idea that the pleasures of the town demanded a horrible price in flesh and bone and sinew from their bodies.

POLITICAL CHARACTERISTICS OF THE GENTRY

Since the gentry were the educated group, government officials in China were recruited mainly from this class. This was true of imperial China and is also true of the officialdom of both the Kuomintang and Communist governments. The few officials drawn from the peasant or other classes were automatically incorporated into the gentry class when they became scholars and officials.

Scholars and educated men stood on the summit of Chinese society. The Chinese placed the scholar first on their social scale, the peasant and farmer next, then the artisan and merchant, and the soldier and others, like actors, at the bottom. The position of the soldier at the bottom of the Chinese social scale has caused both Nationalists and Communists much difficulty in recruiting good men for their armies. Both governments have been forced to wage widespread propaganda campaigns to make the soldier a man of distinction in China.

The gentry, through the scholar-officials, controlled the intellectual life and ideology of the country. The scholar-officials administered the civil service examinations which had to be passed before an applicant could become a recognized scholar and be accepted for government service. The questions which the scholar-officials asked determined what the budding scholar and official must study before taking these all-important examinations. Of course, these questions concerned the traditional philosophy, attitudes, values, ideals, and beliefs. Young minds were thus indoctrinated early with the traditional and controlling ideology of China. So effective was this system of perpetuating an ideology that, even now, the traditional ideologies continue to have a strong hold on millions of Chinese.

Teachers all over China were also drawn from the gentry class. They were held in such high respect as to be considered one of the five objects worthy of worship; the others were, heaven, earth, emperor, and parents. Even today, the Chinese use the term "teacher" as a courteous form of address equivalent to our term "Mr." Because Chinese teachers indoctrinated their students with the same concepts and values that were featured in the civil service examinations, even those students who did not take the examinations but merely learned to read and write were taught to revere and respect traditional values and ideals.

Politically, the gentry functioned in two ways: they checked the absolute power of the emperor, and they acted as an extension of the central government on the local level.

Theoretically the political power of the emperor of China was great. All power in the country was lodged in his person; there was no command he could not give, no veto of his laws, no appeal from his judgment. When he was a strong figure, he often made use of his tremendous power in awesome and terrible ways. Most of the time, however, the emperor was not a very strong figure, and it was then that the power of the gentry-scholar-officials to check imperial ambition was most evident. Even during the regimes of the stronger emperors this power was quite effective, for the gentry controlled the machinery of government. When the emperor gave orders that were detrimental to gentry interests, they evaded, delayed, and choked those commands in the red tape of their administrative machine.

Moreover, gentry families tightened the bonds among themselves through expedient marriages. Connections among the gentry were extremely important, and marriage was a convenient method to arrange alliances between strategically placed families. Since all the gentry families engaged in such practices, the web of interconnected families eventually covered most of the officials in administrative posts.

When the people of any given locality in China were threatened with exorbitant demands from the central government upon their goods and services, the gentry of that locality immediately swung into action to soften these demands. The local county representative of the central government, the county chief, was informed that the gentry of the area thought the requests extravagant. Often this information was sufficient to cause the official to find ways of moderating the demands without impairing his own position in the administration. If the county official stubbornly insisted upon the full measure requested of the people, whether it be taxes or conscription, then the gentry used their web of alliances to reach his superior. Since the county official himself was a part of this web and since he was dependent upon his superior for advancement and other favors, this action was usually sufficient to moderate the orig·inal demands.

The gentry class had most to lose from the unchecked power of an emperor or his followers, for they possessed the money, land, and other objects of value that ambitious emperors might covet. To protect their property, wealth, and high economic status, the gentry sent an unceasing stream of candidates to fill the high and low positions of government. Thus, between the emperor and his subjects there was interposed a deep layer of self-perpetuating bureaucrats who were dedicated to the purpose of checking and modifying the demands of an "all-powerful" emperor.

Until very recently the chain of formally appointed administrative officials reached down only as far as the head of the county, who was usually called the magistrate or mandarin. The mass of people lived in numerous villages scattered throughout the country. With the small staff at his disposal, and the lack of any formally appointed village officials to serve as his assistants, it was only natural that the magistrate should turn to the gentry to aid him in carrying out his duties. The gentry were in a unique position to act as an extension of the central government and as assistants to the magistrate. They were well connected with the government administration through their web of alliances; they were regarded by the peasants as the leaders of the community since they were the larger landowners, the politically connected families, and the arbiters of fashion and morals; and they were concerned with the problems of the peasantry and knew well the intimate affairs of the people of their countryside. Moreover, the gentry were pleased to act in this capacity since it strengthened their position in relation to both the administration and the peasantry. They were needed by both. The administration needed them to aid in such duties as collecting taxes, erecting public works, and preserving the peace. The peasants needed them to mediate for them when taxes were oppressive, conscription was heavy, and other demands were troublesome. The gentry also acted as informal arbitrators in land quarrels, feuds threatening lawsuits, and the thousands of matters with which the local governments dealt. Thus, the gentry were the administrators of an informal countryside government which considerably reduced the formal functions and services of government and kept government interference in local affairs at a minimum.

POLITICAL CHARACTERISTICS OF THE PEASANTRY

The peasant has traditionally thought of the people of China as being divided into two classes—the ruler and the ruled.

During the imperial period the ruling class consisted of the emperor, the royal family, and the gentry class from which the government officials were recruited. Today, the ruling class comprises the

members of the two parties, Communist on the mainland and Kuomintang on Formosa, and their sympathizers and supporters. Those
ruled are the peasants, who make up 80 to 85 per cent of the population, and smaller groups such as laborers, artisans, merchants,
servants, and soldiers.

Thus, the peasant sees no real change in the political structure of
his country. The government is a closely-kept organization with
power concentrated in the hands of a few who stand at the top
of Chinese society. This organization rests upon a broad peasant
base which produces the wealth of the land. Many peasants feel
that modern governments are worse than previous ones in that they
are more prone to interfere in their affairs and more insistent upon
their taking part in government activities.

In imperial China the peasants shied away from government and
governmental activities and scrutiny. They regarded government
with deep suspicion, associating it in their minds with evils such as
taking their scarce food for taxes, taking their needed strength for
public works, taking their sons for the army, and often taking their
land by means of lawsuits. As a result they worked on the assumption that the less they had to do with the government, the better off
they were. In present-day China many of the peasants still cling to
this view of government. However, both Nationalist and Communist propaganda is striving to change this attitude of suspicion and
aversion. Both are attempting to give the peasant a feeling of participation in government and to convince him that this is *his* government, *his* policies, and *his* administration. Still, the great mass of
the peasants want little to do with government, any government,
and the present Communist regime in China has been repeatedly
rebuffed by peasant inertia and stubbornly held peasant belief that
no government is really in their interest.

The peasant is a conservative force in the community. The rural
environment in which he lives provides little stimulation, reason,
or means to change his ways of thinking or acting. This conservatism is one of the greatest barriers to those who seek to remold
China. The peasants are generally content to live in their accustomed pattern of life, even when they have given their support and
help in overturning a dynasty or regime. In the past the peasants
rose many times when their lot became unbearable and there was
no other way to alleviate their condition. During these uprisings

they were as fierce, as cruel, as unyielding, and as devoted to their cause as any modern revolutionaries. But they were interested primarily in throwing out their incompetent and unjust rulers, not in changing the political system itself. Once the rulers had been changed, the injustices remedied, and the country was calm and peaceful again, the peasants resumed their customary traditional way of life.

The Chinese peasant was an independent individual. His political, social, and economic environment compelled him to be self-sufficient and self-reliant. Few people were available to help him financially, physically, or politically. He depended upon his own initiative, his own labors, his own spiritual and physical resources. He did not have the united strength of the large joint family which was characteristic of the gentry. He tried to solve his many problems without recourse to government. He found other ways to settle his disputes with others over land and money. His social security came from his sons, and his daily living from his own foresight and labors. He cared for and built his own irrigation ditches, planned and carried out his own flood-control measures, and made his own fertilizer. When problems arose which he could not handle alone, he sought the help of the gentry or the village elders and not the government.

SOCIAL CHARACTERISTICS OF THE GENTRY

The gentry lived in large families that sometimes included four or five generations. A patriarch ruled over the family much as an emperor ruled over the state. A definite social hierarchy within the family ranged from the lowest female member to the male patriarch himself, and an elaborate and rigid code spelled out the relationships between the various members. A great amount of time and attention was given to teaching and disciplining the younger members so that they might know and practice the ceremonies and etiquette required of them. Stress was laid on ritual and proper behavior toward both the dead and the living.

Large families gave the gentry the unity and solidarity necessary to maintain their position at the top of Chinese society. Family property and family wealth was preserved as a unit and not scattered over a dozen small families. Within the large family all worked in supporting and maintaining the economic and social status of the household. Each depended upon the other. There was no necessity for individual self-reliance and no urge to be independent, such as existed among the members of smaller families.

But forces of division also worked within these large families. The presence of so many different interacting personalities under one roof, living on a common budget and holding common property, gave birth to continual bickering, envious comparisons, jealous maneuverings, and malicious intentions. Very often the wives of the male heirs, insecure and ambitious, worked through their husbands in an effort to have the property divided and the families independent. Generally, the patriarch of the family was able to hold the diverse families together, but after his death those seeking division of the property often won out over the forces of unity.

SOCIAL CHARACTERISTICS OF THE PEASANTRY

Although they aspired to live in the gentry manner, few peasants could afford to do so.

They lived in small families. The tiny bits of land they cultivated could not support a large number of people, and many found it difficult even to support aged parents. In order to preserve intact this small piece of land they often permitted only one son to inherit the property, in contrast to the gentry practice of permitting all male sons to inherit equally.

The peasantry did not have the time, education, or means to follow the elaborate code of etiquette practiced by the gentry. They respected these rules of social intercourse, and they practiced them when they could, but they could not adopt them as fully and completely as the gentry. They offered sacrifices to their ancestors when they could, at least once or twice a year. They stretched their resources to the utmost to follow the wedding and funeral rituals and regulations, and they tried to make their festivals, especially New Year's, as gay and correct as their economic condition would permit. They still do.

Economic necessity forced the peasant to place more importance on obtaining a strong helpmate than upon obtaining important and influential relatives. His almost complete preoccupation with the matter of making a living determined his major concern—the efficiency of the family as a working group. The physical makeup of a wife was very important to the peasant and his family. She needed a strong back, sturdy legs, and firm hands. Her relatives were important, of course, but her health and strength were more important. The peasant had no reason to make strategic political marriages because he had no high position in Chinese society to protect.

He respected the ideals of kinship, and he paid at least lip service to the formal requirements of etiquette in relation to sex, age, and generation. He, too, was a formal member of the clan, and he had a wide number of relatives to whom he was connected by marriage and blood, but he did not require these relatives as much as the gentry did, who needed the web of kinship and marriage ties to shore up their power in the community and in the nation. With little, if any, power to lose, the peasant regarded such ties as relatively unimportant and sometimes even troublesome.

Both peasantry and gentry were bound by the same code of ethics and the same philosophy of life. Both were more interested in stability and the status quo than in changing a political system. Both were more interested in their own particular families and kinship groups than in a national unit called a state. Both required supplementary incomes to maintain themselves. Both were more loyal to their locality and neighborhood than to the ruler. Both held to the same ideals and tried to follow the standards imposed by these ideals to the best of their ability.

During the past fifty years the spirit of nationalism, foreign ideas, aggressive actions by foreign nations, lack of a strong central government, and recurring crises such as famines, floods, and wars have forced both the gentry and the peasantry to rebel and to take other drastic measures in order to protect their interests. The majority were primarily interested in solving their immediate problems and not in changing the traditional social order of China. Many were dismayed when it became evident that a solution to their problems involved radical and unwanted changes in their traditional way of life.

CHAPTER 25

THE CLAN IN CHINA

Practically all the families in my village bear my surname. We are all descended from the same ancestor and the lines of descent can be clearly traced in the genealogy. . . .
—HSIEN CHIN HU

The clan includes all classes of Chinese. Membership is determined by ties of blood and marriage rather than by the economic and educational considerations which distinguish the gentry and the peasantry. Thus class conflicts are often harmonized and class divisions often spanned by the blood-links of the clan.

The clan is an organized and united group of people who trace their ancestry back to a common ancestor. The group is often very large, some clans having thousands of members. Descent is patrilineal, that is, traced back to the father's ancestor rather than the mother's. Some clans trace their first ancestor back to a legendary figure in the mythical period of Chinese history, others to some prominent emperor or official; but few genealogies go beyond the Sung Dynasty. Generally, the clan is limited to the descendants of that ancestor who came to the region first. It does not embrace all those people in China who bear the same surname, but only those of the same surname who are descended from a common ancestor who settled first in a given locality.

Chinese names are generally made up of three characters. The family or surname is written first, the second character is common to all cousins and brothers of the same generation, and the third character is unique to the individual. The importance of the family name is stressed by putting it first. The ties of blood indicated by the same surname are emphasized by the custom of prohibiting marriage between those of the same surname even if the individuals concerned are of different clans and come from widely separated parts of the country.

The relationship between the members of the clan was demonstrated by means of a genealogy, the chart and written history tracing the clan's descent from a common ancestor. In drawing up a genealogy the Chinese did not confine themselves merely to tracing the descent lines of all present descendants from the original paternal ancestor. Genealogies also included the age of the individuals at death, the number of their sons and daughters, the family names of wives, and the family names of sons-in-law. Biographies of prominent men and women, and outstanding achievements of individual clan members were also given. Maps and diagrams showed the location of the clan graves. The history of the ancestral hall, moral and ethical statements, pertinent data with regard to the common property, and any other items which the clan leaders thought important were also included. Keeping clan genealogies up-to-date required long hours of research, meticulous labor, and often much travel. In 1937 there were over 180,000 descendants of Confucius scattered in more than 246 communities, and divided into 60 branches. One clan in Kwangtung is now composed of 118 divisions. The genealogy of this clan traces the movements of these 118 different divisions from the time of the Sung Dynasty to the present. When it is remembered that much more than a genealogical chart is incorporated in these genealogies, the true magnitude of compiling and maintaining a genealogy can be appreciated. In recent years 109 members of the Tseng clan in Hunan worked on the last edition of its genealogy.

THE ANCESTRAL HALL

The ties of blood and kinship were strengthened by ancestral ceremonies, common property, and a common interest in preserving and increasing the prestige of the clan and the welfare of its members. There usually was a clan center where the ancestral hall was built and where most of the ancestral graves were located.

The ancestral hall, like the clan itself, served many functions. It was a convenient place for the clan leaders to discuss clan matters. Records of births and deaths and other personal data concerning the clan members were stored in the hall which thus served as a bureau of vital statistics for the clan. The hall was sometimes given a personality; gifts were sent to, and cases judged by, the "ancestral hall." Most important, however, was a ceremonial hall where the tablets of the dead ancestors were kept and where the so-called ancestor worship was carried out. Each ancestor possessed a tablet, a rectangular piece of wood, upon which was written his name, title, and birth and death dates. While ancestor rites were performed, the spirit of the dead ancestor was supposed to be in the tablet. For this reason these tablets were known as "spirit tablets." More recently, portraits are sometimes used instead of tablets.

Once or twice a year, in the spring or autumn or both, the clan met to honor their common ancestors. Termed "ancestor worship" by most Western commentators, it is actually more a memorial service which indicated, by means of ceremonials, the respect and reverence of the descendants for their ancestors. There was no intent to worship the ancestors in the sense that Christians worship God.

The Chinese believed that the ancestors continued to live in another world as spirits and that they depended upon their descendants for certain necessities of life. These ancestor spirits had the power to help their descendants if the proper rites were rendered them. Otherwise the ancestors would cease to live or might roam about as hungry ghosts. The descendants would then suffer misfortune. It was most important, therefore, that the Chinese have male descendants who would carry on the proper rites for them after their death. Mencius, the most famous disciple of Confucius, stated that the most unfilial act was to leave no posterity. This feeling was engraved so deeply on the Chinese mentality that an individual, if he had no children of his own, would adopt a son to carry on his line and conduct the ancestral rites.

Memorial service was one of the reasons why the Chinese paid such great respect to the aged. Since they were only a step away from becoming ancestors themselves, the aged were felt to be entitled to great honor and homage. The clan supplemented the family in carrying out the ancestral ceremonies. The family usually honored the preceding four or five generations only, but the clan rendered memorial service to all the ancestors, even the remotest ones. Consequently, no ancestor was deprived of the rites, and all clan members were blessed by the help of the comforted ancestors.

The location of ancestral graves was important. A favorable location helped insure the prosperity of the descendants, while an unfavorable location might very well result in their ruin. A location was selected by someone who had a gift for picking a lucky site. This person was versed in the art of *feng shui,* which is literally translated "wind and water." *Feng shui* is founded on the assumption that everywhere there are forces and spirits which affect people for good or bad. The *feng shui* expert was skilled in the art of finding the places where these forces were most favorable. In picking a spot, the patterns of mountains and waterways and many other factors were carefully calculated. The best site for a house, a place of business, or a farm was determined by the same influences. The Chinese have long felt that nature has a vital bearing upon their pattern of life and were willing to go to extreme lengths at times to insure a favorable location. The author knows of a case in China where the mother of a governor of a province tore down and rebuilt her house four times in order to correct the *feng shui.* The rational Confucianist was opposed to such superstitious practices and attributed them to the pernicious teaching of Taoism. The Confucian philosopher Chu Hsi commented perceptively when he said that "divining the auspiciousness" of a place is merely "to divine the beauty or ugliness of the location. If the place is beautiful, then the spirit will be happy and the sons and grandsons prosperous." He advised the Chinese that the only consideration in choosing a grave site was the likelihood that at some future date a road or a wall might be built on the site, a ditch dug there, or some farmer's plough might turn up the bones.

Graves had to be kept in good condition. Once a year, on the Ch'ing-Meng festival in the spring, the descendants sweep and tidy up the graves. Here they offer up sacrifices of food and wine to their ancestors. The clan kept maps of these graves and set aside suitable burial land for its members. This was especially intended to help those members who had insufficient funds to bury their dead in a suitable place.

RITUAL LAND

In addition to the ancestral hall, which was built and maintained by contributions of clan members in the form of money, labor, or kind, the clan often held in common productive land, bequeathed by wealthy members, which provided a regular income for the support of the clan activities and the continuance of the required sacrifices and memorial services. Such land was called ritual land and was sometimes referred to as the "property" of the ancestral hall. The rents from this land were used in part for clan charities which embraced a wide range of welfare activities. The clan provided for orphans, indigent widows, childless members, and those unable to work. In times of crisis, during wars, floods, famines, droughts, and other man-made or natural calamities, the clans did what they could to help out their members. It was a common practice in traditional China to provide for the proper burial and marriage of clan members. Sometimes clan funds were used to further the education of the youth.

Nothing enhanced the prestige of the clan so much as the number of its members who received a formal education. Many clans, both in the imperial period and under the Republic, established schools and engaged tutors to educate their promising youngsters. Some of them set aside a certain amount of land called "school land" to support these schools and tutors. They often paid the traveling expenses of their scholars when they went to Peking to take the final examination. Both clans and government favored these welfare activities, the clan because they helped unify its members, and the government because it believed these welfare services were necessary to maintain order and stability in the community.

Sometimes abuses crept into the administration of clan property, and it was used to further the economic interests of the clan leaders and administered as if the property were their own. The poorer clan members resented the exclusive character of the supervision and use of the common property. Moreover, when the lands were tilled by members, friction sometimes developed over the amount of rent. Clan members insisted that the rent should be low because they were, after all, part owners and entitled to preferential treatment. The clan leaders, on the other hand, argued that if the tillers did not pay the going rate the entire clan would be the loser. Consequently, in order to avoid constant bickering and obtain the fullest amount possible, clan leaders commonly rented the common lands to people outside the clan. This practice, of course, incensed the poorer members and increased their hostility toward the wealthier clan leaders.

GOVERNMENT OF THE CLAN

The gentry were the leaders of the clan because they were men of education and wealth and knew the proper ancestral rites. They were the spokesmen for the clan in dealing with the outside world of government officials and the leaders of other clans. They wielded the same moral influence and enjoyed the same prestige within the clan as in the society at large outside the clan.

Clan members were usually physically concentrated in the neighborhood of the ancestral hall and the ancestral graves. Even when living in distant places, they were spiritually attached to the ancestral neighborhood. Old scholar-officials who had given years of their life to public service and government work looked forward to the time when they could retire to their ancestral homes and spend their remaining years honored and untroubled in the protecting shadow of their ancestral hall. Chinese living in America, Europe, South-East Asia, and elsewhere, still think of themselves as attached to an ancestral home somewhere in China. From time to time they visit these ancestral homes and often request that they be buried there. These attitudes are especially true of the Chinese who come from Kwangtung, Fukien, and other parts of southeast and central China. It is in these areas that the clan organization developed most extensively and put down the deepest roots.

The ancestral hall sometimes served as a courtroom where civil and criminal cases affecting clan members were judged. Traditionally, the Chinese government left the teaching of moral and ethical doctrines, and punishment for crimes against them, to the family and the clan. The government reserved to itself the power to step in and take over whenever it seemed necessary, but this was rarely done. The government was seldom called in even when the dispute was between clans rather than within them. Clan leaders considered it better to compromise and to settle the matter by informal discussions and in committees than to call in even the local government.

Each clan had regulations which the members were expected to follow. They concerned unfilial conduct, property disputes, thefts, and other offenses. Sometimes these regulations prohibited the members from gambling, smoking opium, consorting with prostitutes, drinking excessively, wasting money on luxuries, and other practices considered harmful to the solidarity of the family and the clan. When members offended against these regulations they were subject to judgment by the clan leaders in the ancestral hall. Punishment varied with the offense, ranging from verbal reproofs to expulsion from the clan, either temporary or permanent. The latter was a serious punishment because the expelled individual could not participate in the ancestral rites, enjoy the common funds, and have his tablet in the ancestral hall or his name in the genealogy. A man without a clan in China was in many ways like a man without a country.

THE CLAN TODAY

The Nationalist government, under the leadership of Sun Yat-sen and, later, Chiang K'ai-shek, did not attempt to remove the clan institution from China. They wanted the Chinese to give their loyalty to a state as well as a clan, but it was not their purpose to abolish this cherished Chinese tradition. The Nationalists are in this, as in other matters, more traditionally Chinese than the Communists.

With the coming of the Communist government to mainland China the power and influence of the clan have decreased. In Communist philosophy no rivals to the power of the state can be tolerated. The government must control the activities of the people at all levels. There can be no sharing of political power with social units and social institutions like the clan. Such sharing of power, the Communists believe, can only further the process of decentralization that has been characteristic of China's political history. Consequently, the clan has been shorn of many of its functions, its power and influence decreased, and its leaders—the gentry, the wealthy, and the aged—have been removed or deprived of their prestige.

Nevertheless the clan group, though less organized, continues to exist wherever there are Chinese. The ties of blood cannot be sundered overnight. The clan still lives, and ancestral rites are still practiced in thousands of ancestral halls inside and outside China. The welfare, educational, and judicial functions of the clan have been curtailed, but clan sentiment based on genealogies and ancestor reverence still exists. As long as it exists, there will be clans.

CHAPTER 26

THE FAMILY IN CHINA

The root of the empire is in the state. The root of the state is in the family.

—MENCIUS

The family, the basic social unit in China for thousands of years, was so important that not only the clan but even the state was regarded as an extension of it. A Chinese thought of the interests of his family as the basis for all his judgments and decisions. What was advantageous and good for the family was permitted; what was disadvantageous and bad for the family was prohibited. The individual thought of himself as a member of a family, and he was viewed by others in the same light. The success or failure of an individual reflected upon the family and increased or decreased its prestige. The family was responsible for the acts of its individual members and was held accountable for them by the community and the government. In this sense traditional China was composed of a large number of families rather than of individuals.

Confucian philosophy emphasized the fundamental importance of the family. Of the five basic social relationships necessary to the right functioning of Chinese society, three were family relationships—the relationship between father and son, elder brother and younger brother, and husband and wife. It was in the family that the individual learned his role in Chinese society, or not at all. "Inside the smaller doors leading to the inner apartments are to be found all the rules [of government]. There is awe for the father, and also for the elder brother. Wife and children, servants and concubines, are like the common people, serfs, and underlings."

Economically, the traditional Chinese family was a joint productive effort. All members were supposed to do what they could for the common family, and they were supported from the common funds. There were three important variations of this economic family in China: the small or conjugal family, the middle-way or stem family, and the large or joint family. The small family usually consisted of the parents and their unmarried children. It was similar to the family common in America and the West. The middle-way family was composed of the parents, all their unmarried children, and one married son with his wife and children. The large or joint family included the parents, both married and unmarried children, and all the wives and children of the married children. Sometimes other close relatives, such as grandparents, uncles, aunts, cousins, and nephews, might live in this family. The head of the family, usually the father but sometimes the elder brother, supervised the common property and watched over the moral life of the members.

IDEAL AND PRACTICE

The large or joint family was the traditional ideal family. From the time of the T'ang Dynasty until very recently, the large family system was praised and encouraged by the leaders of society as the ideal family arrangement. The presence in one family of six or more generations who functioned together as one economic unit was the highest expression of this system. Few families achieved this aim. Most large families never included more than three or four generations, and only certain wealthy families were able to achieve this goal.

There are a number of reasons why the Chinese were seldom able to realize the ideal of living together in a large family. Members of the families of the poorer classes were subject to a higher mortality rate than the richer classes and few of them lived very long. Malnutrition, diseases of one kind or another, natural calamities which destroyed their crops and brought famine and starvation, were the common fate of the poverty-stricken peasants and artisan families of China. Only the very strong and the very lucky lived to a ripe old age. Many children died young; it is thought that, prior to the coming of modern health practices, over half of all the children in China died before the age of five. Owing to unsanitary conditions, many mothers died at childbirth. Furthermore, the small amount of land which the poor possessed was insufficient to support large numbers. Even in gentry families, the frequent division of wealth kept the number of members down. As a consequence the vast majority of the Chinese people lived in small and middle-way families which numbered on the average from five to seven members.

Probably a typical Chinese family on the mainland today would include the two parents and up to three or four children. After the advent of the Communist government in China the members of the former gentry class, who most frequently lived in large or joint families, disappeared from Chinese society. Their land, which was the source of their wealth, was redistributed, and they could no longer support the practice of large families. As a result, the small family, so common in America and the Western world in general, is also becoming typical in present-day China.

FAMILY RELATIONSHIPS

Until recent times the parents had almost complete authority over their children. Society sanctioned whatever steps parents took to enforce their commands, and public opinion permitted harsh and prolonged physical punishment when the children rebelled against parental edicts.

However, when the grandfather retained headship of the family, he often protected his grandchildren from the arbitrary dictates of the father and mother. It was common for the grandchildren to scurry to the loving shelter of a grandparent when the father threatened or attempted to punish his children. Others in the older generation, such as uncles and aunts, were also in a position to protect the child from discipline. This was true even when the old one had relinquished formal supervision of the family. The aged were revered and their wishes and desires granted whenever possible. Thus, love for the child was diffused over a wide range of relatives. He found early that he often received more warm affection from his grandparents, uncles, and aunts than he did from his own father.

Traditionally, Chinese fathers were regarded by the sons with a great deal of fear. Since untrained and undisciplined sons gave the community a bad impression of the father, Chinese fathers were often severe and inflexible in training their sons to assume their future role in society and the family. Since the father did not have the same responsibility to discipline and indoctrinate the daughter in her future family duties, the relationship between father and daughter was usually warmer and closer. In some of the more wealthy families it was not uncommon for the father to teach his daughter to read, write poems, and compose music.

The relationship between the mother and her children, both girls and boys, was generally one of warm love and affection. She acted as an intermediary between the children, especially the son, and her husband, and often protected them from his wrath. In poorer peasant families, the love of the daughter for her mother was so great that, many times, the daughter would take something from the family of her husband in order to give her mother a few more material comforts. This act of "borrowing" was one of the seven valid causes for divorce in traditional China.

Parents were obliged to train their children to assume their proper stations in Chinese society. For each generation, for each age, for each sex, there was an accepted pattern of behavior which each Chinese individual had to be taught. Thus, from about four to fifteen or sixteen years of age, the children were taught their future duties. The boys of gentry families were sent to schools or put under the guidance of tutors, to start the long and difficult task of scholarship. The boys of the peasant families were taught field work at an early age and instructed in all the arduous tasks demanded of the farmer-peasant in China. The boys of both gentry and peasant families were taught the ancestral ritual. Both peasant and gentry girls were taught the household duties of sewing, cooking, washing, and cleaning. The peasant girl, in addition, learned to help in the fields during the planting and harvesting seasons. It is a common sight in China to see a long row of bending women planting the delicate rice shoots in the water-covered rice fields.

Arranging marriages for their children was one of the primary obligations of the parents. The boys must be married in order that the family line might be continued and descendants created to perpetuate the ancestral rites. Girls must be married so that they might fulfill themselves as women and strengthen the family fortunes. Gentry families were interested in making a strategic family alliance. Peasant families desired money for their daughters and were reluctant to marry them to families who owned or rented little or no land. Marriages were arranged by the families concerned. The prospective bride and groom had little to say about either the choice of their mate or the marriage arrangements. In fact, they rarely saw each other before the marriage. A meeting of the two be-

fore marriage was sufficient reason for calling off the ceremony, because it violated the custom of separating the sexes and compro-
mised the girl. Marriages were contracted between families on the
basis of convenience. The social and financial position of the families concerned was carefully scrutinized before the marriage contract was signed.

A middle-man always negotiated the marriage. He or she—the
middle-man could be either male or female—did the talking and
bargaining, carried messages, and conducted all the many delicate
but necessary negotiations required to bring the marriage preliminaries to a successful conclusion.

When the bride's parents agreed to the proposed match, they
sent, via the middle-man, a card bearing the girl's eight characters
to the boy's family. These eight characters, which represented her
name, and the hour, day, month, and year of her birth, were then
compared with the boy's personal data by one skilled in such matters. If the comparison indicated future harmony and happiness
for the two individuals, negotiations to connect the two families
through marriage began in earnest. One of the most important questions to be settled, especially for the poor peasant families, was the
size of the dowry to be paid by the family of the bridegroom to the
family of the bride. The girl's family used part of the dowry money
to purchase the bridal outfit and, if there were unmarried sons in
the family, often used the rest as dowry money again, to obtain
wives for them. The wealthier gentry families used all the dowry
and much more besides to outfit the bride. The more furniture,
chests, household equipment, clothes, and other articles that were
carried in the bridal procession when she was escorted to the home
of the bridegroom, the greater the prestige that devolved upon
her family.

Marriage preliminaries were concluded with the fixing of the date
of marriage and the signing of the betrothal contract by the family
heads. The marriage day was selected by an individual skilled in
the choosing of lucky days for important events. On that day the
bride was carried in a long procession, together with her personal
property and bedroom equipment, to the home of the bridegroom.
She usually stayed there for the rest of her life.

When she entered her new home, she was obliged to adjust to a
new environment and a new set of relationships. Usually, she had

not seen any of the family members before, including her husband. She was surrounded by unfamiliar objects, unfamiliar faces, and unfamiliar mannerisms and expressions. The sudden and sharp change from a secluded, familiar life to this rather public, unfamiliar life frightened and confused her. Her most difficult adjustment was to her mother-in-law. Chinese mothers-in-law were often awe-inspiring individuals within the family. They were the rulers in the home, especially with regard to the daughter-in-law's training, discipline, and duties. Since the men of the family were not supposed to give their wives any undue attention beyond the bedroom door, a public show of affection between husband and wife was frowned upon by Chinese society. Consequently, the young bride was forced to spend most of her time in the company of her mother-in-law, trying to meet all of her demands and to bear her scoldings with tact and patience. Stories are told of some mothers-in-law whose nagging and cruelty drove their daughters-in-law to flee from the home or even commit suicide. Filial obligations required the son not to interfere in his mother's treatment of his wife. Both husband and wife stood in a subordinate position with relation to the mother-in-law. Should the husband support his wife against his mother, he aroused jealousy that only intensified the harsh treatment of his wife. Moreover, Chinese society did not favor such action by the son against the mother, to whom he owed loving obedience no matter what the provocation.

In Chinese thought children must do everything possible to ensure the comfort and happiness of the parents. The lives of the son's children, and even his own life, should not be valued over the lives of the parents. Chinese children are told stories of filial sons who cut off portions of their living flesh in order to provide their parents with food and medicine. One of the strictest and most important filial obligations was the support of parents in their old age. Another important duty was faithfully to carry out ceremonial rites to them after their death. Confucius said, "When the parents are alive, serve them with propriety; when they die, bury them according to propriety; and sacrifice to them according to propriety." Greatly prized and respected, the aged in traditional China were valued even over children. Children could be had again, but the aged could not be duplicated, and they soon would become powerful ancestors who could be of great aid to the family. The most important birthdays in an individual's life were at sixty, seventy, eighty, and up. To reach the age of one hundred was the crowning achievement for both the person and the family.

The Chinese lived in anticipation of old age, for growing old was pleasant. Age was respected. It was a time of leisure and of little responsibility. There was no superior over the aged except the dead ancestors, who rarely spoke. The aged were supported and not requested to support anyone else. There were only two periods in the life of a Chinese male when he possessed maximum security and minimal responsibility—infancy and old age. Of the two, old age was the better because one was conscious of the pleasure to be derived from such an almost perfect period.

The woman also achieved respect and superiority with increasing age. The young bride, cowed and afraid, grew into a mother-in-law or female head of the household. She was no longer a stranger and she had sons and daughters-in-law of her own. She was an authority in the family and her position was buttressed by the whole weight of Chinese society. All members of the family owed her respect, obedience, and support.

NEW ATTITUDES TOWARD THE FAMILY

Traditional attitudes toward the family are being modified in China in response to the changing pattern of modern life. Individuals are now encouraged to think in terms of loyalty to the nation rather than to the family alone. This is especially true of Communist China. The welfare of the state is the final basis for all decisions and acts, and when there is a conflict of interest between it and the family, the Chinese are taught to place the interests of the state first. The relationship between the individual and the state is of more significance than the one between the family and the state. The individual's failure no longer reflects upon the family, but solely upon himself. The Nationalists, however, continue to feel that the family is also responsible.

Though families are still held responsible for teaching their members their new roles in society, other institutions are beginning to perform this function. More and more nurseries, schools, clubs, discussion groups, committees, indoctrination courses, party work, unions, co-operatives, and other groups and institutions outside the home and family are molding the character and values of the modern Chinese. He is becoming a different person, oriented outside the family rather than inside.

Modern Chinese no longer give the same respect to the aged as formerly. Yesterday's China admonished the young to be quiet listeners at the feet of her ancient sages. Today's China admonishes the old to be quiet since the ancient learning is no longer applicable. The young in China are hailed as the forerunners of a new society; they are lauded, showered with attention, and placed in positions of authority. This is more true of the Communists than of the Nationalists, who continue to respect and honor the aged.

Marriage laws promulgated by the new regimes express another conception of marriage. The sexes are equal. Each spouse may retain his or her family name and personal property. Each may freely work in any occupation and engage in political and social action. The two people concerned may choose their own mate without interference from a third party. There shall be no compulsion on the part of either party. The interests of the children shall also be safeguarded. "Children born out of wedlock shall enjoy the same rights as children born in lawful wedlock." Husband and wife shall live together as companions and one will not be dominant over the other. Husbands shall have only one wife.

In old China most Chinese were monogamous by economic necessity. But many of the wealthy possessed concubines. Secondary wives were often introduced into the house when the first wife proved barren or had not borne any male offspring. The introduction of a number of wives under the same roof was generally the signal for the beginning of disturbances for the household. Furthermore, many secondary wives under one roof was another instance of the traditional subordination of women. Most women shunned the prospect of becoming concubines. For these and other reasons, the modern Chinese have forbidden more than one wife per husband.

Marriages need no longer be arranged by the families concerned. When a boy reaches the age of twenty, and the girl the age of eighteen, they can legally marry voluntarily. There are still, in many instances, certain ceremonies attached.

Whereas marriage was formerly a family affair, it is now often an ideological affair, especially if one or both persons are party members. One of the members of their party cell, or their discus-

sion or work group, may act as a middle-man in the marriage preliminaries. Instead of judging the marriage from the point of view
of the family, the suitability of the match is discussed in terms of
the advantages that their union will bring to the party and the state.

Where formerly the marriage ceremonies took place in the family
household of the male, today they are often conducted in a public
hall decorated with flags and the pictures of Mao Tse-tung and
other important political dignitaries. The couple, if they are laborers
or workers, frequently wear their regular work clothes and publicly
announce at the ceremony what they intend to do after their marriage to benefit the community. This is a Communist practice and
not true of Nationalist China. The Nationalists rarely interfere in
family matters such as marriage.

Divorce has always been permitted in China. Generally speaking, however, it was a family and clan matter; the wishes of the individual were secondary. Furthermore, divorce was a privilege enjoyed almost exclusively by the man. The wife was practically help-
less when her husband decided to put her away, and it was almost
impossible for her to divorce her husband.

However, she was not entirely defenseless. The husband was not
supposed to divorce his wife except for the following reasons: disobedience to his parents, failure to bear children, adultery, overt
jealousy, a repulsive disease, loquacity, and theft from the family
(in order, usually, to help her mother). Moreover, divorce was
rather rare. Public opinion did not approve of it, and it was usually
more convenient for the man to take other women into his home
than to brave public opinion and the anger of his wife's relatives
and family.

Divorce is also permitted in modern China. It is now a matter to
be decided by the husband and the wife, not by the family. The
new attitude is that divorce shall be granted only when both the
husband and wife want it. Should it be the desire of only one of
the parties, then the state becomes a party to the divorce affair. The
new Communist law states explicitly: "In the event of either the husband or the wife insisting upon divorce, it may be granted only
when mediation by the subdistrict people's government and the
subdistrict judicial organ has failed to bring about a reconciliation."

Although the Chinese society is undergoing change, it has not
completely changed everywhere. The most radical changes have

taken place under the Communists. Elsewhere, in Formosa, Hong Kong, and Southeast Asia, many Chinese still retain the old customs. The importance of traditional attitudes in shaping Chinese families today varies with the individual, the circumstance, and the locality.

CHAPTER 27

POLITICS IN CHINA

For forty years I have devoted myself to the cause of the people's revolution with but one end in view, the elevation of China to a position of freedom and equality among the nations. My experience during these forty years has firmly convinced me that to attain this goal we must bring about a thorough awakening of our own people and ally ourselves in a common struggle with those people of the world who treat us on the basis of equality.

—SUN YAT-SEN

Marxism should not be applied subjectively and dogmatically. . . . The point is to grasp the general truths of Marxism and apply them to the concrete practice of the Chinese revolution. . . . Chinese culture must have its own form, that is, a national form. . . . During the long period of its feudal stage of development China built up for herself a glorious ancient culture. . . . We should respect our past and never deny our history. But to respect our history is to give it a certain scientific esteem; to respect our cultural past is not to negative our present with a view to praise everything in the old including the poison of feudalism. Therefore, it is important for us to teach the people and the young student, in the main, not to look backward, but to look forward.

—MAO TSE-TUNG

Today two governments claim to be the only lawful government of China. One, officially known as the Republic of China, is the Nationalist government, headed by Chiang K'ai-shek, and is located on the island of Formosa. The other, officially called the People's Republic of China, is the Communist government, led by Mao Tse-tung, and controls the mainland of China.

Both of these governments represent a compound of native and foreign elements. The native elements were inherited from the traditional political system of China; the foreign elements were re-

---

Excerpt from Sun Yat-sen reprinted from *Three Principles of the People*, translated by Frank Price (London: Routledge & Kegan Paul, Ltd., 1928). Used with permission.

ceived from the West. The resulting political system has the appearance of Western politics and institutions but is permeated with spiritual and political conceptions from old China. These conceptions date back to very ancient dynasties which ruled China many hundreds of years before the birth of Christ.

HISTORICAL BACKGROUND

The Shang Dynasty, 1600-1028 B.C., had a monarchical form of government, and the king combined both religious and political duties in his person. The succeeding Chou Dynasty, 1028-221 B.C., is famous for three important events in Chinese history: (1) the beginning of feudalism in China; (2) the promulgation of the doctrine of the Mandate of Heaven, or the right of the people to overthrow a wicked ruler; and (3) the initiation of the traditional major Chinese political philosophies—Confucianism, Legalism, and Taoism.

After the defeat of the Shang Dynasty, the country was divided into many territorial units ruled by loyal retainers of the Chou emperors. This arrangement gradually grew into a feudal system in which the loyal retainers had more power than the emperors themselves. The House of Chou justified the overthrow of the Shang Dynasty by teaching that it was right to depose an emperor who had lost his virtue. The Chou ruler was merely carrying out the will of heaven when he threw out the wicked Shang ruler. This idea was later incorporated into Confucian teaching. According to this (Mandate of Heaven) doctrine, the emperor ruled by reason of heaven's favor. If he lost this favor because of a lack of virtue, the people had the right to revolt. The mandate to rule was then given to a more righteous person.

The three philosophies of Legalism, Taoism, and Confucianism first made their appearance in systematized form at this time. These philosophies, especially Confucianism, formed the ideological foundation upon which the Chinese built their political institutions.

Legalism, a totalitarian philosophy that justified any act a ruler thought necessary for the retention of his power, was the first of these philosophies to be used as the official ideology of a Chinese government. It was the orthodox political doctrine of the Ch'in Dynasty, 221-207 B.C. Styling himself "First Emperor," Ch'in conquered the warring states of China and united the country. By destroying the feudal organization that had grown up during the Chou period and concentrating all power in his person, he laid the foundations of a united, centralized, bureaucratic Chinese empire, which, with some modifications, continued to the present. He also showed future Chinese leaders the advantages of using ideology as an instrument of control. Finally, to ensure conformity and centralization he standardized everything he could, including language, currency, weights and measures, and even the size of the wheels of the carts that traveled over Chinese roads.

But when Ch'in, First Emperor, died, his empire fell apart. During the Han Dynasty, 206 B.C.-220 A.D., that followed, a modified form of Confucianism became the state philosophy. From this time to the twentieth century, Confucianism was the controlling social and political ideology. It became a political cult used to support the continuation of such political institutions as the monarchy. The government was administered by scholar-bureaucrats steeped in Confucian knowledge and practice.

After the Han Dynasty fell, there followed a rather long period of general unrest and disunity which was marked by invasions and civil wars. This period, known as the Dark Ages, lasted for about four centuries. The country split into rival kingdoms, some in the north ruled by barbarian tribes, though even these barbarians gradually adopted Chinese culture and forms of organization. This ebbing of power from the emperor continued until China was reunited under the Sui Dynasty, 581-618 A.D. With the beginning of the T'ang Dynasty, 618-907 A.D., power began to flow back again to the emperor.

During the T'ang Dynasty—the golden age of China—much attention was given to improving the administrative machinery of government. The principal improvement consisted in placing the civil service system on a merit basis. The passing of civil service examinations became the main avenue for obtaining government posts. In order to provide the civil service with an adequate supply of trained men, the educational system of the country was reorganized and expanded. The Imperial University at Ch'ang-an was given the emperor's patronage and encouragement, and prefectural preparatory schools and provincial colleges were expanded. Thus the administration of government was given into the hands of educated men who gained their official posts through merit rather than by way of political patronage or corruption. The T'ang rulers separated the civil and military administration and introduced a new supervisory administrative unit at the local level called the "circuit." It was designed to assure a closer connection between the local and central government.

The remaining dynasties, the Sung, 960-1279 A.D., the Yuan, 1279-1368 A.D., the Ming, 1368-1644 A.D., and the Ch'ing, 1644-1911 A.D., which was the last of the imperial dynasties, continued the process of concentrating power in the person of the emperor.

The civil service system was further developed, expanded, and refined. The scholar-officials who staffed the civil service rarely attempted to usurp the emperor's power, though they protected the interests of the gentry class which they represented. Only scholars indoctrinated with Confucianism could become a part of this system. Since the content of the civil service examinations was almost exclusively Confucian, government administrators were completely indoctrinated with this philosophy, and they saw to it that these teachings were transmitted to the people. Confucianism buttressed the imperial government of China. Attempts were also made to bring about a closer tie between the local and central government. During the Yuan Dynasty, headed by the Mongols, closer supervision of local government was obtained by the establishment of provinces. With some modifications, this provincial system continues today. During the Sung Dynasty, a rather effective means of local control called the *pao chia* system was established. Originally devised as a defense measure against foreign invaders, this system became an effective method for internal control because it made neighbors responsible for the acts of one another.

Efforts to enforce greater control over the local units of government were counteracted by strong forces working for decentralization. This tug of war between central and local governments runs throughout Chinese political history. There are several reasons for this struggle. China is a large country. Prior to the modern age there were no quick means of communication between the central government and faraway provinces. Thus a certain amount of autonomy had to be given to the local government officials. The degree of local autonomy varied from time to time, depending on the strength, or lack of it, of the current dynasty. Moreover, the central power was inherently weak because government itself was mini-

mized in the daily life of the people. Most of the daily affairs of the
Chinese were carried on by nongovernmental institutions such as
families, clans, villages, and guilds. Land disputes, suits, quarrels between villages, the collection of taxes, and most of the everyday activities of life were taken care of by the leaders of these units. The
magistrate, the central government's representative at the lowest
level of local government, the county, had only to make sure that the
taxes were collected and forwarded, the peace kept, and public
works maintained.

IMPACT OF THE WEST

China's native political evolution was drastically modified by
the intrusion of Western influences. These began in the sixteenth
century and continue to the present. The Chinese, proud of their
old culture and civilization, struggled long to resist this cultural
penetration by the West, but internal weakness coupled with strong
pressure from the West broke down their defenses and permitted
Western science and philosophy to spread throughout the land.
Their rapid sweep left the Chinese confused, upset, bitter, and desperately groping for a synthesis that would tie the old and the new
together in some effective but understandable form.

The establishment in 1912 of the Republic of China marked the
beginning of almost fifty years of political confusion and discord
as the Chinese struggled to formulate a political philosophy and
establish political institutions which would combine both Western
and Chinese elements.

Dr. Sun Yat-sen, the father of modern China, was chosen president of the new republic. Because he lacked organizational back-
ing, he resigned his office to a strong military leader of the
old regime, Yuan Shih-k'ai. Yuan mocked the new republican institutions by ruling as a dictator until his death in 1916. After his
death, warlords rose all over China. They kept the country in a state
of turmoil for about ten years as they struggled with one another
for control of the nation. Patriotic Chinese were frustrated and em-
bittered by the weak and chaotic condition of the country, and
throughout this period more and more Chinese intellectuals and
students turned to the study of Western ideas and practices for a
solution to their national problems.

Under the leadership of Dr. Sun Yat-sen and his followers, this knowledge and bitterness of the people were channeled into a nationalist movement which eventually succeeded in uniting most of China under one government. Dr. Sun's Kuomintang Party, founded in 1912, and the Chinese Communist Party, founded in 1921, banded together from 1924 to 1927 in a loose association for the purpose of defeating the warlords and uniting the country under one head.

During this period the organization of the Kuomintang was revised along Communist lines. Student, labor, and peasant, organizations were formed, and soldiers were trained. At the time of the split between the Kuomintang and the Communist parties in 1927, a large part of China had already been brought under the control of the associated groups. Under the leadership of Chiang K'ai-shek, who assumed control of the Kuomintang Party after the death of Dr. Sun, most of China was gradually united under one government.

Neither the Nationalist nor the Communist government has ever controlled all of China. From the time of their breakup in 1927 until the present, with the possible exception of the brief United-Front Period beginning in 1937, there has been constant conflict between these two groups. The Communists were never completely destroyed, although they were forced to retreat from the south of China to the sparse northwest, where for some time they struggled to survive as an independent state within a state. Today, the Communists control most of China, and the Nationalists have been compelled to retreat to the island of Formosa off the southern coast of China.

POLITICAL LEGACY OF TRADITIONAL CHINA

From traditional China both Nationalists and Communists inherited the conviction that society is divided into two groups, the ruler and the ruled, that the best method of governing is through a bureaucracy, that collective responsibility should be enforced, that government should be centralized, that government is personal in character, that the individual should be judged in a social context, and that control by means of ideology is essential to the proper functioning of the government.

Both Nationalists and the Communists operate on the theory that the common people do not really know what is best for them and that consequently it is necessary for an educated elite to rule on their behalf. Both governments justify such rule as being in the best interests of the people, the same principle by which Confucianism justified the rule of the scholar-official. With this conception of politics, there is no democratic basis of government in China as the term democratic is understood in the West. The ruled have little share in their government, little chance to participate in policy-making, and few opportunities to make their will felt.

The belief in the right to revolt is still implicit in the political system of China. Both Nationalists and Communists proclaim that their revolutions were justified by the wicked behavior of the former rulers. The Nationalists condemned the Manchus as rulers without virtue, and the Communists condemned the Nationalists as unworthy to continue governing the people. According to this modern application of the Mandate of Heaven doctrine, the present governments are entitled to the power they hold because they carried out the will of heaven when they expelled their predecessors.

The device of collective responsibility, known formerly as the *pao chia* system, has been taken over by both Nationalists and Communists to ensure greater control of the people by the central government. Groups of households watch one another because they are held responsible for one another by the government.

But the historical tendency toward political decentralization in China still hampers the efforts of the Communists to centralize their control of the mainland—it also hampered the Nationalists when they were in control—and they are using all sorts of administrative devices to counter this tendency. In addition to using the collective responsibility method of "people's associations," which is similar in purpose and principle to the *pao chia* system mentioned above, the Communists have experimented with a new administrative unit intermediate between the provinces and the central government. They have also established a commune system which attempts to regiment the life of the rural population.

Government in China remains personal in character, though this characteristic is more evident in the Nationalist government than in the Communist one. Relations between people and officials, and between members of the bureaucracy and their leaders, are extremely important to the proper working of government. Bureaucracy is not yet a cold, impersonal machine; it is a group of human beings performing their duties on the basis of personal relations as well as on the basis of the administrative regulations. Emphasis is placed upon personal leadership, personal virtue, personal contacts. In this kind of atmosphere, judgments are often made on the basis of feelings, sympathies, and obligations rather than on the basis of detailed regulations. The personalities of Chiang K'ai-shek and Mao Tse-tung are vitally important in shaping the character and spirit of their respective parties and governments. To understand Chinese politics it is essential to understand the personalities who make Chinese policy and the relations among them.

Government in China is also concerned with social conduct. Under the Confucian system, only right conduct gave the emperor the power to govern. Since the Confucian scholar knew the rules of right conduct, he was important to the traditional system of government. The worth of the individual continues to be measured in social terms. Has the individual benefited society? Has he conformed to the rules of right conduct? Does he play his role well in relation with others? These are important questions when the character and worth of an individual are being discussed. Government in China is dedicated to the improvement of society.

The use of ideology as an instrument of social control has been carried over from the traditional system to the present. Political indoctrination is considered essential by both Nationalists and Communists. Though such indoctrination is more widely used and effectively administered under the Communist regime, both regimes have bolstered their rule by championing an ideology and indoctrinating the Chinese with its principles. The Nationalists have, for the most part, founded their political system upon the "Three Principles of the People" formulated by Dr. Sun Yat-sen. The Communists, of course, base their government upon the ideology of Marxian Communism as interpreted by Mao, Lenin, and Stalin. The Communists have also, at various times, interpreted the "Three Principles of the People" to harmonize with their Communistic beliefs.

THE THREE PRINCIPLES: THE GREATER SYNTHESIS

The doctrine of the "Three Principles" is an attempt to synthesize the best of traditional China with the best that the West has to offer. The core of this philosophy is made up of three principles commonly translated nationalism, democracy, and people's livelihood.

Sun Yat-sen received his inspiration for these principles from Lincoln's Gettysburg Address which speaks of government of the people, by the people, and for the people. Dr. Sun interpreted this statement to fit the Chinese scene. Government of the people meant national independence or nationalism; government by the people meant a democracy; and government for the people required that the nation use its power to ensure the people's livelihood, to ensure that the needs of all are supplied by the efforts of all.

Nationalism. Nationalism, the first principle, was primarily an appeal to the Chinese to think of themselves, not only as members of a family, clan, and race, but primarily as members of one large political state to which they owed their loyalty and devotion. This was a Western thought.

Dr. Sun insisted that the Chinese people become patriotic; otherwise the nation-state of China would never become independent and strong. The signing of unequal treaties with foreign nations, the establishment by outside powers of spheres of influence, and many other limitations on China's sovereignty were due, in large measure, to the lack of a unifying feeling of patriotism. Chinese independence and continued self-rule depended upon the rapid growth of Chinese patriotism. He believed that China was in imminent danger of being overrun by the Great Powers and feared that the Chinese race would be swallowed up and absorbed by the rapidly increasing white hordes. He looked forward to the time when the Chinese would relieve China's neighbors of the white imperialist burden that now lay so heavy upon their lands and replace this burden with the civilizing influence of China.

Chinese nationalism was to be preserved by a revival of the old Chinese ethical philosophy, which was to be broadened by the addition of Western techniques and science.

As a Confucianist and a Christian, Dr. Sun stressed virtue and high ideals. He believed in the natural goodness of man and his reasonableness. He emphasized loyalty, filial devotion, kindness, love, faithfulness, justice, harmony, and peace as the motivating forces of the revolution. He hoped that this ideological nationalism would make China a leader among the nations of the world, capable of fostering the kind of peaceful cosmopolitanism that prevailed in earlier days in East Asia.

Democracy. Democracy or popular sovereignty, the second of the three principles, defined liberty in a special manner. To be sure, it provided for a representative form of government, with the administration of government by elected officials and with the power of election, initiative, referendum, and recall in the hands of the people. But it stressed the duty of each Chinese to subordinate his interests to the interests of the state. The individual did not need liberty in China; it was the state that needed liberty.

Dr. Sun held that the Chinese historically enjoyed a large measure of local autonomy and personal freedom. Generally speaking, the only interference with individual freedom in traditional China came from either the family, the clan, or the guild, not from the government. Theoretically, the central government was all-powerful, but it rarely used this power at the level of the people's daily life.

On the other hand, Dr. Sun thought that the Europeans and Americans prized personal freedom because, until comparatively recently, they had been oppressed by feudal lords and despotic kings. As a result Western tradition emphasized the concept of natural freedom and the right of every man to do as he pleased provided he did not infringe upon the rights of someone else. In the past the Chinese had enjoyed too much of this kind of freedom; what they needed in the future was freedom to work on behalf of the Chinese nation-state.

Dr. Sun felt that men are not equal, that they can be divided into three classes: (1) "those who know and perceive beforehand," the creators and inventors, the men of wisdom and insight who think independently; (2) those who "know and perceive afterward" and cannot initiate or create; and (3) those who "do not know and perceive" and, like the blind, must be led by the more knowing and perceiving people. They act but do not think. The great majority of mankind is in the last group. With this conception of the inequality of mankind, Dr. Sun, quite naturally, followed the practice of the Confucianists in separating the people into two classes—the ruler and the ruled. The acting but unthinking mass should be governed by the wise and creative thinkers.

Yet the masses should be given an opportunity to participate in politics so that they could learn to practice democracy and become a progressive force in China. Dr. Sun believed that the people were capable of learning and felt that there must be some check on the elite ruling class lest it become despotic and unresponsive to the requirements of the common good.

Dr. Sun distinguished political power from administrative power. Political power or sovereignty, expressed specifically in terms of election, initiative, referendum, and recall, was lodged in the people. An elite ruling group checked by the sovereign power of the masses, formed the essence of what he called popular sovereignty. He compared the government to a factory or corporation which is managed by competent men but in which the final power is retained by the owners—the shareholders. "This general manager is an expert who has the ability; the shareholders simply keep a supervision over him. The people of a republic are shareholders, the president is general manager, and the people should look upon the government as an expert." Government by experts, and the division of the society into the rulers and the ruled followed Confucian tradition rather closely.

Although this political system was ultimately subject to the will of the people, the people were not yet trained in the art of government. Therefore, Dr. Sun proposed a tutoring period during which the Kuomintang Party would teach the masses about the "Three Principles of the People" and constitutional government. When the people became capable of governing themselves, the Kuomintang would abdicate its position as sole acting head of the government, and the people would then elect their own officials. The authoritarian but competent government of the Kuomintang would be replaced by democratically elected but competent representatives of the people. The period of tutelage was divided into three stages: the military period, which would last only as long as military operations continued; the political period, during which the people would be taught the art and the theory of government and their new powers; and the final period of democratic and constitutional government.

Sun Yat-sen crowned his proposals with regard to democracy with the recommendation that there be five separate and distinct departments of government—the legislative, the executive, the judiciary, the examination, and the censorate or control department. The first three departments are customary in Western political systems; the latter two—the examination and control departments—were customary in the traditional Chinese political system. Dr. Sun was convinced that this combination of Western and Chinese institutions would make the finest and most complete government in the world.

Livelihood. Livelihood, the third principle, embodied the idea of providing the Chinese people with a decent standard of living in terms of food, clothing, shelter, and transportation. It was also designed to enrich and strengthen the entire nation-state. Dr. Sun recommended two programs that he believed would meet both needs —equalization of land ownership, and government regulation of capital.

The first was important because China was predominantly an agricultural country and there was a grave inequality of land holdings which was a primary cause of many of China's economic evils. Sun Yat-sen recommended that the government purchase land at a fair price and equalize its ownership. After the land had been divided, its value should be fixed, and any future increase in its value which did not stem from the owner's own efforts should revert to the community. He also urged a number of reforms to increase farm production.

Sun Yat-sen thought that the government should regulate capital. He favored state action to develop industries and enterprises that the country needed. He desired the nationalization of heavy industries and the communication and transportation system, the development of consumer co-operatives, and improvements in the condition of the laboring classes. He also mentioned progressive income and inheritance taxes. He believed the people should be protected against exploitation by the regulation of private industrial capital. He wanted Western nations to invest in China, although he opposed any Western exploitation of the Chinese people.

The principle of "livelihood" in its broadest sense is summarized in the Nationalist Constitution of China, which states that the "national economy shall be based on the principle of the people's livelihood for equitable distribution of land ownership and control of capital in order to obtain a well-balanced development of public economy in private livelihood."

COMMUNISM: A LESSER SYNTHESIS

Chinese Communism represents a more radical departure from the political philosophy of imperial China than the "Three Principles of the People." Less effort is made to synthesize traditional Chinese thought with Western Communism as interpreted by Lenin and Stalin. Chinese Communists theoretically accept the major Marxist assumption that economic factors determine the political and cultural organizations of any society, but they have had to adapt Communist theory and practice to the special political and social conditions prevailing in China. "We are not idealists," Mao Tse-tung declared. "We cannot place ourselves above the conditions of present-day life."

Mao accepts the orthodox Communist theory that for China and other undeveloped nations there must be a dual revolution, one from feudalism to capitalism and one from capitalism to socialism, but does not believe that the revolutionary transition from feudalism to the new democratic stage must be led solely by a dictatorship of the proletariat, or factory workers.

He taught, prior to the Communist victory in China, that the first stage of new democracy in China should be led by a "combined dictatorship of all revolutionary classes." Of these the peasants were the most important. Mao early recognized their key value by shifting the Communist base in China from the urban proletariat to the peasantry. He held that other progressive groups were the proletariat, the *petit bourgeoisie*, and the national capitalists. The *petit bourgeoisie* embraced government employees, professionals, intellectuals, handicraftsmen. National capitalists were Chinese industrialists who operated production facilities and who desired the development of China's industry free from foreign domination. Enemies of the state were the imperialists, feudalists, and bureaucratic capitalists. They were called reactionary groups who could not be assimilated into the socialist society.

The government based on a coalition of anti-imperialist and anti-feudal elements was termed a "democratic dictatorship." It was democratic, according to the Communists, because these groups understood the "real interests" of the people. It was a dictatorship because they controlled absolutely the imperialist and feudal groups of the nation. In practice this stage ended by 1956 when all trade and industry was nationalized.

This new "democratic republic" practices *democratic centralism.* Generally speaking, democratic centralism means that the people are permitted to discuss policy and elect representatives of each level of political life, but that once a decision has been made, and the election certified from above, complete obedience is demanded. The people may criticize and discuss the manner of implementing a policy, but the policy itself is immune from any adverse comments. Discussions and elections form the democratic content of democratic centralism; the requirement of absolute obedience represents the centralist content. Up to the present time the centralist aspect appears to be dominant.

Mao tried at one time to harmonize Communist theory and practice with Sun Yat-sen's "Three Principles of the People." He declared that "the principles of the minimum program of the Communist Party are fundamentally and consistently the same as those of the Three Principles of the People." He advocated control of capital and equalization of land, two basic ideas of Sun Yat-sen's third principle of "people's livelihood." Land was to be divided and given to the peasants as their own property; state ownership was to be limited to banks, industries, and commercial organizations too large for private owners to handle. This was another example of Mao's policy of not placing himself "above the conditions of present-day life."

Since Dr. Sun's teachings had become widely accepted and understood throughout China, Mao's "acceptance" of them has undoubtedly helped him in spreading Communist doctrine.

THE DRIVE TOWARD A POWERFUL STATE

Theoretically, supreme authority in Communist China rests with the National People's Congress, which is elected every four years. In fact, the members of the Congress, numbering over a thousand, merely serve to provide a united front for the decisions of the Communist party. Administration is carried on by the State Council, which is headed by the Premier of China; but actual power is concentrated in the Communist party.

The party includes 17–18 million Chinese, although millions more support its principles and programs. It is controlled by a Central Committee that is elected by national party congresses. The Central Committee, in turn, elects a Standing Committee that is composed of the most powerful leaders of the party and that is the real focus of power in China. All state organs are subject to the commands that issue from a few top leaders of the party. Usually, the top officials of the government and the leaders of the Communist party are the same persons. The authority of the party is evidenced by the person of Mao Tse-tung, who holds no official post in the government but controls the state through his position as head of the party. Wherever there is a government official who is not a member of the party, there is near him a deputy or a secretary who is a member, and this arrangement carries downward through the various levels of government to the basic administrative units of the communes at the local level.

In 1949, the Communists gained control of a country made desolate by years of war. Gradually, they curbed inflation and restored and improved the transportation system. By confiscating the properties of businessmen, industrialists, and foreign investors, they brought under their control much of the industrial production of the country and increased the revenues of government. By 1952, the Communist leaders had rehabilitated the economy of China, but they lacked the capital and skilled manpower needed for rapid industrialization. To implement their First Five-Year Plan, they therefore turned to Russia for financial and technical aid. The Soviets advanced a credit of 130 million dollars that, together with 300 million advanced earlier, made a total loan of 430 million, part of which the Chinese had to start paying back in 1954. Another aspect of the First Five-Year Plan that was to plague the Chinese at a later date was its emphasis on heavy industry at the expense of light industry and agriculture.

During the period of the First Five-Year Plan, the Communists began to collectivize agriculture. Beginning in the spring of 1953, they began to organize the villagers into temporary mutual-aid groups, then into permanent mutual-aid teams, and then into agricultural producers' cooperatives. The farmers worked on the basis of joint ownership of their pooled property, were paid in proportion to what they contributed, and had the right to withdraw their property from the cooperatives if they wished. Soon after, joint ownership became common ownership; they could no longer withdraw their original property; and they were paid on the basis of their work rather than on their capital investment in the common holdings. By the end of 1957, the Communist leaders reported that over 95 per cent of the peasant households were members of collective farms.

Although food production barely kept ahead of the rapidly increasing population between 1952 and 1957, industrial production during this period increased at a yearly rate of around 4 per cent. Emboldened by this success and convinced that collectivization was right, the Communist leaders announced a Second Five-Year Plan for the period 1958–1962. In February, 1958, they proclaimed "a great leap forward."

To accomplish this "leap," thousands of party cadres were sent into the fields to mobilize the masses. Workers labored fourteen or even sixteen hours at a time to meet production goals. Peasants worked in the fields from dawn to dusk and then tended backyard furnaces far into the night, producing inferior iron and steel. To mobilize labor more efficiently, the leaders changed the cooperatives into communes, each commune including about five thousand households. The peasants were required to give all but a few personal belongings to the commune, and to eat, sleep, and bathe in common buildings. Since the communes permitted labor allocation on a massive scale, millions were mobilized to repair roads and build railroads, to the accompaniment of clashing cymbals and stirring music.

As a result of the great leap forward, new cities sprang up overnight near industrial centers. At the same time, the people were driven to exhaustion, and food shortages began to plague the cities and the countryside. The people became resentful, and the leaders were finally forced to relax their pressure. The commune was decentralized into three levels of ownership. It continues to own factories, public buildings, and power plants to which all in the commune have contributed. The production brigade, a subdivision of the commune, owns its own land and tools and whatever factories and public buildings have been constructed with brigade funds. The production team, which is a subdivision of the production brigade, about the size of a peasant village, owns its own animals, houses, and local property. The leaders of the commune and its subdivisions are elected. They need not be Communist party members, but they must be sympathetic with the party's agricultural objectives.

Since 1960, the Communist leaders have tempered their almost inhuman demands on the energies of the Chinese people. They have devoted more attention to agriculture and have emphasized light as well as heavy industry. Because of a shortage of arable land, they have just managed to keep their agricultural production on a level with their growing population. At times, they have had to buy millions of tons of grain from such countries as Canada and Australia in order to feed their people. There is some evidence of malnutrition in certain areas, but in general the food supply appears to be adequate, though not abundant. Industrial expansion remains a primary goal. Vast natural resources have been discovered, and industrial complexes have been built near these resources. It has been estimated that within twenty years China will rank behind the U.S.S.R. and the United States as a great industrial power.

The Chinese regard the United States as their principal enemy. They point to U.S. soldiers in Korea, Japan, Taiwan, Vietnam, and the Philippines and to the powerful American fleet that patrols the waters between mainland China and Taiwan, the seat of Nationalist power. Insisting that Taiwan is an integral part of Chinese territory, they declare that there can be no peace between the United States and China until the Nationalist forces are withdrawn. They demand an equal voice in the higher Communist councils of the world. Though they desire Russian aid, they will not play a subservient role or compromise their ideological principles. The rift between Russia and China has widened in recent years, and they have become rivals for the allegiance of the Communist world.

CHAPTER 28

KOREA

Korea, "Land of High Mountains and Sparkling Streams," has the more ancient name of Cho-son, which was given to it in the twelfth century B.C. by the first Chinese to govern the country. Cho-son means "Land of the Morning Calm" or "Morning Radiance." Because the country isolated itself from the rest of the world for many years, outsiders often referred to it as the "Hermit Kingdom."

Korea is a mountainous peninsula jutting out from the eastern coasts of the Eurasian Continent. It lies between the Yellow Sea, which separates the peninsula from China on the west, and the Sea of Japan, which separates it from Japan on the east. Chinese Manchuria covers most of the northern boundary of Korea with the exception of a narrow strip in the northeast which is bordered by Soviet Russia.

The Korean peninsula is approximately 85,000 square miles in area and about 600 miles long and 135 miles wide.

There are two political Koreas today—North and South Korea. North Korea is officially known as the Peoples Democratic Republic of Korea and is ruled by a Communist government. South Korea is officially named the Republic of Korea and is now ruled by a military government.

The population of Korea is approximately 33 million. Of this number roughly 23 million live in South Korea below the 38th parallel, and the remainder in North Korea above the 38th parallel. More than 80 per cent of the people derive their living from agriculture, and the great bulk of the population is rural in character. P'yongyang, located on the mouth of the Tadong River, is the capital of North Korea. Seoul, located on the mouth of the Han River, is the capital of South Korea.

Because of her location Korea has served as a bridge connecting Japan with the religious, political, and social ideas of China. Korea was originally settled by various families of men, but it was the Chinese who most influenced the Koreans' language, culture, and customs. But over the centuries the Korean people have evolved their own unique language, culture, and customs from this original heritage. The Japanese owe a great debt to the Korean people for having transmitted to them so much of the wealth of Chinese philosophy, religion, art, and architecture.

The location of Korea has influenced both her own historical development and the political relations between Korea, China, Japan, and Russia. China, Russia, and Japan at one time or another have sought to control Korea because of the country's unique geographic position. Japan has thought of Korea as a dagger pointed at her heart. China thinks of Korea as a nation uncomfortably close to her industrial area of Manchuria. Russia believes that control of Korea would help to secure her position in East Asia. Because all three have long felt that Korea is necessary to their security, her land has been saturated by the blood of many armies.

Unfortunately, the travail of the Koreans has not yet ended. Most Koreans had looked to a period of peaceful independence and greater prosperity after the defeat of the Japanese who had ruled their country as a colony since 1910. This was not to be. The Allies were victorious in 1945, but Korea was divided. The Russians occupied northern Korea down to the 38th parallel, and the Americans occupied the land from there southward. After prolonged and strenuous efforts by the Americans and others to bring into being a United Korean government had failed, the Russians established a Communist government in their area, and the Americans encouraged the formation of a democratic form of government in South Korea. In June, 1950, a few years after the establishment of the two governments, the North Koreans invaded South Korea, thereby initiating a war which eventually drew into its vortex many of the nations of the world. The Communist bloc of nations poured military supplies, advisors, and many thousands of soldiers—mostly Chinese soldiers—into supporting North Korea's aggression. Defending South Korea were a number of nations, headed by the United States, who fought under the banner of the United Nations. After the fighting and bombing stopped three years later in July, 1953, both Koreas lay ravished and still divided; two economic, political, and social wrecks which even now, more than a decade later, have not recovered completely from the agonies of this war.

The fate of South Korea was most deplorable, and the lament of her people still echoes in the land. Much of the war was fought on her soil. Her fields were mined, her crops destroyed, her cities leveled, and her people killed in droves by pestilence, starvation, bullets, and bombs. The fear of further invasion and rape by her enemies in the north has necessitated the maintenance of an expensive defense establishment. She has had little chance to recover from her serious wounds because the resources that are urgently needed to rehabilitate the country are required to support an army, navy, and air force. She has few industries and a paucity of employment outlets for her people. Life goes on somehow, but frustrations grow as hope recedes and morale drops. These frustrations have shown up on the domestic political scene within the past several years. Syngman Rhee, the aged, paternalistic first president of the republic, was forced to resign his position after the April Revolution of 1960 and leave the country. In May, 1961, the democratic government which succeeded the Rhee regime was taken over by the military who were profoundly disgusted by the inefficiency and corruption they observed at every level of government. Today, a hard-working and dedicated band of officers is attempting to lift the country from the economic, political, and social depths and restore to the people confidence in their leaders and hope for the future. In October, 1963, one of these officers, General Chung Hi Pak, was elected President of the Republic.

From the inception of an independent South Korea, America has given massive economic aid to Korea which, for the most part, has been spent in defense measures. Koreans and their friends everywhere live in expectancy of the day when, once again, they can rejoice in a prosperous and viable country.

Stubbornly independent, the Koreans have sometimes been described as the "Irish of the Orient." Although the North Koreans have received economic aid from both China and the U.S.S.R., they remain quite determined to preserve their flexibility of policy and action within the Communist bloc of nations. No small nation bordered by giants can preserve complete political and economic autonomy, but the North Koreans are striving to remain as independent as possible.

The North Koreans have had some success in increasing their industrial output since the end of the war with South Korea. Traditionally, North Korea has been the industrial part of the peninsula, dependent upon the half now called South Korea for agricultural products, textiles, and light-industry products. Now they must rely upon other countries and their own efforts to supply these products. They are stressing increased agricultural production, and they aim at exporting steel, other metals, and machinery to less developed countries and, possibly, to the West. Most of the trade is with the U.S.S.R., for China cannot supply their industrial needs; but they side with the Chinese in the Sino-Soviet quarrel. Like the South Koreans, they would prefer a united Korea, but on terms unacceptable to the South Koreans.

Apparently, there will be two Koreas in the foreseeable future, to the detriment of both.

JAPAN

The Japanese call their country Nippon, which means "Land of the Rising Sun." Geographically the country is an island group of approximately one thousand islands. The major part of the area is included in the four main islands of Honshu, Hokkaido, Kyushu, and Shikoku.

Japan is one of Asia's most important countries. During the past hundred years it has practically lifted itself from among the least known countries in the world, to one whose influence is felt throughout Asia and the world. Despite its meager land area—slightly smaller than California—and the relative paucity of its natural resources, Japan has become one of the world's great industrial countries. Japanese products are to be found in every country in Asia and are familiar to most Westerners. The quality of these products has improved over the years, and today their cameras, lenses and motorcycles are regarded as among the best in the world. Japanese technicians are to be found in many Asian countries helping in the establishment of small industries and sharing their technical knowledge with their Asian neighbors.

The Japanese are assisting today in the rehabilitation of many Asian countries which two decades ago they had conquered by force of arms. Twenty years ago the Japanese were regarded as one of the great military powers of the world; they occupied and controlled, for a period of time, a great part of Asia. The combined power of the Allies eventually wrested these areas from the Japanese, but not before Japanese actions and ideas had changed the political face of Asia by destroying the underpinnings of Western colonialism in this region.

The Japanese have been accused of excessively imitating others and described as lacking in originality. It is true that the Japanese have taken ideas from others and copied products produced by others, but they have also originated concepts and products which have been widely accepted and imitated by others. Nor have they imitated slavishly, for in many instances they have practically and esthetically improved the original foreign product through additions created by their own inventive and artistic minds. Ideas which have flowed in upon them over the centuries from Asia, particularly from China via Korea, have been modified to fit the Japanese scene. Their present great industrial complex, which was rebuilt so rapidly from the rubble of war, is a tribute to the skill, persistence, intelligence, and imaginativeness of the Japanese people.

It is essential to understand something of the thought and way of life of a people who have created a key country in Asia, who have since the late nineteenth century shaped the destiny of so many millions of Asians and non-Asians through their military and political activities, and who will continue to play a major role in the evolving life of mankind.

CHAPTER 30

JAPANESE IDEOLOGY

Japanese thought is a composite of indigenous beliefs grouped under the name of Shinto, or "Way of the Gods," and a number of foreign ideologies of which Confucianism and Buddhism are the most important. From the fusion and interaction of these concepts has come what the Japanese like to refer to as the spirit of Japan, a spirit which they believe has made the land and people of Japan unique. Because it has a mystical character and includes the whole corpus of sentiment and belief that moves the Japanese people to action, it is impossible to define this spirit, but certain of its aspects can be described.

REVERENCE FOR NATURE

Shinto, the native religion, and Taoism, an ideological import from China, have given the Japanese a deep and reverent feeling for nature which is revealed in the tender, patient care they lavish on their islands. These resemble gardens that have been trimmed and trained to be natural scenes of beauty. Trees have been shaped to serve as frames for islands, lakes, and mountain tops. The forest paths ramble gracefully, the brooks murmur in soft, pensive tones, and even the small stone is perfectly placed to give an artless but harmonious appearance of grace. The beauty that is Japan is the result of an abiding love and respect for nature and for the divinity which lives within it.

The mingling of Shinto and Buddhism has stimulated the holding of many festivals which bring added gaiety and charm to an already lovely group of islands. Nature, festivals, and joy are intimately related. The great festivals are occasions for celebrating the changes of season or the generous harvests that divine nature has bestowed upon the Japanese people. The emperor of Japan participates personally, as an intermediary between his people and the gods of nature, in both the spring and autumn festivals. He seeks the blessings of the gods for the new planting, and he gives thanks for the benefits the people have already received in the form of food.

There are many festivals. There are the flower festivals which are celebrated once a month, there is the doll festival, the children's festival, which honors Gautama Buddha as a child, the moon festival, and the New Year's festival, which lasts for a month, and many others. These festivals are not merely Shinto or Buddhist—they are Japanese festivals.

BUSHIDO

Bushido, or "the Way of the Warrior," is the name for a code of behavior and morals which had its origin in the military history of Japan. It developed from the intimate relationships that existed between the early landholder and his armed retainers. Gradually it evolved into an expected pattern of behavior that governed soldiers under the stress of war. From vague beginnings in the early feudal and prefeudal period to the seventeenth century, this creed of Bushido served as a well-known social guide, rule of life, and set of ideals for the *Samurai,* or military class.

With the establishment of the Tokugawa shogunate in 1603, Bushido was codified and given a definite philosophical base. It became a system of practical ethics which was to serve not only as a guide for the samurai, but as a set of high ideals for all good Japanese citizens. It was an ambitious attempt to apply the code of the warrior to civilians. Taken from the context of war and battle, it became somewhat elaborate, ceremonial, and complex, but the ideal and spirit of Bushido still remains a part of every Japanese.

Bushido incorporated elements from Confucianism, Buddhism, and Shinto. Confucianism stressed the quality of loyalty which should exist between the inferior and the superior in social and family relations. The "five relationships" predominated. The son owes obedience and loyalty to his father, the younger brother must be loyal to the elder brother, the subject must be loyal to his emperor and to his lord, the wife to her husband, and a friend to a friend. The Japanese taught that the loyalty of the vassal to the lord transcended all other loyalties and that this loyalty passes on from father to son and from generation to generation. For a mother or father to substitute their son for their lord's son who was threatened by an assassin, and to watch him being killed with no show of emotion, was not only ethical but an act highly praised. The Japanese people possess a strong sense of obligation and generally subordinate their individual desires to the claims of society. The struggle between obligation and natural affection is a common theme of Japanese tragedy.

"The Way of the Horse and the Bow," another name for Bushido, also incorporated qualities from Zen Buddhism and Shinto. Zen teaches that enlightenment is achieved only through one's inward efforts, and consequently it stresses self-discipline, self-control, and self-conquest. These were the qualities that military men made an essential part of their code. Shinto bequeathed to Bushido its great reverence for nature, its simplicity and lack of ostentation. From Shinto, Bushido also obtained its strong attachment for the land of Japan and all that it stood for, and this sentiment still grips the people and leaders of Japan.

From earliest times to the present, Japanese rulers have typically made use of religion to serve their own political ends. The Yamato rulers, the dominant clan of early Japan, fostered a belief in the superiority of their divine ancestress, Amaterasu, the sun goddess, in order to justify their assumption of the rulership of all Japan. In the sixth century, the Saigo family used the new religion of Buddhism to further their political fortunes, while the Nakatomi and other clans upheld the native gods as a counterbalance. The Tokugawa rulers stressed Buddhism because it upheld their policies of maintaining unchanged the Japanese social and political structure. Later, the group of samurai who overthrew the Tokugawa rulers used the ancient religion of Shinto to justify the revolution and to strengthen their right to rule. All political leaders stressed those elements of loyalty and obedience found in Confucianism and emphasized the superior-inferior relationships which were an integral part of Confucian doctrine. In modern times, those types of Western constitutions and ideas found favor with the Japanese authorities which gave a great degree of power to the ruling executive body.

The Japanese have often been accused of being mere borrowers, slavish imitators of the ideas of others. This is not true. Japan has received much from her neighbors in the East and, more recently, from the countries of the West, but in each instance the Japanese have shaped these ideological imports to fit their own unique environment and needs.

CHAPTER 31

SHINTO

The roots of Shinto, "the Way of the Gods," are deeply embedded in the legendary past of Japan. For centuries Shinto teachings were handed down by word of mouth; it was only in the eighth century A.D. that Shinto beliefs and observances were put into writing. Basic works are *Kojiki*, "Record of Ancient Things," and *Nihon-shoki*, "Chronicles of Japan." The *Manyoshu*, or "Collection of a Myriad Leaves," an anthology of eighth-century verse, contains some parts of Shinto ritual and faith. A handbook of Shinto prayers and sacred rites entitled *Engishiki*, or "Origin of Rites," was written in the tenth century.

The *Kojiki* (712 A.D.) and the *Nihon-shoki* (720 A.D.) are our principal written sources of information about early Japanese beliefs and customs. Both works are written in Chinese characters because the Japanese had not yet evolved their own script at this early period.

They were written primarily to strengthen the dynasty of the reigning Yamato sovereigns and the social position of the seventh-century aristocracy. Early myths, legends, and events were chosen which tended to buttress the legitimacy and prestige of the ruling king and his clan; genealogies were included to provide the emperor and the important clans and families with gods for ancestors. The compilers planned well, because these two books have been used throughout Japan's long history as documentary proof of the divine origin of the Japanese people and their leaders. In the nineteenth century these same two works provided a firm foundation for the growth of Japanese nationalism.

THE SHINTO STORY OF CREATION

The *Kojiki* and the *Nihon-shoki* relate the story of the creation of the land and people of Japan. Out of chaos came heaven and earth, and then a succession of divine beings ending with the god Izanagi and the goddess Izanami. These two deities stood on the bridge of heaven and dipped a spear into the waters beneath them. The drops that dripped from this spear piled up and formed the islands of Japan. Then these two divine beings descended to this land, married, and produced such offspring as the mountains, rivers, and forests of Japan. Izanami gave birth to Amaterasu-o-mi-Kami who shone so brightly that her parents sent her to heaven where she rules as the sun goddess. Thus the sun was created. A younger brother was also sent to heaven where he shared power as the moon god with his sister Amaterasu. Thus the moon was created. Izanami then gave birth to Susa-na-wo who was so fierce and cruel that he was sent to rule the world of darkness. Izanami then gave birth to the fire god who burned her so seriously that she died. This did not stop the creation of gods and nature, however, for from her excreta and the tears of her husband more gods were born.

Japan's earliest history continues with the uncouth behavior of Susa-na-wo in his sister Amaterasu's palace. He so shocked and angered his sister that she fled and hid herself leaving the whole world in darkness. The gods tricked her into revealing herself again by having one of their female members perform an indecent dance in front of her hiding place. Hearing the laughter and shouts of the gods watching the dance, she looked out to see what was taking place. They seized her, pulled her out into the open, and light shone again upon the world. Susa-na-wo was banished from heaven to his land of darkness, but before he returned, he went to Japan where he begot many offsprings who ruled over these island lands.

A decision was made in heaven to send Ninigi-no-Mikoto, the grandson of the sun goddess, to rule Japan. He came first to the island of Kyushu bearing three treasures given him by his grandmother Amaterasu—a jewel, a sword, and a mirror. Ninigi married, and had children and grandchildren. One of his great-grandchildren, Jimmu Tenno—Tenno literally means "Sovereign of Heaven" and is the common name for emperor in Japan—moved eastward from Kyushu to central Japan where he is said to have set up the state of Yamato on February 11, 660 B.C. This is considered the foundation date of the empire of Japan, and Jimmu is regarded as the first emperor.

As the Yamato clan gained supremacy over other Japanese clans, the legendary stories became accepted as true and the three treasures—the jewel, sword, and mirror—given by Amaterasu to her grandson Ninigi became symbols of imperial authority. These legends also formed the basis for popular belief in the divinity and natural superiority of the Japanese people. The origins of most modern Shinto deities and much Shinto ritual are traced by the Japanese to the *Kojiki* and the *Nihon-shoki*.

NATURE IS DIVINE

Shinto teaches that nature bears divinity within itself. Shinto deifies all natural forces and regards all things animate and inanimate as divine and the product of deities. Mountains, trees, stones, winds, lightning, birds and plants, are reverenced and worshipped as carriers of a divine spirit. This kind of religion—usually called animism—is very widespread and may at various times have been universal among early mankind, but in Shinto the Japanese have brought animism to its most civilized and sophisticated form.

The Japanese gave the name *kami* to the gods of heaven and earth and to the spirits that dwell within natural objects. *Kami* literally means "superior" or "above," and the Japanese applied this word to all things they thought superior regardless of whether they were living or dead. The early Japanese, impressed by such natural forces as raging seas and frightening storms, and awed by the majesty of mountains and the vast sweep of forests, thought of these expressions of nature as something superior and above them. Kami implies respect and reverence, and it came to be applied to anything that was mysterious, awesome, and strange. The Japanese gradually endowed all nature's manifestations with the divine presence referred to as kami.

In order that the awesome expressions of nature might be more approachable, the Japanese gave them an anthropomorphic character. The sun became the sun goddess, the moon the moon god, and Japan's beloved mountain Fujiyama became Fujisama—"the Mountain Goddess." Besides these well-known deities there were the earth god, the food god, the fertility god, and other gods and goddesses who were members of the Shinto pantheon.

Ancient Shinto has no images. The mountain, valley, stone, or tree was worshipped in its natural state. Later, objects thought to be bearers or symbols of divinity were enclosed in a crude manner with sticks or branches of trees. Still later, under the influence of Buddhism, Shinto housed the symbols of divinity in more elaborate and colorful structures. However, for the most part, the religion retains much of its original simplicity. The great Shinto shrines at Ise are torn down and erected every twenty years in their original form with unpainted wood. These are the national shrines of the sun goddess and the food goddess. They are merely large huts, with no place for congregants to sit, and the people simply stand outside the shrine to worship. After washing his hands and rinsing his mouth, the worshipper generally stands outside the shrine, makes an offering, claps his hands, bows, claps his hands again, and leaves. Sometimes the ringing of a bell substitutes for the hand clapping.

None of the gods and goddesses of the Shinto pantheon are sharply defined, for Shinto has little speculative and philosophical content. The obscurity and vagueness which surrounds Shinto deities continues even today as new functions and new identities accumulate. This vagueness does not worry the Japanese worshipper. It is enough for him to know that the shrine encloses a divinity which brings the good things of life to himself and his country. Except in the case of the more prominent deities, Shinto shrines are essentially a means by which the worshipper gets in touch with the unseen.

Shinto is much concerned with natural processes. Birth, growth, and life are blessings which should be sought from the gods and for which thanks should be given when obtained. Death, decay, sterility are to be shunned and guarded against in every possible way. The chief evils are those that interfere with the productive forces of nature; the chief blessings those that encourage them. The prevalence of phallic symbols in trees and stones is due to this emphasis upon the constructive processes of nature. The greatest and most joyous festivals in Japan are those that deal with the planting and harvesting of crops.

Shinto is a religion of love and thanksgiving, but it is more—it is a religion which shows a striking appreciation of nature's beauty. Nature provides a feast for the eyes as well as food for the stomach. The Japanese felt that anything so beautiful must be godlike, and they honored the valleys, mountains, rocks, and streams of their land by making them divine. The earth and sky, the land and sea, the sun, moon, and stars are bearers of a beauty beyond the power of man to express, and the Japanese considered them to be among their greatest deities. The gods of nature were givers of life and beauty, and the Japanese could only love, praise, and be greatful. There was little need for fear; there was a great need for thanksgiving.

An example of the appreciation of beauty which permeates the

Shinto religion is the lovely setting of its shrines. They are often set in a serene landscape and surrounded by ancient trees. Some Japanese have stated that the real spirit of Shinto can be felt best among the old whispering pines that girdle and shelter their shrines. Often these shrines are framed by a torii (p. 239) which separates the secular from the divine and is a sign that one approaches a sacred place.

This love of beauty which fills the Shinto religion is found everywhere in Japanese life. An attractive simplicity is revealed in the arrangement and service of food and in the tea ceremony which is carried out in a very clean little room surrounded by a miniature garden. Many homes in Japan have carefully planned gardens, which may sometimes be small but are always tasteful and show the work of patient, artistic hands. A home is so designed that it becomes a part of the surrounding scenery; there is no jarring note, only a harmony of man and landscape.

RITUAL PURITY

Ritual purity is the heart of Shinto ceremonial. Before a person can worship, he must be purified. Pollution is offensive to the gods, and the avoidance of anything that will defile a person is an integral part of Shinto observances. Some of the many things that can soil a person are uncleanliness, menstruation, sickness, and wounds or injuries of all kinds. This is an actual physical impurity. The uncleanliness that needs to be washed away is something that can be seen, something that is physically repulsive. There is no sense of sin or feeling of guilt such as Westerners might possess. In the moral sense the problem of evil does not exist for the Japanese. The early religion of the Japanese was almost completely free from abstract ideas of morality. The Shinto worshipper has to be purified of his physical uncleanliness; there is no abstract guilt to be forgiven. It is a ceremonial matter rather than an ethical or moral compulsion.

Purification is obtained in three ways—through exorcism, cleansing, and abstention. An unclean worshipper can be cleansed by a priest who waves a wand and pronounces a formula of purification. An offender is cleansed of defilement by washing or by sprinkling of salt and dirt. Abstention is practiced most often by the priests and consists of the avoidance of anything that might defile a person, such as sickness or certain kinds of food.

CHINESE INFLUENCES

Shinto has been influenced by foreign imports. From Confucianism it obtained ancestor worship, emphasis upon loyalty to the emperor, and a guide for social behavior. From popular Taoism it received magical practices and sorcery. Other Chinese imports were the theory of the dualism of the *yin* and *yang*—*yin* represents a female or negative element, while *yang* symbolizes the male or positive element—and the theory of the five elements of wood, earth, fire, metal, and water which influenced divination, fortune-telling, and augury. The greatest influence was Buddhism, which overshadowed Shinto from the ninth to the nineteenth century. These foreign ideas brought ethics and philosophy to Shinto, added foreign gods to the Shinto pantheon, and sometimes veiled the original simplicity of Shinto shrines and objects by introducing a tendency toward ornateness and complexity.

From the moment these foreign ideas entered Japan there began a process of harmonization which has continued to the present day. This process was so successful that today the Japanese can, and often do, consider themselves at the same time Shintoists, Buddhists, and Confucianists. A good example of this process can be seen in the early harmonization of Buddhism and Shinto.

When Buddhism first entered Japan around 552 A.D., it clashed with Shinto, not because of doctrinal differences, but because they were both used as a justification for strife in a struggle for power between several Japanese clans. When the clans upholding Shinto were finally defeated, support for Buddhism in Japan was guaranteed. Buddhism spread very rapidly, especially in the court circles. The native cult of Shinto continued strong among the common folk. Then the eclecticism of the Japanese and the assimilative quality of Mahayana Buddhism became manifest.

The Buddhists declared that the native gods of Shinto were really incarnations of Buddhist deities, and they frequently and specifically identified these deities. The Japanese monk Gyogi reconciled the two religions by stating that they were merely two different forms of the same faith. Acting upon this theory Buddhist priests took part in Shinto rites, and an empress of Japan publicly proclaimed that the cardinal duties are "first to serve the Three Treasures—Buddha, the doctrine, and the order (Buddhism)—

then to worship the gods (Shinto), and next to cherish the people."
She saw no objection to the participation of Buddhist nuns and
priests in the important Shinto feast of the Great Festival of the First
Fruits which is celebrated at the beginning of each reign. On one
occasion a prominent Shinto deity was conveyed from western Japan to the capital, Nara, where he was installed in a special shrine
and attended by a priestess who was also a Buddhist nun. For seven
days, forty Buddhist priests prayed at the shrine of this Shinto
deity.

Today shrines and temples exist peacefully together, representing to the Japanese mind not contradictions but only differences of
function. Today in Japan a new baby may be taken to a Shinto
priest for a religious service, but should he die, his funeral will be
conducted by Buddhist priests. Many homes have both Buddhist
altars and Shinto sacred shelves.

POLITICAL ASPECTS

The ascendancy of the Yamato clan raised its clan deity, the sun
goddess, to the pre-eminent position of ancestress of all other clans.
Gradually she became regarded as the ancestress of the entire race.
More and more Shinto became a vehicle for official ritual and
stressed the functions of the emperor as the intermediary between
the people and the ancestral gods. It became an institutional religion supported by the ruling classes and tied closely to the political
system of Japan, and a national cult developed centered in the sun
goddess who was the ancestress of the ruling family.

In 1882 Shinto was divided into Shrine Shinto, often referred to
as State Shinto, and Sect Shinto, the traditional native religion. State
Shinto was the official cult sponsored by the government for the
purpose of inspiring in the Japanese single-minded obedience and
loyalty to the emperor and, through him, to the state. Although it
was placed above all other beliefs in Japan, officially it was declared
not to be a religion. This distinction was somewhat artificial, because the same deities were worshipped and the same shrines honored in both sects; the division between the two Shintos was more
political than religious.

The administration of about 100,000 shrines was placed under
the Home Ministry. Certain family shrines were taken over by
the government, and officials placed in charge. Often there was no

change of personnel, merely of title. Priests were graded and given court rank according to the shrine they served. The government also gave detailed instructions with regard to the performance of rituals and ceremonies. This nationalist trend affected some shrines more than others, but in most cases emperor worship was added. The shrine of Ise, which is dedicated to the sun goddess, became the greatest shrine in Japan. The emperor and government officials traveled to the shrine of the sun goddess on important occasions.

The aim of this movement was to revive loyalty to the emperor as over against the shogun and feudal lords. *Shogun* literally means "Barbarian-Conquering General" and was the title given the military dictator of Japan during the feudal period. State Shinto was a means of obtaining national unity and stability. The ruler was viewed not only as a political head but also as the chief priest of the nation—the main intermediary between the sun goddess, his ancestor, and the people. Article III of the 1889 Constitution declared: "The Emperor is sacred and inviolable." The Emperor possessed divine virtue and had the quality of infallibility. The emphasis placed upon divine rule led many Japanese to think that the emperor was destined by heaven to rule the world.

Prior to the war there were numerous Shinto sects and subsects with a total of about 17 million members. Although all the sects teach certain common doctrines, such as ritual purity and divinity in nature, they differ in their emphasis upon such things as the tradition of ancient Shinto, Confucian elements, worship of sacred mountains, purification, and faith healing.

State or Shrine Shinto, abolished in December 1945, is attempting to become Sect Shinto, a religion with an ethical content and an organized priesthood. Most of its individual shrines are now incorporated as religious bodies, and thousands of them have formed an association with headquarters in Tokyo. Shrine Shinto is also giving a good deal of attention to social work of all kinds.

Shinto is not dead in Japan. It continues to grow and change and influence the lives of the Japanese people.

CHAPTER 32

BUDDHISM IN JAPAN

> *No matter how many beings there are,*
> *I vow to rescue them;*
> *No matter how endless the passions,*
> *I vow to destroy them;*
> *No matter how great the depths of the Dharmas,*
> *I vow to know them;*
> *No matter how much beyond my reach the truth of Buddha,*
> *I vow to know them;*
>
> —THE "FOUR GREAT VOWS,"
> recited by the Zen monk after every service

Buddhism was carried to Japan from Korea around the middle of the sixth century A.D. At first it was not graciously received, but it soon took root and flourished under the protection of the Soga family and the patronage of Shotoku Taishi (593-622 A.D.). As a result, Shotoku, the prince regent during that period, is often called the founder of Buddhism in Japan.

By and large Buddhism was supported and encouraged by the ruling group in Japan. In 685 A.D. the court instructed the people to set up a Buddhist shrine in their houses which would serve as an object of worship and to which food might be offered. Even now most Japanese houses contain such a shrine. During the Tokugawa Period (1603-1863) the shogun patronized Buddhism as a stabilizing force in the country, and every household was required to belong to some Buddhist sect. As a result of this requirement, the temples became storage houses for the vital statistics of the nation, because each temple recorded the births, marriages, and deaths of its members.

Buddhism entered Japan as both a bearer and an aspect of Chinese culture and is fundamentally the same as in China. It is divided into various sects, of which the largest and most popular today is the Shin-shu. Shin-shu follows the Chinese type of Mahayana Buddhism and teaches salvation by faith in Amitabha Buddha. It is a ceremonial and pageant-loving sect. The second largest Buddhist sect in Japan is Zen, which differs radically from Shin-shu because it teaches that salvation is the result of one's own efforts rather than the outcome of a faith in some supernatural deity. Zen traces its origin to Ch'an Buddhism which started in China around 400 A.D.

ZEN BUDDHISM

Zen teaches that the Buddha-nature is everywhere, not only in some Western Heaven or Pure Land. All living things possess the Buddha-nature, and all men may attain Buddhahood. Zen belief in the universality of the Buddha-nature is vividly exemplified in the story of a Buddhist monk who entered a temple and spat on the statue of Buddha. When he was reproved for this insulting behavior, he answered: "Show me a place to spit where there is no Buddha."

Man has the power within himself, says Zen, to discover this Buddha-nature. When he comes to understand the true character of his own nature, he will be enlightened. But he must achieve his own salvation; no one can achieve it for him. Thus Zen differs from the general teaching of Pure Land and Shin-shu Buddhism, which stresses dependence upon others, and more closely resembles the original teaching of Gautama Buddha who stated that each man must reach enlightenment by his own efforts.

The followers of Zen believe that enlightenment comes suddenly, but only after a lengthy and rigorous period of meditation sometimes lasting for many years. The story is told that Bodhidharma, an Indian sage who first brought Zen doctrines to China, sat for nine years in meditation facing a blank wall. Because of the prominent place of meditation in Zen Buddhism, it has been poetically described as "the Philosophy of Silence."

Because it believes that absolute truth cannot be expressed in words or analyzed by means of sacred scriptures, Zen Buddhism has little use for books, scriptures, discussions, and writings of any kind. Neither good works, nor faith, nor prayer can substitute for meditation in reaching a knowledge of the Buddha-nature that is the foundation of life. Meditation is helped by simple and self-disciplined living. In Japan, Zen monks feel that such pursuits as tea drinking, gardening, and contemplation of nature aid in some manner to the final goal of enlightenment. The simplicity, austerity, and self-conquest that is required of followers of Zen appeals to the tastes of many Japanese, especially those of the military class.

Meditation is preliminary to the final goal of sudden enlightenment. Zen masters often hit or shout at their students when it seems that they are on the verge of the intuitive flash which signifies a sudden comprehension of the Buddha-nature. This enlightenment has been described as a sudden revelation in which the bottom seems to fall out of everything and in which the mystery underlying all things is revealed in a blinding flash. Although outwardly the enlightened one continues to act like an ordinary man, he is no longer attached to this world. He is sometimes described as one who continually eats but swallows not a single grain, who always clothes himself but touches not a single thread.

Buddhism showed the same adaptability in Japan that it showed elsewhere in Asia. It penetrated all levels of Japanese life, influencing and being influenced in a re-enactment of the same process that took place in China. Shinto deities, for example, were referred to as Bodhisattvas and Buddhas, and ancestral worship became a part of Japanese Buddhism. Prince Shotoku stated that Shinto was the roots of the tree, Confucianism the stem and branches, and Buddhism the fruits and flowers. Japanese Buddhism differs from that of China not so much in doctrine as in the strong position it continues to hold in Japan in contrast to its decline in China.

The religion founded by Gautama Buddha continues to be an inspiration to the Japanese people. Although it was relegated to a secondary position by the government from 1868 onward, and although its resources and prestige were crippled by the war and by postwar occupation reforms such as religious freedom (hundreds of temples seceded and became independent), land reforms, and the separation of church and state (many temples were deprived of their principal income), Buddhism is still a major force in Japan. The monasteries do educational work ranging in level from the kindergarten to the university; the people still flock to the Buddhist temples and priests for funerals and memorial services; and the Buddhist monk remains a common sight. One Buddhist sect, the Soka Gakkai, has recently become influential in politics and religion. Claiming around 15 million members in many parts of the world, it is militant, conservative, and nationalistic.

CHAPTER 33

THE JAPANESE FAMILY

The Japanese belongs to his personal family, which, in turn, belongs to the national family of which the Divine Emperor is the kind father.

—HELEN MEARS

The Japanese have long been taught to regard themselves as one large family headed by a divine emperor. Since the same duties and loyalties that bound together the members of a Japanese family were regarded as also serving to bind together the members of the state, the nation literally became an extension of the family, and Japan was viewed as populated by a number of families ruled by fathers who in turn were subordinate to the great father of all—the emperor. This conception was reinforced by religion, for primary in the life of the community was the religion of the family rather than any personal faith or belief. All Japanese thought of patriotism as involving the worship of Shinto deities through household Shinto. Japan became a family state.

The individual exists mainly to ensure the preservation, continuity, and good name of the family. Though physically a separate entity, the individual Japanese is looked upon as an extension of the larger group. This attitude often works great hardship upon the Japanese individual. In school, boys and girls work with the stern eyes of their families fixed upon them. Failure to pass injures the reputation of their entire family. The family, not just the boy and girl, has been discredited. In all his relations with outsiders, the individual child bears the full weight of family responsibility. The accelerating tempo of modern life in Japan has increased the anxiety of individuals by introducing greater competition among them and thus providing them with many more opportunities for failing their

From *Year of the Wild Boar* by Helen Mears, published by J. B. Lippincott Company, copyright 1942.

families. The individual is reminded over and over again that he is an inseparable part of the family; whoever laughs at him laughs at the family, and this must never happen.

It is within the family system that the Japanese learn how to live in Japanese society. Within it a Japanese finds the whole social pattern of Japanese society. Boys and girls learn early from their elders the proper ceremonials before the domestic shrines; the stern precepts of unquestioning obedience which govern relations between children and parents, husband and wife, and young and old; and the external forms of family etiquette demanded by Japanese society. The head of the family possesses all authority, assumes full responsibility for the status and continuity of the family, and is given the complete respect and obedience of all members. The young owe respect to the old, and the women owe loyalty and submissive service to the males. Wives are subordinate to their husbands, younger brothers to older brothers, and servants to the masters of the household. To a certain degree this same hierarchical pattern is found elsewhere in Japanese society. The political leader often stands toward his party members as the family head or elder brother toward the subordinate members of his family. Labor bosses are regarded as fathers of the laborers or as heads of great union families. Even large business firms, industrial plants, and military organizations are regarded as great family organizations, within which relationships are similar to those within the immediate family. Ultimately the entire Japanese nation is regarded as one large national family whose head is the emperor, and the whole Japanese people owe him the same loyalty, respect, and obedience which they owe to their personal family and household head.

STRUCTURE AND ECONOMY OF THE FAMILY

The traditional family, still widely prevalent, includes the head and his wife, the eldest son either by birth or adoption, his wife and children, and any unmarried children. This family might also include a retired head of the house and his spouse, that is to say, the surviving grandparents. Thus, there are two and sometimes three American-style families in each basic Japanese family. The household may also include uncles, aunts, cousins, and nephews; in well-to-do families servants may also live under the same roof. In all these cases, those living under the same roof are considered as belonging to one household.

Modernization has affected the size of Japanese families. The modern marriage group commonly found in the cities consists of husband, wife, and children. Continued urbanization is bringing about smaller families. Other reasons for smaller families are the late marriages of younger sons who cannot afford to marry earlier, economic advancement, a high degree of literacy, a knowledge of birth control, and abortions.

In 1948, the Japanese diet passed a law which permitted abortion when the health of the woman "may be affected seriously by continuation of pregnancy or by delivery, from the physical or economic point of view." There are probably more than a million abortions each year. The law also provided for the dissemination of information about contraceptives, and the aim of the government is to make available one person trained in family planning for every 500 families. Japanese women are realizing in growing numbers that fewer children may result in better health for the mothers, better education for the children, a higher standard of living, and fewer financial worries.

Japan is the one Asian country which has taken effective action to meet the problem of overpopulation. There has been a real decline in the birth rate. It is more evident in urban areas than in rural ones, which are less affected by modernization. Because of excellent medical services, the population continues to increase, but a projection of present trends suggests that the population may actually start to decline after the 1990's.

The household is the basic social unit of Japanese society. The size of a community is often computed in terms of households. The household head represents the members at important community meetings and activities, and to him all official documents and messages sent to the household are addressed. He is responsible for the acts of the members of his household and, at times, has even been arrested when a criminal from his household could not be apprehended. A member of the household represents it at all the occasions in which it has an obligation to participate, such as weddings, funerals, and religious ceremonies.

A series of households of the same kin-group comprises the extended Japanese family. It consists of the main family house called a *honke,* and the branch family house or houses called *bunkes.* In the *honke* or main house the eldest son stays with his family and parents. The *bunke* or branch house is founded by the younger brother when he leaves his parents' house, marries, and raises a family of his own. The extended family also includes all the brothers and sisters of all male members of the house and children of the family head who may have married or been adopted out.

The Japanese family is primarily an economic unit. It has a common budget and holds property in common. The family head, who acts as the trustee for the property and not as the owner, controls and is responsible for all the finances of the household, doling out the money as members need it and carefully scrutinizing all expenditures. In many Japanese households the family head deputizes his wife to supervise the daily household expenses. Often he consults with other prominent members of his family before he makes major and sometimes minor financial decisions. In this way he shares his financial responsibilities with other members of his family, and if the decision turns out badly he cannot be blamed alone.

The Japanese family, particularly the rural family, plays an important role in spreading scarce resources and in cushioning its members against economic shock. Owing to the delicate balance that exists between the Japanese people and their resources, if there were no mutual aid on the part of the family members many persons would starve. Since the Japanese are somewhat averse and unaccustomed to receiving charity from the state, they depend upon their families to tide them over critical periods. During the depression of the 1930's, Japanese living in the cities hastened by the thousands back to their ancestral homes in the country where they shared the food of their families. After the Second World War, returning soldiers and repatriates also went to the countryside because there was little for them in the cities. In both cases the Japanese government was spared the trouble and expense of providing food, shelter, and clothing for millions of its people.

In the rural areas occupations still continue to be traditional. The families in the country are tied to the soil, and the planting of wet rice or other grains is their main occupation. Generally, the eldest son carries on his father's occupation, whether it is farming, fishing, artisan work, or a combination of all three. Both in the cities and in the rural areas numerous manufacturing processes, retail marketing, and other economic activities are still carried on in family households. In many cases the hired workers are still regarded as members of the family.

But here too some change is occurring. Whereas co-operative family enterprises were once the rule, today the breakdown of the extended family is leading to other forms of economic association. Industrial and agricultural co-operatives and voluntary organizations composed of people who do not belong to the same family, either immediate or extended, are becoming more and more common. Increasing numbers of younger sons are leaving the family homes and going to the city where they are employed in work which keeps them separated from their ancestral home. As a result, in certain parts of Japan today there is no sharing outside the small immediate families which must depend upon their own efforts to the same extent and in much the same way that American families do.

Marriages. Marriages are arranged between families, not between individuals. Since the Second World War there has been more individual choice in the selection of mates, but even in these instances the families still negotiate the marriage contract and make the necessary preliminary arrangements. For most Japanese, families still play a major role in selecting the prospective mate.

Usually they try to pick someone from the same social level. A family friend undertakes the job of go-between for each family; these middle-men meet together to discuss such delicate matters as the character of the family, police records, social and economic status of the families involved, health of the intended mate, and other touchy questions that it might be impossible to speak about in face-to-face conversations between the two families.

When the preliminary arrangements have been negotiated to the satisfaction of both families, a date is set for the wedding. It is often chosen by astrologers who recommend a lucky day. The bride's family prepares various articles, such as a chest of drawers, trunks, clothes, and toilet articles, which the bride may need. The quantity and quality of the gifts the bride receives depend, of course, upon the wealth of her family. Some wealthy brides have very elaborate wedding gifts costing a great deal of money. The bride's family provides her trousseau, but no dowry.

Wedding ceremonies consist in part of a formal exchange of *sake*, a rice wine, between the middle-men, the immediate relatives, and the bride and groom. There is usually a wedding banquet at which the relatives of the bride and the groom are introduced to each other. Also, at some time during the first few days of her marriage, the bride is introduced to the village and to the leading members of the community.

Sometimes the marriage was not officially registered immediately. If the marriage did not work out well, the bride could be sent home more easily if there were no official record of the marriage. Of course, when a child was expected, the marriage was registered immediately in order to legitimize the child. The birth of a child strengthens the marriage and secures the position of the wife in her new home.

Children and Adoption. Children are wanted and loved in Japan. Above all the Japanese couple want a male child, because the family line is continued through the males. If there are no sons born, they can ensure the continuation of the family by adopting a son.

A couple may adopt the younger son of the brother of the family head. If this is not possible, then a child of one of their other relatives is adopted. Occasionally, when a couple have had a daughter but no son, they will adopt a boy who then marries their daughter and assumes their surname. He thereby becomes their son, and he will inherit their property when they die. Adoption is sometimes carried to great extremes in Japan. There are cases of families adopting a niece and then adopting a son to marry her. Elder brothers have adopted younger brothers as sons, especially when there has been great disparity between their ages. Some of Japan's great business firms are headed by men who were adopted into the family when other sons were lacking or when the natural son showed no desire to carry on the business.

Because the continuity, preservation, and reputation of the family depend largely upon these adopted sons, they are usually chosen very carefully. Their character, health, attitude, and other pertinent characteristics are investigated thoroughly before they are officially adopted.

Adoptions are legalized when they are recorded in the *koseki*, or family register, which is kept in the police station of the village to which the family is attached. This all-important family register indicates the legal and social status of the family members. It is necessary for identification, and a man without a koseki is regarded with suspicion because he must be a scoundrel if he is without a family. Legal marriage in Japan consists in the formal transfer of the bride's registration by her father to the koseki of the groom's family. Both adoptions and marriages can be dissolved when they turn out to be undesirable.

FAMILY RELATIONSHIPS

Parents and Children. The Japanese attach more importance to the relationship between parents and children than to the relationship between husband and wife. Theoretically, Japanese parents have almost unlimited power over their children, but, practically speaking, they are restrained by custom, society, relatives, and the law. The Japanese in general are usually sensitive to the dictates of public opinion, and most parents are careful not to exert their powers too harshly. On the other hand, children are subject to these same pressures, which require them to be obedient and respectful in all cases to their parents. Filial piety is regarded by the Japanese as the foundation of all virtues, and indeed it is the fundamental virtue upon which the Japanese have built their social patterns. The worst statement to make about a child is to say that he or she is unfilial. Parents have definite duties to perform in connection with their children. They must teach them the difference between right and wrong, punishing them when they do wrong and commending them when they do right. They must provide their children with an academic as well as a moral education, and modern Japanese law requires them to send their children to school. They must find mates for their sons and daughters. They must support their children and provide them with the necessities of life. They must instruct the children in the duties and ceremonies that they will later perform as adults. Girls should be taught to assist in offering sacrifices at the domestic shrines and in the care of the household. Boys should be taught whatever occupation they are expected to undertake, whether it is farming, business, artisan work, or a professional career.

Although traditional attitudes toward the relationship between parents and children still pervade Japanese thought and practice, modern forces sweeping Japan are making children more independent of their parents. They do not always accept their parents' interpretation of what is right and wrong. The conflict between traditional and modern concepts of life, and the new knowledge to which children are exposed in school, weakens the power of the parents. Younger sons who are forced to leave the family and go elsewhere in search of a living become indifferent to the influence of their parents. The growing preference for small families and the increasing number of Japanese living in the cities are other circumstances contributing to the decline of patriarchal power.

Husband and Wife. The new Civil Code which went into force in January, 1948, states expressly that "husband and wife shall live together, and shall co-operate and aid each other." It also states that "any property in regard to which it is uncertain whether it belongs to the husband or the wife, is presumed to be property in their co-ownership." Further, the Code says that "husband and wife may effect by agreement divorce."

These are recent laws made under the pressure of American occupation personnel who were attempting to Westernize the relationship between husband and wife. Traditionally, and to a large extent even today, the loyalties of the husband are directed toward his parents and blood-relatives rather than his wife. His kin come first and his wife second. If necessary, the dutiful Japanese son would give up his wife if his father or mother disapproved of her. It is the wife's duty to prove her worth to the boy's parents. Most Japanese marriages still take place for the benefit of the man's house. It is in the man's house that the wife must live and work, and it is to the success of his family that she must devote all her energies. He generally controls the family property, and he is thought to be mentally and physically superior to the woman. The traditional attitude toward the married woman is expressed in the *Great Learning for Women* written during Tokugawa (1603-1868) times by Kaibara Ekken (1631-1714).[1]

> When a woman is divorced after once marrying, she is disgraced all her life, even if she is married again to a rich husband, for it is against the way of women. . . . A woman has no master but her husband whom she should serve with respect and humility, never with a light attitude and disrespect. In a word, the way of woman

---

[1] Baroness Shidzue Ishimoto, *Facing Two Ways: The Story of My Life* (New York: Holt, Rinehart and Winston, Inc., 1935). Used with permission.

is obedience. To her husband she should be submissive and harmonious, serving him with gentle and humble expression of the face
and speech. Never should she be impatient and willful, proud and
impertinent. This is her first duty. She should absolutely follow the
husband's teaching and wait for his direction in everything of which
she is not sure. If the husband gets angry and acts accordingly, she
should fear and be ruled by him; never contradict him. The husband
is Heaven to the wife. Disobeying Heaven only incurs righteous
punishment. . . .

This attitude is being modified in modern Japan to the same extent that other traditional social attitudes and customs are being
modified. Increasing urbanization is creating smaller families in
which the orientation of the husband is toward the wife rather
than toward blood relatives who do not live with them. Under
these conditions there is more companionship between husband
and wife, greater emphasis upon the advice of the wife, and more
and more freedom of association and intimacy. Baroness Shidzue
Ishimoto stated in her autobiography that there was no privacy in
the Japanese house, "for the rooms are not locked and usually the
sliding doors which separate the rooms are kept open even on cold
winter days. So my husband and I behaved like strangers to each
other while we lived in the midst of watching eyes. It was a life in
which individuality was completely killed in order to create harmony for the family." This is true of the traditional Japanese family where the parents live with the married son, but in the modern
Japanese family husband and wife act more freely and more intimately, without fear of criticism. This kind of environment tends
to give the wife greater freedom and greater influence in the home.

THE FAMILY COUNCIL

Rich and noble families have for generations possessed family
codes which govern the behavior and activities of the family members. Of more practical importance is the family council which
makes decisions on all matters which the family head considers important enough to bring to the council's attention. Such matters are
marriages, adoptions, investments, the education of family members (especially beyond the compulsory levels), funerals, and other
weighty occasions. The family head usually determines whether
or not a subject is important enough to be considered by the coun-

cil. But since responsibility lies so heavily upon him, he tends to use the council when in doubt.

The membership of the family council varies from family to family. Usually it includes the older family heads of the chief and branch families, and sometimes even the widows of the dead family heads, especially if they are competent. Paternal relatives, however, predominate.

Each household has a family council. Members of one family council may belong to other family councils at the same time, and thus many households are tied together by the members of the family councils. In these overlapping kinship groups members intimately related to one family may be peripheral to another. Because of this web of interconnected councils staffed by blood relatives, it can be said with some truth that the Japanese are tied together in one large family.

Family councils are solicitous about the good name of the families they watch over. Formerly, only samurai and nobles had family names, but now everyone has a family name of which he is proud. The name must not be tarnished in any way. One of the common ways for a family to acquire a bad name is to have some black deed recorded against it on the official register. The family council is careful lest this occur, because the living, the dead, and the still unborn are all affected by such an act.

Family councils have functions besides those of decision-making with regard to important family matters. These councils provide the kinsmen with mutual support, even though members may be scattered throughout the countryside and in the cities. Branch houses are tied to the main houses, and scattered blood-relatives to each other. This system tends to preserve the older forms of Japanese social life and slow up the process of change which is being felt throughout Japanese society. Members of the family council are generally conservative and reluctant to modify the established patterns of social life.

Even though extended families are decreasing in importance in Japan, the family council still retains its significance, and in most cases is still the court of last resort.

CHAPTER 34

THE JAPANESE WOMAN

*What is the use of developing the mind of a woman or of train-
ing the power of her judgment when her life is to be guided at
every step by a man? Yet, it is highly important that she should
be morally trained, so that she be always gentle and chaste,
never giving way to passion inconvenient to others, nor ques-
tioning the authority of her elders.*

—THE GREAT LEARNING FOR WOMEN

*Japanese women are best in the home either as housewives or
daughters. I came to realize this during my sojourn abroad. The
cream of our womanhood is to be found in the country and the
modern girls who go about wearing Western clothes in the city
are the worst examples of our fair sex.*

—MR. FUMIKO HAYASHI IN 1936

*Art. 14. All of the people are equal under the law and there
shall be no discrimination in political, economic, or social relations because of race, creed, sex, social status or family origin.*

*Art. 24. Marriage shall be based on the mutual consent of both
sexes and it shall be maintained through mutual cooperation
with the equal rights of husband and wife as a basis.*

*With regard to choice of spouse, property rights, inheritance,
choice of domicile, divorce, and other matters pertaining to
marriage and the family, laws shall be enacted from the stand-
point of individual dignity and the essential equality of the
sexes.*

—THE CONSTITUTION OF JAPAN (1947)

For over a thousand years Japanese women have been taught that
they exist to serve men faithfully and well. They have been carefully indoctrinated with the idea that women are subordinate to

Passage from *The Great Learning for Women* reprinted from *Year of the
Wild Boar* by Helen Mears, published by J. B. Lippincott Company, copyright
1942.

men. The traditional ideal woman of Japan is one who unquestioningly and dutifully follows the old Japanese rule of "obedience to a father when yet unmarried, to a husband when married, and to a son when widowed."

This subordination of woman is expressed in many social attitudes and practices. Boys are valued more than girls, and the birth of a male is hailed with greater joy than the birth of a female. Boys are rarely disciplined and often outrageously spoiled; while girls are treated with affection, but firmly disciplined in preparation for their future role of submissive service in the household. Brothers rank ahead of sisters in the family hierarchy. Good wives are meek and subservient in the house, deferring always to the desires of their husbands. On public streets a well-trained wife walks several paces behind her husband, and she frequently carries the packages. She generally does not share in his social evenings out, nor should she reprove him no matter what the provocation.

The following two stories illustrate the traditional attitude toward women. Lafcadio Hearn tells in one of his stories about a Japanese wife who served her husband with unflagging energy and dedicated her life to making him happy and contented. She was obedient in all things and completely loyal. After some years of happy married life, the husband fell under the spell of a lovely geisha girl. (Geishas are highly trained in the art of pleasing men. They sing, play musical instruments, recite poetry, and are capable of conversing on a great variety of subjects with intelligence and wit. The Japanese man often finds in the geishas the companionship that he misses in the faithful but stiff and proper wife at home.) The woman's husband began to come home later and later at night, but, as a dutiful and thoughtful wife, she was always waiting up to greet him when he came in and to serve him tea and perform any other service he might require. Some nights he did not come home at all, and on those nights the wife got very little sleep.

She wondered why her husband stayed out so many nights, but she dared not ask him. Eventually, her servants told her about the husband's affair with the geisha. Though deeply wounded by a loved one to whom she had dedicated her life, she could not express her grief; such action would be un-Japanese. Lafcadio Hearn describes her in the early morning hours, sleepless but still awaiting the return of her erring husband.

She waited through all the morning hours, fearing for him, fearing for herself also; conscious at last of the wrong by which a woman's heart can be most deeply wounded. Her faithful servants had told her something; the rest she could guess. She was very ill, and did not know it. She knew only that she was angry—selfishly angry, because of the pain given her—cruel, probing, sickening pain. Midday came as she sat thinking how she could say least selfishly what it was not her duty to say—the first words of reproach that would ever have passed her lips.[1]

Helen Mears relates the story of Akiko, the modern young Japanese girl who had given up her family and her prospective adopted parents in order to marry a man of her own choice. She served him loyally both as a working companion and as a wife. Then, he too became involved with another woman. One night the police came to their house and arrested him on suspicion of Communism. Akiko was arrested at the same time on the theory that the wife must necessarily derive her opinions from the husband. After she was questioned, it became clear that she was not a Communist, and she was released. The husband was kept in jail.

Although he had caused her great unhappiness by his affair with another woman and his radical activities, Akiko remained loyal. She visited him every two weeks, bringing him her small earnings. The trip to the jail was long and tiring. The wait in a dirty anteroom where she was confronted with an atmosphere of fear, suspicion, and dejection was an experience she dreaded.

[1] *The Selected Writings of Lafcadio Hearn*, edited by Henry Goodman (New York: The Citadel Press, 1949). Used with permission.

Then one day she reached the prison just as her husband's mistress was leaving. She was shocked and hurt at learning that even in prison her husband was faithless. That day Akiko was told she must wait in the prison anteroom until evening visiting hours because the prisoners were allowed only one visitor each afternoon. Finally, after much persuasion the prison officials permitted her to see her husband. Somehow she found the courage to question him in un-Japanese fashion about this other woman. He admitted that the other woman came to see him frequently and brought him presents and implied that he enjoyed these visits.

Angry and upset, Akiko returned home and poured out her troubles and complaints to the two Western women, one American and the other English, with whom she lived and worked. The American woman described the scene. "The pressure of Akiko's tension seemed to fill the room with an oppressive weight. She leaned forward to us. 'You,' she said, 'you are Western women. Give me advice then. Do you think I am justified in taking him by the kimono collar and shaking him just a little?'" [1]

FROM COMPANION TO SERVANT

The Japanese woman has not always occupied such a low position in Japanese society. In the very early period of Japan's history she was the man's equal, his companion and not his servant. The *Manyoshu,* written in the seventh and eighth centuries, the oldest Japanese anthology of ancient poems, speaks of young men and women dancing and singing together in the springtime. They married in those days by mutual agreement and they did not need the services of a middle-man. The woman was the equal of man, and she fought, governed, and led armies to war. A famous empress, Jingo, about 200 A.D., led a powerful army into Korea. Women then were judged, as were men, on the basis of merit, since they were regarded as individuals with the same rights and privileges as men had.

Circumstances began to change about the sixth century A.D. At that time Buddhism and Confucianism, bearers of Chinese and Indian ways of life, carried other ideas, attitudes, and customs to the Japanese people. As the cultural influences from the mainland

---

[1] Adapted from *Year of the Wild Boar* by Helen Mears, published by J. B. Lippincott Company, copyright 1942. Used with permission.

came to dominate the Japanese social scene and as Japanese social patterns evolved, woman's intelligence was questioned and her talents were ignored. She began to be considered a follower rather than a leader, and a servant rather than an equal, with a place only in the home. It was no longer possible for her to dance with men in the warm light of spring without being considered an immoral woman, nor could she lead armies or govern the country. She finally was transformed into the woman who thought it an extreme act of defiance to think of taking an erring husband by the kimono collar and "shaking him just a little."

Training of the Ideal Woman. The training of the traditional type of Japanese woman began in childhood. She learned early in life that obedience, devotion to duty, patience, good nature, self-sacrifice, and submissiveness were the virtues expected of her and that her goal in life was to become an acceptable wife and a respected mother. She was also given practical training. She was taught to be an efficient housewife. She learned to sew, clean mats, wash clothes and woodwork, cook and serve meals, and performed all other household chores.

Certain variations in her training depended upon the social level that she occupied. The farm girl learned to help in the planting and harvesting of rice and other crops and to work at other tasks required by a farming family. The daughter of a higher-class family was taught ritual etiquette—the proper way to open and close doors, to enter and leave a room, to greet superiors and inferiors, to speak to relatives and friends, and to perform a thousand other formalities accumulated over a period of fifteen hundred years. Many were also taught the elaborate conventions that governed the serving of tea and the making of flower arrangements and trained to play some musical instrument.

The restrictions placed upon upper- and middle-class women were more onerous and more strictly enforced than those placed upon women of the farming and laboring groups. The latter, particularly if they were married, were much freer in their associations; they frequently smoked and drank together with the men of the house. Women on the upper levels rarely acted so freely, even with men who were close relatives. There were a number of reasons why this situation arose. The attitude regarding women that originated in the sixth century A.D. had less effect on lower levels of society.

Women who worked on farms and at other physical tasks were much more important economically to farming and laboring families than the women of the upper classes were to their more wealthy families. It was more difficult for the poorer families to subsist without the help of their women. Men on this level could not afford to pay for the outside companionship provided by the geishas and other women, and looked toward the home for the informality and relaxation to be found in mixed company. Wealthier men, on the other hand, could find companionship with the geishas and at the same time impose strict limitations upon the behavior of their wives at home.

GRADUAL EMANCIPATION OF THE
JAPANESE WOMAN

With the opening of Japan to Western penetration in the nineteenth century the status of the Japanese woman slowly improved. She gradually began to regain the equality she had lost centuries before.

At first her progress was almost imperceptible. After the Meiji Restoration in 1868, the new rulers of Japan wanted a new political order and a new economic system, but not a new social system. They kept the Japanese woman out of politics by refusing her the right to vote and the opportunity to occupy political office. Girls were permitted a small amount of formal education, but this schooling remained an extension of their home training. They were taught that the Japanese people were one family, that their fathers and husbands were the representatives of the emperor, and that to disobey them was to disobey him. They were taught that the purpose of their education was only to make them better Japanese wives and mothers. However, the fact that they received six years of compulsory education widened their horizons and exposed them to influences which encouraged their efforts to resist an inferior status.

Although the new rulers were successful in keeping Japanese women out of politics, it was impossible to keep them out of the new economic system. They were needed to provide the cheap and efficient labor that Japan required to maintain a competitive position in world markets and to fill the many jobs that mushroomed in a rapidly industrializing nation. By 1936 Japanese women were engaged in all kinds of economic activities. Dressed in either Western or Japanese clothes they operated the telephone exchanges and served as conductresses on the motor buses. They worked as stenographers and typists in large business firms. They worked as "gasoline girls" in the service stations, clerked in large department stores, and waited on customers in tea shops and restaurants.

In all these cases, the new rulers made a determined effort to utilize the services of women without exposing them to dangerous thoughts of equality or to the social ways of Western women. The treatment of textile workers is a good example of how women were employed in a useful occupation and yet shielded from alien influences. Made to dress in a uniform consisting of a white middy blouse and black shirt, they worked in large textile factories surrounded by high walls which kept them penned in until their contracts expired. Sometimes these contracts ran for three years or more. The workers were usually recruited from the farms where their indoctrination in womanly obedience and submission was already almost complete. When the textile management contracted with the head of the household for their services and wages were agreed upon, the girls were ordered by their fathers or the heads of their households to enter the plant. The management then assumed responsibility for them. It was supposed to continue their education along traditional lines. In the better factories, classes were conducted in sewing, flower arrangement, reading, writing, and arithmetic. The girls were encouraged to use their spare time in making trousseaus and in preparing themselves for their future married life. Most of their wages were either taken for their support within the factory walls or sent home to their family heads. They were rarely permitted outside the walls. Some never went outside until their contracts had expired and they returned home to be married.

Still, the Japanese leaders were not successful in isolating Japanese women completely from the social currents sweeping in from the West. Once they had experienced the adventure of reading and the satisfaction of receiving a wage, women began to function independently and to enjoy the fruits of self-reliance.

The most obvious and superficial break with tradition was in make-up and dress. Narrow eyes, a small mouth, demure lips with very faint artificial coloring, natural eyebrows, a willowy frame, and delicate curving lines were the traditional marks of a beautiful

Japanese woman. A high and well-shaped nose was considered a woman's most important facial feature. She "enhanced" this beauty by applying a dead-white make-up and painting her teeth black.

This traditional conception of beauty was modified by the impact of styles from France, England, and the United States. Although, traditionally, curly hair was regarded as unnatural, permanent waves became the fashion. Large and deep-set eyes enhanced by mascara became the most striking facial feature. Former dead-white cheeks were now enlivened with pink rouge. Lipstick followed the contour of the lips, and teeth came to be polished white instead of blackened. Many Japanese women adopted Western dress. They wore hats, dresses, suits, and sometimes Western-style shoes and silk and nylon stockings. The latest fashions from abroad were displayed in large department stores.

However, the Japanese woman could not throw off the traditions and attitudes of centuries as easily as she changed her make-up style. In fact, she never completely gave up her Japanese dress. Even though she liked and wore Western-style clothes, she also retained a Japanese wardrobe. Kimono manners and kimono customs continued to persist though she dressed in Western clothes and used Western make-up.

With the coming of the Second World War and the occupation of Japan by American forces, the Japanese woman made significant gains in raising her status and increasing her freedom of action. The war speeded up the hiring of women in industry. More and more women were required to man the machines and take over the jobs that had formerly been performed by men. Women became essential for the full and efficient operation of the Japanese economy. They started to realize their importance to the war effort and to the economy of the nation, and their self-respect grew with this realization. Many Japanese women were now ready for the reforms and legal freedoms which the Occupation and the new Constitution granted to the woman of Japan.

In October, 1945, the Japanese woman was given the right to vote and to hold political office. The new Constitution, which became effective May 3, 1947, guaranteed these rights and gave women legal equality with men. A Japanese woman can now vote, pursue a career, run for office, and become the legal guardian of her children. Legally, divorce is no more difficult for her to obtain than it is for her husband. In addition, the Civil Code was revised to grant women full civic rights, and a law was passed extending compulsory education from six to nine years and establishing co-education in secondary schools and universities. Labor laws were enacted which promulgated the principle of equal pay for equal work and provided for special maternity benefits.

In many instances the Japanese women have made good use of these rights. In the first three general elections since they acquired the vote, six women were elected to the Diet. When the Peace Treaty was signed in 1951, twelve women were in the Lower House and twelve in the House of Councillors. There were 961 women in various local assemblies, and five held the office of village chief. Women's organizations multiplied; membership in these organizations is estimated to be over 6 million today. Large-scale educational programs in political and social matters are being sponsored and undertaken by the Y.W.C.A., Japan's League of Women Voters, and the League of Democratic Women. The government has established a Women's and Minor's Bureau in the Labor Ministry to promote the interests of women and children.

Nevertheless, the gains made by women are still mostly confined to the statute books. Japan is still largely a man's country, the father still remains the head of the household, and sons are still more welcome than daughters.

The Japanese woman remains traditional in her attitudes, customs, dress, and low status. This is especially true of the rural woman. Although she has felt some of the alien currents brought in by the Westerners, especially the Americans, she has not felt them deeply or applied them to her daily life. The farm woman's marriage is still arranged for her, her modesty and obedience still praised, and her subordination to the male emphasized. Nor are arranged marriages confined to rural women. The husbands of Emperor Hirohito's two daughters were picked by the emperor's mother, the Dowager Empress Teimei. The court officials, at the request of the emperor, chose an eligible wife for the Crown Prince Akihito.

The impact of freedom-conscious America upon Japanese attitudes toward women is most felt by the women of the upper and middle classes, who live mostly in the cities. They had been traditionally the most restricted and therefore the most eager to escape. These women were educated and hence susceptible to outside influences and interested in them. They had the leisure time to think about these Western currents and to work in women's organizations. Today they are among the most progressive women in Japan.

There is no question but that the women of Japan will eventually regain the equality with men which they held in the early period of Japan's history. The women of the city and the upper and middle classes will reach this goal before the women of the country, but in time all will attain equal status.

CHAPTER 35

POLITICS IN JAPAN

Art. I *The Empire of Japan shall be reigned over and governed by a line of Emperors unbroken for ages eternal. . . .*
Art. III *The Emperor is sacred and inviolable.*
Art. IV *The Emperor is the head of the Empire, combining in Himself the rights of sovereignty, and exercises them, according to the provisions of the present Constitution.*
        —THE CONSTITUTION OF THE EMPIRE OF JAPAN (1889)

Art. I *The Emperor shall be the symbol of the State and of the unity of the people, deriving his position from the will of the people with whom resides sovereign power. . . .*

Art. III *The advice and approval of the Cabinet shall be required for all acts of the Emperor in matters of state, and the Cabinet shall be responsible therefor.*

Art. IV *The Emperor shall perform only such acts in matters of state as are provided for in this Constitution and he shall not have powers related to government.*
        —THE CONSTITUTION OF JAPAN (1947)

Politics in Japan are being pulled in many directions by forces of the past and the present. In the short period of eighty years, Japan was torn from centuries of isolation, forced to put on the institutional trappings of Western democracies, and transformed from a semifeudal association of lords into a centralized modern nation.

During this period, aided by modern technology, Japan expanded into one of the greatest empires on earth. She defeated China in 1895, routed Russia in 1905, shared in the victory of the First World War as an allied power in 1918, and annexed Manchuria in the 1930's. Her widespread empire disintegrated with terrible suddenness at the conclusion of the Second World War, and her own homeland was occupied and governed by American troops.

The Americans launched a determined effort to change the political system of Japan into one patterned after Western models.

To have all this happen within the short space of eight decades to a country which had long been isolated from world events left most Japanese mentally and emotionally gasping. If permitted, the Japanese would probably have tried to retire from the world for a time to meditate on their recent history and to make plans for a slower pace in the future. But they were soon caught up again in the vortex of domestic and world crises. They have had little time or opportunity to plan their political evolution in a leisurely way, and they have been forced to search for suitable political institutions that will enable them to face the future with some degree of security and stability while at the same time coping with the daily complexities of government.

Whatever the outward appearance of their evolving political system, it will be permeated with a spirit that comes from deep in Japan's past. The Japan of tomorrow will be a product of the Japan of yesterday, and there will be no understanding of it until there is some understanding of old Japan's political life.

THE RISE OF THE IMPERIAL SYSTEM

The Clan of Yamato. The early political life of the Japanese was organized around a clan system. About the beginning of the Christian era there were a number of clans in central and western Japan, each presided over by a high priest or priestess. One of these clans lived in the Yamato Plain just south of the present-day city of Kyoto in central Honshu and was called the Yamato clan. Loosely speaking, a clan is a division of a tribe which traces its descent from a common ancestor and the members of which bear the same surname. In China and in Japan a feeling of brotherhood and a spirit of co-operation characterized the clan institution.

The Yamato clan prospered and expanded until, by about the third or fourth century A.D., it was the dominant clan in central and western Japan. The high priest of the Yamato clan assumed first place among the clan chiefs, and worship of the sun goddess—the divine ancestress of the Yamato clan—became an integral part of the worship of the other clans. The descendant of the high priest of the Yamato clan reigns today as Hirohito, Emperor of Japan, and the sun goddess is still the primary deity of the Japanese nation.

The Emperor. The emperor system in Japan is remarkable for its age. For over fifteen hundred years the ancestors of the present emperor have reigned in Japan. Few families of royal blood today can claim such a history of unbroken reign reaching far back into the early centuries of the Christian era. It is true that, during most of this time, the royal family of Japan possessed little actual power, but the emperor as an embodied institution of divine descent has long commanded the reverence and honor of the Japanese people. He does today. The regime of Hirohito is a living witness to the tenacity and ability with which the Japanese have preserved a cherished heritage through all the vicissitudes of time.

This same tenacity and ability is manifested in the worship of the sun goddess. The transfer of her worship from a family to a national cult was completed by the sixth century A.D. From that time to the present this worship has been enshrined in the hearts of the Japanese people and constantly reinforces the right of the imperial family to reign. Just as the sun goddess is first among the gods of Japan, so must her descendant, the emperor, be first among the people of Japan.

Japan Borrows from China. From late in the sixth century until early in the ninth century, Japan borrowed heavily from the magnificent civilization of her neighbor China. Buddhism was instrumental in calling the attention of the Japanese to the wonderful cultural achievements of the Chinese. Its priests carried samples of this culture from Korea to Japan. Gradually, the Japanese awareness of Chinese civilization turned into a desire to imitate, especially since this was the period when the T'ang Dynasty ruled in China. It was one of the finest periods in China's history, and the Japanese were impressed. Convinced that an adaptation of many of the administrative features and political institutions of this dynasty would strengthen the Yamato government, the Japanese leaders began a systematic and purposeful borrowing from China.

At that time Japanese clans possessed a large measure of autonomy. The chiefs of the Yamato or imperial clan ruled more by reason of prestige and by balancing and mediating struggles between clans than because of their own economic and military strength. Prince Shotoku, one of the earliest of those leaders who wanted to establish a strong central government headed by the imperial clan, stated the substance of their desire when he said: "The

Sovereign is the master of the people of the whole country; the officials to whom he gives control are his vassals." These Yamato clan leaders controlled the Japanese sovereign; they schemed to increase his power in order to extend their own control over the autonomous clans.

In pursuit of this aim the Yamato state was reconstructed by its supporters to resemble the Chinese empire. The chief of the Yamato clan was installed as an emperor holding all secular power as well as functioning as the high priest of the country. Under a theoretically all-powerful emperor there was established a complex administration which, with some exceptions, was similar to that of the T'ang government in China. The country was divided into prefectures, approximately like states, and subprefectures, somewhat like counties. The emperor appointed officials to govern these prefectures in his name. This measure, of course, brought the clans under the closer supervision of the central government. The government bureaucracy was financed by taxing each adult who possessed land. The central government was housed in the new capital of Nara, which was especially built for this purpose and modeled after Ch'ang-an, the capital of the T'ang Dynasty. Thus, in the interests of centralization, a new system of local government, of land tenure, and of taxation was imposed upon the Japanese.

Although outwardly and on paper these imposed institutions gave the Japanese government a striking resemblance to the Chinese administration, they were in spirit and in content very Japanese. Adaptation and modification were inevitable, for while the Japanese could borrow the external forms of the Chinese system, they could not borrow the long centuries of evolution that had gone into the making of this system. The Chinese political system flowered from philosophical roots which had first been planted over a thousand years before in feudal China. Even in China it had not succeeded immediately. Not for many centuries did the key figures of the Chinese administration, the examination-tested civil servants, come to occupy the positions formerly held by hereditary rulers. A tradition of loyalty and public service had to be built up over the years; it did not come overnight.

In Japan, family and heredity determined one's position on the social scale. The aristocrat by blood ranked highest. Accordingly, appointment to top positions in the new Japanese bureaucracy was based on heredity and family connections rather than learning. Most of the provincial posts fell into the hands of the local aristocrats. At the capital the hereditary nobles occupied the important positions. The autonomy of the clans continued, though in theory they received their power to govern from the emperor. Instead of developing an administrative system which was staffed by an educated personnel loyal to the central government, as in China, the Japanese devised a system which confirmed the value of heredity and clan loyalties by confining official positions to aristocrats.

Another instance of the Japanizing of Chinese institutions and concepts is found in the emperor system. The Chinese emperor was checked in his use of absolute power by the right of the people to revolt if he should rule badly. This idea was alien to the Japanese because a divine emperor could do no wrong. Therefore, revolt against the emperor has never been condoned in Japan. The result was that the centralization of secular authority, borrowed from the Chinese system, conferred more power on the chief priest of the Yamato clan than had been enjoyed by the Chinese emperors.

EMPEROR'S POWER FLOWS INTO OTHER HANDS

From the ninth to the twelfth century the emperor's power declined until he became almost a puppet in the hands of his court nobles and their allied provincial aristocrats. During this period most provincial posts were filled by local aristocrats, and at the capital hereditary nobles occupied the most influential positions. The ministerial offices of the central administration became hereditary—another example of the Japanese modification of China's administrative system—and the lands of the great court families and monasteries were exempted from taxation. One of the principal reasons for the decline of the emperor's power was the increase of these independent tax-free estates called *shoen,* or manors. As the amount of tax-free land increased, larger taxes were imposed upon the remaining taxable land. This additional tax forced the owners of the taxable land to cede their land to holders of tax-free estates. The holders of these lands would then give them back in return for a share in the produce. The increased wealth and power that came from the possession of tax-free land strengthened the great court families and the monasteries.

The Fujiwara were the greatest of these families. They held

power in Japan by ruling through the emperor and using him as a figurehead. Kamatari, the founder of the Fujiwara family, began to rule Japan in this manner as early as 645 A.D. It was Kamatari who championed the introduction of a Chinese type of administration in order to centralize imperial government control. His son ruled behind six emperors during the period 659–720 A.D. The Fujiwara family maintained control of the emperor by marrying him to a Fujiwara girl and then forcing him to abdicate after he had fathered offspring old enough to carry out the ceremonies required of his office. The head of the Fujiwara family would then assume the office of regent who ruled during the minority of the emperor. In the ninth century the Fujiwara family transformed the regency into the office of civil dictator, which enabled a Fujiwara to rule openly even after the emperor had reached his majority. In effect, this was a dual monarchy, for the Fujiwara could also appoint the highest officers in the land and thus operate an independent and separate government.

In the course of time, the offices and appointing power became hereditary in the Fujiwara family who continued to monopolize them until the nineteenth century. By that time, however, these offices and privileges had become merely nominal. Political power passed from the Fujiwara to the feudal military class. But just as the Fujiwara did not usurp the throne of the emperor, the new feudal leaders did not usurp the offices that had become hereditary in the Fujiwara family. This preservation of an office or institution even after the power it originally held has been lost exemplifies the tendency in Japan for offices to become hereditary and pointedly illustrates the respect the Japanese hold for tradition.

After the Fujiwara family declined in power, other family clans like the Taira, Minamoto, Ashikaga, and Tokugawa established feudal military governments which ruled the country. They continued, however, to maintain the institutions of emperor, civil dictator, and regency and all the other apparatus of imperial government in Kyoto, the capital of the country. The latest example of dual government in Japan was the military government of the American occupation forces. This military government held all the real power in Japan, but the emperor and his civil government continued to reign by the side of the military government.

THE FEUDAL PERIOD OF JAPAN

The period from the twelfth to the nineteenth century in Japan was the Feudal Period. The three main periods of Japanese feudalism were: (1) the Kamakura Shogunate (1185–1333), which was founded by the Minamoto clan; (2) the Ashikaga Shogunate (1333–1568); and (3) the Tokugawa Shogunate (1600–1868).

Prior to the Kamakura Shogunate there arose in Japan a military class which was supported by tax-free manorial estates. Territorial holdings, the most important source of wealth in Japan, could be retained and expanded only by the use of force. Under these circumstances the military class became the most important class, and in the twelfth century two associations of knights headed by the Taira and Minamoto clans respectively emerged as the strongest military forces in the country. The military association headed by the Minamoto clan was ultimately victorious and a military government, called the Kamakura Shogunate, was set up at the city of Kamakura. The tax-free manors of the Taira clan were confiscated and given as grants to the loyal vassals of the Minamoto clan. Its chief, Yoritomo, was given the title of *Shogun,* or "Barbarian-Subduing General," which gave him command of all the military forces in Japan. Thus began a feudalistic type of government in Japan which characterized Japanese government from this time until the entrance of Japan into the modern world system in 1868. It is frequently called *Bakufu,* or "tent government."

Another example of the Japanese political custom of ruling through a figurehead is to be found in the early years of this shogunate. The Hojo family was a member of the Taira clan, but Tokimasa, its head, early joined the association of knights headed by the Minamoto clan. After Yoritomo's death, he became regent for Yoritomo's second son and thereby established a rule by Hojo regents who continued to use the shoguns as figureheads for over a hundred years.

Obviously, things are not always what they seem in Japanese politics. A noted modern authority on Japan, Mr. Edwin O. Reischauer, observed in his book *Japan Past and Present:*

> Thus, one finds in the 13th century Japan an emperor who was a mere puppet in the hands of a retired emperor and of a great court

family, the Fujiwara, who together controlled a government which was in fact merely a sham government, completely dominated by the private government of the Shogun—who in turn was a puppet in the hands of a Hojo regent. The man behind the throne had become a series of men, each one in turn controlled by the man behind himself.[1]

The Kamakura Shogunate started a feudal type of military government which was uniquely Japanese in character. The military generalissimos called shoguns were aided in their rule of Japan by a number of powerful lords who held their land as grants from them. Though vassals of the shoguns, they were supreme within their own domains. This was feudalism in the sense that the right to govern was conceived of as a property right which belonged to anyone who possessed a manor or fief. The reciprocal relations of a military, social, and political nature which existed between the lords and the shogun, and between the lords and those who peopled their domains, were also feudal. The lords owed the shogun loyal and obedient service in return for the granting of their fiefs or domains. Those who lived in the lords' domains owed them also loyal and obedient service in return for their protection and livelihood. Thus Japan, alone among Asian countries, developed something very like European feudalism. The first British ambassador, Sir John Alcock, after seeing the daimyo with their armed retainers, remarked that it seemed like England in the time of the War of the Roses.

The period of the Ashikaga Shogunate was marked by more fighting among the military men in the provinces, by the emergence of the peasant as a foot-soldier succeeding the knight on horseback, and by the rise of the great feudal lords called *daimyo*. These daimyo divided all of Japan among themselves, leaving nothing to the emperor or to the court nobles. Their well-defined territories were the foundation of the political system from about the fourteenth century to the Meiji Restoration of 1868.

These powerful daimyo were ultimately subdued and united by the efforts of three very famous military men—Oda Nobunaga, Toyotomi Hideyoshi, and Tokugawa Ieyasu. The last founded the famous Tokugawa Shogunate which continued until the nineteenth

---

[1] Edwin O. Reischauer, *Japan: Past and Present* (Second Edition; New York: Alfred A. Knopf, 1953). Used with permission.

century and was Japan's ultimate feudal government prior to its emergence as a modern state.

The Tokugawa Shogunate. The basic political objective of Tokugawa Ieyasu, the founder of the Tokugawa Shogunate, and his successors was to preserve the political power of their house forever. To this end Tokugawa established a political system which might be described as a centralized feudalism. It was feudal in that the basic political unit of the country was the daimyo's sharply outlined territory which he held as a grant from the shogun. The daimyo, within certain limits imposed by the shogun, was the absolute ruler of his land, and the office of daimyo was hereditary. The granting of these domains by the daimyo gave rise to the reciprocal obligations characteristic of feudalism.

The Tokugawa Shogunate was centralized in that a strong central government was set up at Edo, the present Tokyo. It carefully scrutinized the words and actions of the daimyo and limited drastically their power and scope of action. Rigid controls were imposed upon these great lords, such as requiring them to keep their families in Edo as hostages, discouraging visits from one daimyo to another, and surrounding the domains of less loyal daimyo with those persons more loyal to the Tokugawa family. The Tokugawa government even produced a crop of spies who reported daily to the shogunate about the various activities of the daimyo and their supporters. Furthermore, visits of the daimyo or their supporters to the emperor in Kyoto were forbidden except with the express consent of the central government, because the Tokugawas did not want anyone else to control the imperial government at Kyoto. Change of any sort was frowned upon and the social structure of society, with the warrior class at the top and the merchants and artisans at the bottom, was frozen. Finally, to prevent any possible threat from outside the country, Japan was sealed off from the world and no one, Japanese or foreigner, was permitted to enter or leave the country. The only exceptions were the crew of a Dutch ship once a year and a few Chinese traders.

This centralized feudalistic system of government worked well for the Tokugawa Shogunate, and for more than two centuries the Tokugawa family remained in power. It was only after a long evolution of economic and social forces, which exploded shortly after the forcible penetration of Japan by the West in the nineteenth century, that the Tokugawa Shogunate fell. It was succeeded by a type of government more Western in form, but similar to the Tokugawa government in spirit and attitude.

MILITARY DOMINANCE IN JAPAN

The spirit and attitude which characterized the Tokugawa Shogunate are revealed in the continued dominance of the military class of Japan. Out of the stress and uncertainty of war in feudal Japan the military emerged as the dominant group with a special code of behavior and morality. First came the knight with his armor, horse, and sword, who introduced the ideals of mental and physical conditioning. He was succeeded by the *samurai,* or "one who serves," who carried on the military ideals and held a prominent place in Japanese political life well into the twentieth century. The code of the samurai warrior is called *Bushido,* or "Way of the Warrior," which values loyalty to the overlord above all else and teaches that bravery and obedience are the fundamental qualities of the good Japanese soldier. For over seven hundred years these ideals were glorified. Personal loyalty, reciprocal obligations, mental and physical discipline, courage, and obedience were the criteria by which the Japanese judged themselves and others. Since it was the military class which best exemplified these virtues, the Japanese, even in modern times, have generally looked up to it. The military set the pattern by which the people lived. Their words were to be listened to with respect; their commands carried out without question.

It is not surprising that the modern political life of the Japanese has been greatly dominated by military leaders. It was a group of young samurai who started the revolution against the Tokugawas and replaced feudalism with a modern centralized state.

Encroachment by Western powers set the stage. In 1853-54 Commodore Perry, an American, forced the closed gates of Japan by means of his black warships. In 1863 the English bombarded the southern city of Kogashima in revenge for the murder of an Englishman. In the following year a fleet of allied Western warships fired on Shimonoseki, a city in southwest Japan, in retaliation for an attack on some Western merchant ships. In each case the Japanese were powerless to reply. This was a military lesson they never forgot, and from that time onward a small group of samurai leaders determined to make Japan as strong as possible.

They worked towards a strong state in two directions: they strengthened the central government by domestic reforms, and they started a systematic and intensive study of Western nations for the purpose of borrowing those qualities of Western culture which made Western nations strong.

DOMESTIC REFORMS

In 1868 the Tokugawa Shogunate was removed and a government bestowed upon the people which, at least theoretically, centered around the emperor. He was brought from the obscurity of the old capital of Kyoto and installed as the head of the state in the new capital of Tokyo. The divinity of his ancestors and his absolute right to rule Japan were emphasized. The shogun was now pictured as a usurper of the emperor's power. Ancient Japanese mythology was revived in order to give further support to his divine authority. The sun goddess, ancestress of the imperial family, was honored as the primary deity of Japan. The emperor was made the main prop of the new Japanese government, and all religious and secular power was concentrated in his person.

There was precedence for this restoration, for the new leaders were utilizing the emperor in much the same way that the Fujiwara family and the shoguns had used him—as a front for their rule. As in old Japan, the emperor reigned but he did not rule.

Government was centralized even more than formerly. In a few short years, the daimyo were persuaded to deed their land over to the central government in exchange for money and privileges. These feudal domains were then made into prefectures governed by officials appointed by the central government. The samurai or warrior class was stripped of many feudal privileges. Universal military conscription was introduced, which brought all classes of young men into military service instead of only a privileged few. Of course, the military ideals and spirit were retained, but the military was directly responsible to the central authority in Tokyo and not to some feudal daimyo.

Selections from the West. At the same time these vigorous samurai leaders initiated a study of Western institutions and technology that was far more systematic and extensive than the earlier study of Chinese culture. Students were carefully picked. They were then sent to various great nations to learn all they could about the special features for which each nation was famous. Naval students were usually sent to England, army and medical students to Germany, law and education students to France, and business and education students to the United States. One group, headed by Prince Ito, traveled all over the world searching for the Western constitution that would be most suitable for Japan's particular needs. Such a constitution was finally found in Germany.

Within a short time the political and economic face of Japan was radically changed. A constitution was adopted which provided for a cabinet and a parliamentary body consisting of two houses whose members were elected. The courts and law codes were reformed and patterned after those of France. A western type of civil service was organized to administer the government. The tax system was broadened and standardized. A banking system was set up modeled after that of the West. Japan very soon resembled Western nations in many ways, but the resemblance was only surface deep, for Japan still retained her old ways of thought and action.

Control by a Small Group. The small group of men who governed the country in the name of the emperor numbered less than one hundred. From the restoration of the emperor in 1868 until 1918, this small band came mostly from the samurai class. But as time went on, they were joined by others who had amassed wealth in business and controlled great portions of Japan's economy. These men, too, were frequently samurai who had entered business when samurai privileges were removed. This economic clique, which worked closely with the militarists and bureaucrats in making Japan an industrialized and trading nation, is commonly referred to as the *Zaibatsu*, which means "money faction." Led by four big business interests which overshadowed the others, the Zaibatsu controlled the Japanese economy until the end of the Second World War. There is evidence that this same group continues to dominate the economy.

This oligarchy of military, economic, and bureaucratic cliques decided that universal education was required if the country was to make any substantial progress as a modern industrial state. The Japanese leaders soon learned that Japan could not industrialize, nor could her soldiers learn quickly the techniques of modern war-fare, unless the Japanese were taught to read and write. Accordingly, universal education was instituted, and education for a minimum number of years—at that time six—became compulsory. This education was not intended to improve the individual's future standard of living or to meet his individual needs, but rather to serve as a means of training and conditioning the people to be useful and submissive servants of the state. The goal was not to improve the individual but to improve the position of the nation on the international scene.

Although political parties arose during the twentieth century, which on the surface were democratic, they possessed a feudal structure and spirit which were peculiarly Japanese. Japan's political parties were headed by a leader or leaders who were regarded in much the same light by their members as the feudal lord of earlier days was regarded by his retainers. The same obedience was demanded, the same mutual relationship of responsibility and service was expected, and personal relations continued to be more important than law and principle. Here, as in the many other Western institutions borrowed by Japan prior to the Second World War, the form was of the West but the spirit and heart was of old Japan.

In 1868 the Japanese were much more successful in establishing a centralized government than when they borrowed from China back in the seventh and eighth centuries. It was a much more efficient and systematic adoption and took place more rapidly. But in each instance, the new concepts and institutions brought in from the outside were imposed upon the country by a small band of leaders.

THE POSTWAR PERIOD

After Japan's defeat in the Second World War, a third purposive borrowing took place. Emperor Hirohito was persuaded to renounce his divinity and to become a symbol rather than a god to the Japanese people. Religion was divorced from politics, and church and state became separate as in the United States. The rights of the people and the worth of the individual were emphasized in order to offset and counteract the conception that the individual had value and meaning only as a member of a community. Equality of opportunity and equality before the law were stressed. Government by law was made fundamental in the new Japan, in contradistinction to the former concept that law was a guide for the ruler rather than a protector of the rights of the individual. All these innovations were incorporated into a new Constitution granted to the people of Japan by the occupying American authorities. This Constitution continues to serve as the basic legal authority and foundation for the present Japanese government although some of its underlying principles are now being re-evaluated by Japanese lawmakers.

The American occupation troops have now left Japan, but for the most part the institutions they set up continue in force. There are many indications, however, that the innovations are now being modified to harmonize with the Japanese patterns of life. Rarely, if ever, is it possible to make an individual into one's own image and likeness; it is even less possible to remake a country to fit one's political convictions. The American leaders of the occupation tried with vigor and imagination to reform Japan's political and economic attitudes and her institutions, but were only partially successful. Much that was done remains, but centuries-old political traditions bear much weight on the Japanese political scene. Although outside pressures are forcing changes in Japan's political life, they are made within the context of her accustomed modes of thought and practice. The outcome is always something uniquely Japanese.

Since their defeat in 1945, the Japanese have created one of the world's greatest industrial areas. Japan is the largest shipbuilder in the world and the fourth largest producer of steel. The Japanese make transistor radios, cameras, and electronic devices; and they mass-produce refrigerators and washing machines. Real growth rates for the period between 1958 and 1963 averaged 13 per cent, the highest in the world. And the Japanese citizen is able to enjoy the products and the freedom created by his technology. Television sets and washing machines are commonplace; thousands rush to the golf course daily, and thousands more crowd the theaters and department stores.

The Japanese face some difficult questions: How can they move their economy along at the same booming speed, and what should be their relations with China and the United States? But they are confident that they will find the answers to these questions, and nowhere is this confidence more manifest than in their energetic and determined technology.

CHAPTER 36

SOUTHEAST ASIA

Up to this point, it would appear that the countries of India, Pakistan, China, and Japan have been overemphasized. This would be true only if the ideological, economic, social, and political thought and institutions of these countries had no similarity to, or influence upon, the patterns of life and thought in other Asian countries. But this is not true, for many of the traditional beliefs and practices of the people of South and East Asia are embedded deeply in the traditions of all Asian countries. Selected aspects of the life of the people in the larger countries of South and East Asia were stressed in order to provide the reader with a basic knowledge of the life of *all* Asians. An understanding of the thought and life of the people of India, Pakistan, China, and Japan will bring with it a greater comprehension of all Asians and will serve as a firm foundation for more detailed readings on other individual countries and peoples, such as those of Southeast Asia.

Southeast Asia consists mainly of two regions—the Indo-China peninsula on the mainland of Asia, and the two island groups of Indonesia and the Philippines. On the island of Borneo are the Protectorate of Brunei and two parts of Malaysia—Sarawak and Sabah. North and South Vietnam, Laos, Cambodia, Thailand, Burma, Malaysia, and Singapore are located on the Indo-China peninsula.

SIMILARITIES TO OTHER REGIONS OF ASIA

In terms of topography and climate, there is a great similarity between all of the Southeast Asian countries. Mountains are a prominent feature in every part of this region, and the cones of active volcanoes are a common sight in the Philippines as well as in Indonesia. The climate is either equatorial monsoon, with rain most of the year, or tropical monsoon, with periodic rains and a wet and dry season. In either case, rainfall is abundant. The similarity of topography and climate results in similar ways of living.

The general description, given in the early chapters of this book, of where and how most Asians make a living also embraces the people of Southeast Asia. Most of the Asians in this area, like Asians elsewhere, are farmers who depend upon human and animal labor rather than on the machine; water buffaloes and oxen are as intimately related to the people and the landscape as they are in other Asian countries. Like most Asians, the people of Southeast Asia look upon rice, vegetables, and, to some extent, wheat, as staple foods. The cultivation of wet rice creates long vistas of reflecting pools of rice paddies which are so many mirrors of rural scenes throughout Asia. Here too the villages house the majority of the people. Except for any striking differences in physical structure and facial characteristics, the Southeast Asian might find it very difficult to determine that an unidentified picture of a man stripped to the waist and cultivating his rice fields in another region of Asia was not a faithful portrayal of a typical Southeast Asian scene. But the bonds that tie them to other Asians are not merely physical; they are also spiritual.

Religion has played a key role in shaping the cultural heritage of the Asian people. Asians have long believed in the divinity of nature, and offerings to the spirits of the mountains, lakes, and forests are still a common practice. The great religions of Buddhism, Hinduism, and Islam have influenced all Asian cultures. Buddhism influences the life and thought of millions of Asians everywhere and is deeply rooted in the soil of a number of Southeast Asian countries. Hinduism did not have the missionary force that drove Buddhism outside the borders of India, but Hindu teaching and practice did penetrate Indonesia and other parts of Southeast Asia. Pakistan and Indonesia are the largest Muslim nations in the world, and Communist China, Christian Philippines, and Hindu India all possess large minorities of Muslims. Confucianism and Taoism, products of Chinese thought, have influenced the religious and philosophical thought of some Southeast Asian countries for centuries.

Similar social customs connect the people of Asia. The people of Southeast Asia are familiar with the joint or large family system which is found throughout the entire region of Asia. Under this system father, mother, unmarried children, and married sons with their wives and children live together under one roof and generally have a common budget. There are variations of this family system from country to country, but a Thai, a Burmese, a Malayan, a Vietnamese, an Indonesian would immediately recognize and accept this system wherever he found it. He would know too that, with increasing urbanization and industrialization, this system is breaking down and that in Tokyo, Bombay, Osaka, and other large cities he will find increasing numbers of small Western-style families, because the same social change is evident in Djakarta, Saigon, Bangkok, Rangoon, and other large cities of Southeast Asia.

The women of Southeast Asia appreciate the attitudes and problems of women in other parts of Asia. Trudging home from the rice paddies at dusk, the women of Vietnam feel the same fatigue that grips their sisters who must labor in the fields of Japan. The traditional woman of Indonesia would find nothing strange in the attitude of the Indian woman who places the male before herself and grows old before her time in her constant and untiring efforts for the husband and the family. The modern woman of Malaysia and the Philippines sympathizes with her counterparts in China and Japan who are straining to raise their social status and, when necessary, fights with the same determination and spirit for her rights.

The young men and women who study and work in Southeast

Asia share the eagerness of the youth in China, India, Pakistan, and Japan to change some of the traditional customs of their countries. It is still a common practice in Asia for marriage contracts to be negotiated and concluded between families, rather than solely between the individuals concerned. The prospective bride and bridegroom are frequently consulted and asked if they have any serious objection to the boy or girl under consideration, but the final decision is a family decision. The young Southeast Asian has the same longing as his peers elsewhere to be free to choose his own mate. However, even when he has this freedom, the wishes of the family are taken seriously, and their approval of the match is usually sought.

The youth of Southeast Asia, like his contemporaries in other countries of Asia, is impatient with the slow pace of his country's evolution into a modern nation-state. He blames his leaders for their rigidity in holding to the ways of the past. He blames the peasant for his bovine attitude and for his resignation when natural and man-made calamities befall him. He blames the entire social system of his country for not affording him an opportunity to participate actively in the country's affairs, and he becomes frustrated. His frustration, like that of his peers throughout Asia, leaves him receptive to suggestions to work actively in change-overnight schemes presented him by Communists or other authoritarian dogmatists. He may, or may not, become a dogmatic revolutionary, but the conditions and processes that led him to the brink of acceptance are as familiar to the youth of Japan as to those of Laos and Vietnam.

The teachers of Southeast Asia have traditionally been held in the same respect as those of China, India, and Japan. Teaching was, and is, a most honored occupation. But all teachers, no matter where they live in Asia, realize that they are faced with a multitude of common problems. With few exceptions, they are confronted with the massive problem of illiteracy. Nowhere, with the exception of the Philippines, are there enough teachers to man the classrooms. The vast majority of teachers are overworked and underpaid. Honor cannot pay the rent, the food bills, the clothing bills, and the many other bills a position of honor entails. Their social status is declining, their working conditions are deteriorating, their morale is dropping, and their future is rather bleak. But the typical Asian teacher recognizes his responsibility and willingly endures frustration and hardship in order that his country may have the educated manpower base that is essential to any progress. The teachers of Southeast Asia, like their confreres in other Asian countries, are a most dedicated band of men and women.

Similarities between the region of Southeast Asia and other Asian areas could be multiplied many times. The cities of this region are expanding at an extremely rapid rate and becoming the centers of political and economic control. The leaders are exerting every effort to industrialize in order to shore up their economic base and raise the standard of living of their people. Life expectancy does not go beyond forty years of age, and modern medical facilities are limited. Nationalism is rampant everywhere in Asia. In all of Asia, love of country is moving the people to act. Everywhere people are trying to reconcile this spirit with their traditional loyalties to the family, the clan, the caste, and the class. Everywhere the conflicts between old and new values are tearing the hearts and souls of the Asian people. The birth of nations in Asia has brought instability, uncertainty, fear, insecurity, pain, chaos, pride, and hope. The bonds of similar ways of life and thought that tie all Asians together, bonds that have been forged over the centuries, are now being reinforced by the rising expectations of all for a better life and by the advent of independence and nationalism.

DISTINCTIVE CHARACTER OF SOUTHEAST ASIA

Although there is much in the mode and view of life of Southeast Asians that is similar to that in one, or more, or all of the Asian countries outside this region, there is also diversity, sometimes great diversity. Many differences in thought and practice between Pakistan, India, China, and Japan have already been shown. The Laotians, Cambodians, Burmese, and Thai from Southeast Asia and the East Asian Chinese and Japanese all name themselves Buddhists but the Southeast Asian's interpretation of Buddhism differs significantly from that of the Chinese and Japanese. The Indonesians and Pakistanis both profess Islam and both adhere to the same basic doctrines, but the Indonesians have colored Islam to blend with their special environment and supplemented it with treasured indigenous usages of ancient origin. The social life of the Southeast Asians is differentiated from that of some other Asians by qualities that are derived from their own special heritage. There is a basic theme that runs throughout the social life of Asia, but there are variations of emphasis and stress, modifications, and additions which give to the social life of each country its individual character. The political posture and problems of the Southeast Asian countries demarcates them from other countries and, on occasion, from each other.

The accessibility of the area from the sea permitted long-continued Chinese and Indian cultural penetration and, more recently, the introduction of Japanese, European, and American influences. This mixture of Chinese, Indian, Japanese, Western, and indigenous cultures resulted in a special orientation to life. Southeast Asia has a distinctive character which sets it apart from the neighboring regions of Asia.

CHAPTER 37

RELIGION IN SOUTHEAST ASIA

Religion has had a profound impact upon the people of Southeast Asia. Their conception of the good life, their customs, their art, and their literature all witness to the influence of religion in the daily lives of the people. The profusion of temples, pagodas, monasteries, shrines, and mosques reveals to the most casual observer that religion has found a permanent home in this land. The humble shrine housing an unadorned village guardian and the majestic temple enshrining an array of breathtaking Buddhas have a revered meaning and function for the people. Wherever one walks in Southeast Asia, there he will find the spirit and evidence of religion.

Followers of all the world's religions are to be found in Southeast Asia today, but the beliefs and practices of the vast majority of the people stem either from animism, Hinduism, Buddhism, or Islam or from a combination of two or more of these religions. Buddhism, in the form called Theravada, is dominant in Burma, Thailand, Cambodia, and Laos. Islam is the prevailing religion in Indonesia, Malaya, and Borneo and has followers in all of the other countries. The religion of Vietnam is a blend of Mahayana Buddhism, Confucianism, Taoism, and animism. The majority of the Filipinos are Christian. But regardless of which imported religion predominates, certain beliefs and practices indigenous to the various countries of Southeast Asia remain an integral part of the religious life of the people. This is particularly true of animism, which was the original religion of almost all the people of Southeast Asia.

Animism is the belief that all objects, including trees, rivers, volcanoes, and other natural objects, possess a conscious life or are endowed with indwelling souls. In Laos, the people believe that certain spirits, or *phi*, possess great power over the destinies of man and are to be found throughout the material universe. Evil spirits, or *phi*, may cause disease or other troubles, and exorcists must be called in to drive them out of the body. Sometimes a Bud-

dhist priest, who has this special knowledge, may be called upon
to perform the ceremony of exorcism. In Thailand, the two religions
of animism and Buddhism are intermingled. In almost every Thai
village there is a tutelary guardian as well as a Buddhist *wat*, or
compound. In many parts of Burma, the villagers still make their
offerings to the *nat*, or spirit, who dwells in some natural object and
whose favor is important to them and their community. It is an ancient spirit, for it was born in the legendary past of Burma, but it
retains its vigor despite the passage of time. In Indonesia the people
are careful to propitiate the spirits that inhabit their land, and offerings are faithfully laid before the powerful spirits of certain trees
or presented to the spirits of the sea, the rivers, and the volcanoes.
The spirit world of animism is still close to the people of Southeast Asia, and neither the imposition of another religion nor the
introduction of an irreligious philosophy has been able to exorcise
these spirits completely from the land and the people. But religions
from India and China did enter Southeast Asia and gradually
superseded or assimilated most of the original religious beliefs.

BUDDHISM IN BURMA, THAILAND, LAOS, AND CAMBODIA

Through the instrumentality of Indian traders, priests, ad-
venturers, and travelers, the culture and religious ideas of India
were brought to much of Southeast Asia. Indian culture is strik-

ingly evident in the literature, art, architecture, and dances of many countries in this area. The great Indian epic, the *Ramayana*, is well known in Burma, Thailand, Laos, and Cambodia, and although it has been modified to fit its new setting—Thailand has four versions of it—the general outline still remains. The *Mahabharata*, another great Indian story, has been so completely absorbed into Indonesian literature that the Indonesians think of themselves as the descendants of the characters in the tale.

Theravada Buddhism. The religion of the vast majority of people in the countries of Burma, Cambodia, and Laos is Buddhism in the form called Theravada, "the Path of the Elders." From India, and the neighboring island of Ceylon, Theravada Buddhism spread eastward to these countries. It will be recalled that Buddhism eventually split into two major schools of thought known as Theravada or Hinayana ("Lesser Vehicle") and Mahayana ("Greater Vehicle"). Mahayana Buddhism, described earlier in this book, is followed in China, Korea, Japan, Tibet, and Vietnam. The Theravada school of Buddhism teaches the more austere and simple way of life. It is a more literal interpretation of Buddha's teachings and adheres rather closely to his original doctrines. It is more demanding upon the individual than Mahayana Buddhism. To carry out fully the Buddha's requirements, it is necessary to renounce the world completely and enter a monastery.

A person who follows these prescriptions literally and diligently will become an *arhat*, "worthy person," one ready to enter Nirvana. An individual must do this himself; he can expect no help from other men or gods. It is self-purification, salvation through individual effort, not through grace.

In their interpretation of Buddhism, many of the people of Southeast Asia differ from the Chinese, Koreans, and Japanese—Zen Buddhism excepted—for generally these Asians do not emphasize the principle of self-help, but rather rely upon the redeeming merit of saintly men who have refused Nirvana in order to help others achieve it. It is a compassionate religion in that it is more concerned with helping others, and its highest ideal is that person who forgoes his entrance into Nirvana until all have attained it. A story is told of four men who were climbing a mountain. One by one they approached the top of the mountain. The first man to reach the summit stood up, looked, and then with a great shout threw himself out of sight on the other side. The second and third man did likewise. When the fourth man reached the top and looked, he gasped in astonishment and awe, for there awaiting him was a paradise of beauty and eternal life. He had found his Shangri-la. But instead of jumping into it immediately as the others had done, he returned down the mountain and spent the rest of his life showing others the path to this earthly paradise. The first three men were followers of Theravada; the last one, a follower of Mahayana Buddhism.

In Theravada Buddhism, Gautama Buddha is not an object of worship but is regarded as the embodiment of a principle of enlightenment. He is merely an outstanding example of an eternal concept which has been made concrete in Buddhas before Gautama Buddha and will continue to be known in earthly form throughout time. The images of Buddha, which portray an idealized symbol rather than a real human being, are the result of this conception.

Since Nirvana could be achieved only by the unaided efforts of the individual, the gaining of merit became a fulltime preoccupation of the followers of Theravada. It became a monk-oriented religion. Theravada holds that adult males should become priests or monks —sometimes called *bonzes*—and most males put on the robes of a monk for a temporary period prior to marriage. The individual is free to remain a monk as long as he wishes. Even a short period as a monk is meritorious for the individual and an honor to his family. Yellow-robed monks alone, in pairs, or in groups are expected and accepted participants in the daily activities of the countries that practice Theravada, and as they sally forth in the early hours of the morning to seek food in the name of Lord Buddha, they are a constant reminder to the people of their Buddhist heritage and duties.

The Buddhist Wat. Unlike their colleagues in China, Korea, and Japan, who perform only limited functions of a religious nature, the Buddhist priests in Burma, Cambodia, Laos, and Thailand perform services that make them indispensable to the secular as well as religious life of the community. They officiate at religious festivals and ceremonies and pray over the sick. They are invited to birthdays or weddings to pray and speak and are required for funeral ceremonies and the naming of infants. In many rural areas they are the only teachers available, and their compounds the only schools in the neighborhood. They are necessary for almost every important family and community affair. In almost every village of these countries there is a Buddhist wat, or compound—wats are sometimes referred to as *pagodas*—which serves as the educational and social center of the community. Some of the larger cities have many wats. A wat consists of a group of buildings surrounded by a wall or fence. Within the wat there are halls or temples for both laity and monks, a library, dormitories, shrines, and sometimes bath-houses. There may also be a crematorium, for the Buddhists cremate their dead. Almost every wat contains a school, either for the monks or the children of the community, or both. It is estimated that one-half of the primary schools of Thailand are located in wats. The villagers come to these wats to seek the advice of the monks, to relay local news and gossip, to leave their valuables for safekeeping, to rest, and to attend to a host of other secular matters in addition to making merit and undertaking other spiritual duties. Festivals also are often held within the wat, and during these periods it resounds with gaiety and joy. A most highly esteemed member of the village community, the abbot, presides over the wat. Monks of all grades are respected by the people, even by the foremost officials of the country. The abbot's counsel is often sought by the people, especially in matters of some importance to the family or the community, and in many instances his advice is preferred to that of the secular authorities. He mingles daily with the people, giving guidance, information, and assistance.

The people voluntarily support the wat and the monks, for it is the way of merit to Nirvana. It is estimated that in some countries the people spend from 5 to 10 per cent of their income in supporting the wat, not including food and volunteer labor. Their wats and their monks are essential to their life.

Social and Political Aspects. Most of the Buddhists feel that their harmonious relationships within the family and the community are the result of Buddhist teachings and practices. The training of the mind to curb passions, anger, and greed makes them more forgiving and more tolerant. The Thais say that no good Buddhist will despise a person who has different views from his own. They point to the fact that even at their football and boxing matches there are rarely public displays of temper and that at public gatherings of all kinds they are orderly and quiet. The Burmese claim that the teachings of Buddha on the relationship that should exist between husband and wife, parent and child, teacher and student, employer and employee, friend and friend has been a major factor in the preservation of harmonious relationships among the Burmese. These relationships are founded on mutual tolerance and respect.

The imprint of Buddhism is vividly marked in the festivals of the people in the Theravada countries. Many of these festivals have flowered from the seed of Buddhism. In Laos, during the full moon of the month of May, a festival is celebrated in memory of the birth, enlightenment, and death of Buddha. Dances, processions, and puppet shows create an atmosphere of earthly gaiety, but the religious significance of the festival is also present in the blessing of children and expectant mothers and in the offerings made to the priests. Each month of the Burmese calendar has its special festival, as have the wats at various times of the year. In Thailand, the annual Festival of the Great Pagoda, which is held in the middle of the twelfth lunar month, draws throngs of people from all over the country. They come primarily to pay homage to the relics of Buddha housed there, but they stay to enjoy the amusements and the many varieties of food and sweets available in the fairground that surrounds the compound of the Great Pagoda.

Buddhism is not divorced from the political life of these countries. The Burmese have repeatedly stated that Buddhism is the unifying and stabilizing force that welds them into one nation. During periods of chaos, and domination by others, Buddhism has played a major role in preserving them from disunity and despair. The Burmese monks were in the forefront of the campaign for independence from England. In Laos, all nobles are required to take a yearly oath of allegiance to their king in the Temple of Sisaket in the capital. After being defeated by the Thais, the oath to the Thai ruler was taken in the same temple, and the French continued the custom when they assumed power. Buddhism is the state religion of Laos, and the constitution requires the king to be a fervent Buddhist. He is the Supreme Protector of the Faith, and he appoints the head of the church. The political and religious hierarchies are parallel and interdependent. Important official ecclesiastical appointments are generally made only after joint consultation and agreement of church authorities and secular political officials. In Thailand, the Supreme Patriarch of the Buddhists is chosen by the king from the nominations presented him by an ecclesiastical council. Although the monks of Thailand have refrained from political activities, the religious and secular authorities are closely linked.

The only word that properly describes the role of Buddhism in the countries of Burma, Cambodia, Laos, and Thailand is *pervasive*.

There is no aspect of a person's life in these countries which is not affected by Buddhism. Religious instruction is usually mandatory whether the schools are government-sponsored or private. Monks are used to disseminate modern concepts of health and hygiene and other Western learning. Stories on Buddha's life and teachings have motivated and inspired numerous poets and writers, and even the more modern and secular literature has religious nuances. The sometimes overwhelming beauty of the architecture and statues is the result of a passionate impulse to bring divinity to stone, wood, and bronze. Buddhism is of the heart and mind of the people of Cambodia, Burma, Laos, and Thailand.

ISLAM IN INDONESIA

Indians carried Hinduism and Buddhism to Indonesia. They, together with the Arabs, brought Islam to Malaya and Indonesia. There they found an indigenous body of beliefs and practices which substantially stemmed from animism. It was around the first century A.D. that Hinduism and Buddhism began to become known in Indonesia. Indian priests, traders, and warriors introduced the Indonesians to the Sanskrit language, sacred texts, rituals, temples, and Indian literature. These two religions mingled with the original animism, and in the process of acceptance they were adapted by the Indonesians to fit their needs and setting. Hinduism and Buddhism—Mahayana Buddhism—vied for supremacy in Indonesia, and slowly Hinduism prevailed but not completely, for the resulting religious pattern was a combination of Hinduism, Buddhism, and animism plus some other customary beliefs and practices. This fusion of Hinduism, Mahayana Buddhism, and animism endured until Islam became the dominant religion of Indonesia around the beginning of the sixteenth century. The fusion still endures in Bali, but its structure and content is Balinese, not Indian.

Islam started to spread in Indonesia about the thirteenth century, and within two hundred years was the religion of the majority. The process of conversion was a slow but peaceful one. Islam was not forced upon the people at sword point; the Indonesians responded to the attractiveness of the doctrine as described by the persuasive tongues of Indian traders from the west coast of India. These merchants established themselves in the main ports of Indonesia, and Islam radiated out from their headquarters. These Indian Muslims, on the surface at least, bore many similarities to the Indians who had preached Hinduism and Buddhism and, therefore, were not regarded as totally alien to the Indonesian scene. Further, there was much in Islam that appealed to the religious spirit of the Indonesians, and they were inclined to accept it. But again, as in the case of Hinduism and Buddhism, in the process of acceptance they contrived to make it uniquely Indonesian.

Because of the danger of idolatry, Islam frowns upon portrayals of living beings. It does not, however, forbid pictures of natural objects such as flowers, trees, or leaves. Since the Indonesian artists desired to portray living beings as well as lifeless objects, they invented a new form of art by making portraits of animals out of leaf and flower designs. Close up, the drawings appear to be merely leaf designs, but from a distance the image of an animal is clearly discernible. The walls of some mosques in Indonesia are decorated with these leaf designs.

Because shadow-plays were intimately connected with animism, and to a certain extent with Hinduism and Buddhism, Islam prohibited the exhibition of them. But the Indonesians knew that Islam encouraged decorations composed of Arabic passages from the Koran, and they began to use artistic Arabic characters in their compositions. Close up, they are finely written Arabic characters, but from a distance they have the figure of a *wayang* puppet. To make shadow-plays acceptable to all, the puppets were fabricated from tree stems rather than leather, and revered figures from Arabic and Muslim literature replaced the more ancient characters.

The architecture of the mosques is more Indonesian than traditional moslem; it is square rather than circular and often lacks the usual dome for a roof. Mosques and Islamic cemeteries are sometimes entered through a Hindu-styled gate, and names of Muslims are often of Hindu origin. Muslim girls are frequently named after the wife of Muhammed, but many are also named after Queen Sita, the heroine of the Indian epic the *Ramayana*. The amalgam of religious practices is illustrated in the celebrations that are held on important occasions such as the birth of a child and the initiation of community projects. Although a Muslim official might preside on these occasions, some relics of Hindu practices are preserved, and the custom of celebrating these events had its origin in the ancient animistic past of Indonesia.

The Indonesians have the knack of blurring the sharp lines which ordinarily divide religions in other parts of the world. They are, for the most part, Muslims, and they will not easily change their religion—Christianity has had little success in converting Muslims to its faith—but they are also Indonesians with a strong tendency toward harmonizing natural and supernatural forces. They are a tolerant people willing to accommodate rivaling points of view. They have succeeded in shaping animism, Hinduism, Buddhism, and Islam to fit their unique personality and environment.

MAHAYANA BUDDHISM IN VIETNAM

The Vietnamese, like the Indonesians, were open-minded and tolerant with regard to new religious ideas. What they liked, they accepted and blended with other beliefs and ways which they had previously adopted. Both Chinese and Indians introduced Buddhism to the Vietnamese, but the Chinese influence was predominant, and they preached the Mahayana Buddhism that flowered and flourished in China. For centuries Buddhism was patronized and encouraged by the Vietnamese rulers and became firmly rooted in Vietnam. However, the Chinese also introduced Taoism and Confucianism to the Vietnamese, and Taoistic practices have their own special role in the religious life of the people. Confucianism, since it is not really concerned with the after-life, was confined to the more scholarly and to the officials of the country, although it was proclaimed as the official ideology of the state. The majority of the Vietnamese are regarded as followers of Mahayana Buddhism, but their original animism, and various forms of Taoism imported from China, are also vital elements in their religious life.

CHRISTIANITY IN THE PHILIPPINES

Although there are large numbers of Muslims in Mindanao and Sulu, the great majority of the Filipinos are Christians. The Spanish governed the Philippines for almost four hundred years, and since one of their principal aims was the propagation of Catholicism, they made a special effort to convert the Filipinos. They were successful, and today most of the Filipinos are baptized Catholics. Almost every town of any size has a church which often dominates the community physically and socially. Most of the festivals—and there are many of them, for the Filipinos are a gay people—are held to honor some patron saint or to commemorate a religious feast day. Their religious rituals and practices often convey a sense of the dramatic which is characteristic of the Spanish approach to religion. With the assumption of power by the Americans in the late nineteenth century, many Protestant missionaries started to proselytize in the Philippines with some success, but their converts are still far outnumbered by the Catholics.

The people of Southeast Asia have welcomed many religions. Animism, Buddhism, Hinduism, Islam, Taoism, Confucianism, and Christianity have been received with tolerance, listened to with respect, and frequently adopted—if not entirely, at least in part. They have adapted them to fit their own environment and personality, for to most Southeast Asians the cultivation of the spirit is of the essence of life.

CHAPTER 38

SOCIAL LIFE IN SOUTHEAST ASIA

Most of the people of Southeast Asia live in village-centered communities whose members are closely knit by ties of blood and marriage and by a communal spirit of co-operation. Except for certain areas, their land is relatively underpopulated, well-watered, and generous in its response to those who cultivate it with even a little care. Fish and rice can be had by all who apply themselves, and the disruptive evils of near starvation and famine do not persistently disturb the relationships between the members of the community. Their lives are not dominated by the intense and insistent pressure to expend their total energies in the search for food as so many must do in China, India, Korea, Pakistan, and other countries of South and East Asia. Their daily routine is slower and more tranquil, and they have the time and the inclination to meditate, to rest, to visit, and to play.

Characteristically, they regard their fellows as allies, rather than competitors, in the quest for happiness, and their relations with one another are frequently distinguished by mutual assistance and a spirit of helpfulness. They try to resolve conflicts as expeditiously and justly as possible. They base their social relations on the principle that harm to another is to be avoided even at the price of sacrificing one's own interests, and they believe that if all are imbued with the same charitable spirit the community will be at peace.

This distinctive trait of mutual assistance is most marked in the family and the village, but it also extends to the nation and beyond. It is magnificently illustrated by the dikes that contain the waters of the Red River of Vietnam. These dikes are estimated to run for a distance of sixteen hundred miles, and measure as much as sixty feet wide at the base and twenty feet at the top. The beginning of these dikes is unknown because it lies deep in the vague past of Vietnam, but for thousands of years the Vietnamese have continued to rebuild and maintain these monumental barriers against

floods. The construction and maintenance of the dikes was a communal activity that included all within the area nourished by the
river's waters; it still is today. When an alarm sounds warning of a
breach in the dike, the neighborhood swarms to the danger spot to
prevent an onslaught of flooding waters over the land. A striking
example of self-help, this custom also indicates the venerable character and the lasting strength of the co-operative attitude that distinguishes many people in Southeast Asia.

This quality of mutual assistance circumfuses the daily life of the
village and the family. Villagers join together in building schools,
dams, dikes, roads, and secular and religious community buildings.
They assist each other in constructing a house, in planting and harvesting the crops, in healing the sick and burying the dead, in se-
curing husbands for the spinsters and brides for the bachelors, in
celebrating the birth of children, and in all other matters where the
hands and minds of many are needed. The Indonesians considered
this practice of co-operation important enough to be formally prescribed as a part of the customary law, called *adat,* which regulates
their social relations. To most Southeast Asians, however, mutual
help is a natural law, for it is neither debated nor forced but
naturally and instinctively given.

THE FAMILY

The families of Southeast Asia have a tolerant flexibility in
regard to the number of members included. In the Philippines, in
Laos, and in the Southeast Asian cities, the family may sometimes
be comparable in size to those of Western countries, but it is always
prepared to expand and receive aunts, uncles, cousins, in-laws, even
remote relatives, and friends, if they need its security. It is common
to find within the family married daughters and sons, their children,
and other relatives or friends, in addition to the parents and their
unmarried children. There is always room for one more and, indeed, "the more the merrier" is a phrase that aptly describes the
attitude of many families in this region, an attitude which renders
orphanages and homes for the aged largely unnecessary.

There are certain practical advantages in having many members
in the agriculture-focused families of Southeast Asia. Whoever is
regarded as a member of the family is expected to do his or her
share in providing for its support. At an early age the child starts

carrying water, watching the water-buffalo and feeding the other animals, taking care of the babies, and handling other small but necessary chores. The aged help with the lighter field work and do much of the baby-sitting and cooking, sometimes freeing the mother and father for gainful labor outside the home and the fields. Over a long period of time the people have worked on the premise that the greater the number of persons supporting the family, the greater the income in food and kind.

Practical advantages or not, the group living of large families would be unbearable without a degree of concord among the members. The daily living together of large families is made possible by the rather well-defined roles and functions of the members. The roles may be defined differently from family to family because many Southeast Asian countries have large minority groups whose customs are of ancient indigenous origin or were born in alien soil and carried there by immigrants, but there are some general principles which are looked upon by many as basic to their family and communal living.

The young are subordinate to their elders and owe them respect, obedience, and devotion. Youth is a period for acquiring knowledge and learning social roles, for gathering the wisdom, know-how, and experience of the preceding generations. The prevailing theory is that a person cannot teach what has not been learned, or practice what has not been imbibed from childhood. Discord arises within the family and the community only from those who have not been well-taught or well-disposed to receive the instructions of their teachers. The word "teacher" is esteemed throughout Southeast Asia, for it signifies that most important function of preparing the youth for his future role in the family, community, and nation. If the older members of the family fulfill this role with distinction, their kin will be honored, and the reputation of their family enhanced. If they perform it badly, they shame their kin and dishonor their family. The responsibility to prepare the youth adequately for life weighs heavily upon his elders; for in a very real sense, his future is their future.

Generally the child is receptive to what he is taught because it is accompanied by love. Children are wanted and welcomed, and they know it. They are the continuation of the family and the hope of the community. They are individuals destined eventually for the desirelessness of Nivana or the complete satisfaction of all desires with God. Children are loved to the point where they are almost overindulged, but neither they nor the elders ever forget their subordinate place in the family.

The aged too must live up to their respected roles in the family. Their function is to advise, since the wisdom accumulated over the long course of their years must be shared with the family and the community. They participate in the deliberations of village and local councils because, since community projects require the efforts of all, all should be involved in the basic decisions that pertain to these projects. The degree to which decisions are arrived at through free discussions on the village level would amaze most Westerners, and the grass-roots feeling for democracy would call forth the envy of many Western political leaders. The aged are wanted, needed, and made secure, and there is not the onus on them, as in the West, of being expected to make a new life for themselves apart from the family they helped to found and preserve.

Men and women have their special roles in the family. The man is formally the head of the household, and his authority is buttressed by the long-held assumptions of tradition and religion which teach the inherent superiority of the male. The woman's placid acceptance of her lower rank further bolsters his status in the family and in the community where he represents the family in council deliberations and decisions. It is his duty to perform the more arduous work of the family, such as preparing the fields for cultivation, doing carpentry and masonry work, and carrying heavy materials. There are certain religious duties that only a male may perform and, in the Buddhist areas, he often assumes the robes of a monk for a short or long period depending upon his inclinations.

The woman is primarily responsible for the good ordering of the house, and all the domestic tasks that accompany housekeeping. She cooks, washes, sews, cleans, and, if she is the wife of a village farmer, she helps to care for the livestock, carries water, cultivates a garden, and lends a helping hand to her husband in the fields at planting, harvesting, and weeding time. In the care of her children she often has the assistance of older children and old people who cannot work in the fields. Like any mother, she is expected to be always ready to cope with the great and small emergencies that from time to time visit any household.

Although she is formally subordinate to the male, her counsel is sought and frequently followed in making marriage arrangements, planning family celebrations, managing the household, and other important family matters. She has always worked side by side with the husband on the farm and in business ventures, and was commonly seen alone selling her wares by the roadside and in the markets. Now she is even to be found in the professions, and there are growing numbers of women doctors, educators, lawyers, playwrights, authors, radio announcers, and business entrepreneurs. She does not compete with the male, and she has no desire to usurp his established role in the family. She knows her complementary role is essential to the smooth meshing of social relations within the family and the community.

SOCIAL CHANGE

These understood roles are fulfilled today by most of the Southeast Asian people, and they continue to contribute substantially to the agreeable nature of social life in this region, but forces are at work which are altering these roles, often imperceptibly and sometimes significantly. Modern education is conveying novel ideas to the people which are often accepted as better than traditional ones. In some parts of Southeast Asia polygamy was, and is, permitted, but there is increasing pressure from influential segments of the society to curtail and prohibit it. Even where it is legal, many refrain from practicing it because of possible social censure. In much, but not all, of Southeast Asia women have always had inheritance rights in the family property. Now new concepts of women's rights to inheritance are bringing this privilege to women in all areas. Unlike those in other parts of Asia, many women of Southeast Asia have had for centuries the right to secure divorces. This freedom, too, is now being extended to women in the few territories where it was unknown before.

The youth, intoxicated by the unaccustomed wine of social freedom he is obtaining from books, magazines, and movies is beginning to struggle against the restraints of a subordinate position. He is convinced that his new knowledge is far superior to that of his elders, and he prefers to supplant his usual passive role with a more free and active one. The hint of juvenile delinquency now found in the cities could grow into a major social problem if not properly handled.

The accelerating urbanization process is conditioning the social life of the people. The size of the family is being directly affected by this trend. Since cities are being inundated by people, urban land is becoming scarce and expensive and many families are forced to live in restricted quarters. The limitations of space have a direct physical bearing on the number of family members who can be accommodated. Moreover, unlike village-based families whose economy is founded upon an agricultural system that favors many workers, the city-based families rely upon other means of support which do not require the co-operation of many hands. But the traditional welcoming attitude toward those who want to be a part of them still persists in many families who migrate to the cities, and they try to make room for all who come. They may all have to be packed tightly in cramped quarters, but they feel that the spiritual and emotional warmth that results from their close association outweighs their sacrifice of special freedom.

The political chaos prevailing in some countries of Southeast Asia is expediting the breakdown of traditional values. Alien forces are working fanatically and energetically on this troubled scene to sabotage the old mores and replace them with radical dogmas. South Vietnam, one of these disturbed areas, vividly illustrates this threat to traditional social values. The Communists in South Vietnam have made the destruction of the social system one of their major aims. They are creating conditions which place child against parent, brother against brother, and friend against friend. They are sundering families and wrecking old friendships, with the result that traditional virtues are being destroyed.

One favorite Communist technique involves a breaking down of an important three-sided relationship—that between parents, child, and teacher. A young student returns home from school one day, and after performing his daily chores around the house sits down to dinner with his family. Two or more Communists enter the house and demand that the student tell them what he has been taught that day. When the student has finished his recital of the content of the day's teaching—which may not have pleased them—they give him some printed sheets of Communist propaganda and order him to present them to the teacher as the text for the next day's instruction. They then threaten the child with the death of his mother, or father, or both, if he does not follow their command. This action presents the child, the parents, and the teacher with a frightful dilemma. The child has always been taught to respect the teacher in the same way he respects his father and mother, but if he does not obey, his father and mother will be killed. If he asks his father and mother for advice, how should they advise him? If he asks his teacher for advice, how should he advise him? The teacher does not want the blood of the boy's parents on his hands. He knows that such threats have been carried out many times and that he, too, may be killed if he does not teach what has been given him. Under these circumstances what happens to their old values and the truth that has been their guide for living? Incidents of a similar nature can be multiplied many times, all designed to undermine the foundations of the Vietnamese family and social system.

To a greater or lesser degree these new influences are altering the social life of the people in all Southeast Asian countries. In some countries, such as Vietnam and Laos, forces for change are abetted by violence and the implements of war. In other countries social change is occurring more peacefully and gradually, as a result of education, urbanization, industrialization, and other evolutionary factors. The problems created by nationalism and by intermittent political crises of regional or international scope are also drastically reshaping the social life of the Southeast Asian people.

CHAPTER 39

POLITICS IN SOUTHEAST ASIA

Southeast Asia is at present a politically unsettled region. Serious problems of both internal and external origin are perplexing the political leaders of this area. They lack sufficient knowledge of, and experience in, the theory and practice of constitutional democracy; they still lean toward authoritarian leadership and tend to rely upon men rather than laws. The clash of minority groups and the confusing conflict of differing ideological doctrines add to their difficulties. Their external political problems originate in their relationships with their regional neighbors, in the proximity of Communist China, and in the recurring crises that result from the moves of antagonists in the deadly drama of the Cold War.

INEXPERIENCE IN DEMOCRACY

Southeast Asian countries have a long history of authoritarian government at the national level, but a very brief history of the Western-style constitutional system of government. From the beginning of their history, the people have been accustomed to the idea of a ruler who neither sought nor wanted their advice, but demanded their obedience and support. Although at the village level decisions on matters which concerned the community were usually made only after long discussion and the consent of the family representatives, this democratic method was not practiced on the national level. Nor did the villagers want the ruler to be overly interested in their daily affairs—they felt prying officials would be annoying. All they generally asked from their rulers was a minimum of local interference, and few taxes.

Within the past two decades, most of the peoples of this region have been presented with constitutional democracies by their idealistic, revolutionary, educated élite. They were told that this was a new era, that they were now the real rulers of the country, and that their elected representatives would act on their behalf on the national and local levels. Parties were formed and candidates offered to the people for their consideration. In most cases, the people returned to power those who had previously ruled them or the revolutionary leaders who had gained national independence for them.

In the ensuing years, most of the countries of Southeast Asia have been governed according to constitutional provisions, and some progress has been made in educating the people to a better appreciation of democracy. Most of the people are now aware of the external trappings of democracy, but many have not yet grasped its spirit and philosophical basis. This is due in part to the lack of native roots for democracy—it is a recent import of Western origin—and in part to the little time people have had to adjust to it, and it to them. A people cannot be expected to attune themselves overnight to political conceptions which grew and matured within a different environment and tradition. The basic principles of democracy are suitable for all persons, but the manner in which they are worked out in action varies with the character and traditions of the people. Moreover, time and peace are needed for the proper development of democracy, and the people of Southeast Asia have had neither adequate time nor a truly peaceful atmosphere in which to cultivate their new democracies.

Unfortunately, many believed that the establishment of a constitutional system of government would be an immediate panacea for their economic, social, and political problems. When it failed to provide a swift and effective remedy for their ills, some became impatient and turned for quick action to the time-tested, well-known pattern of government by a dictator. As a consequence there have been a number of coups and attempted coups in some countries of this region. In some cases, these sudden take-overs have disturbed the stability of the country, but in other instances, they have not. The latter has been true whenever the assumption of power by force is not alien to the political tradition of the region and, indeed, is more familiar to the people than constitutional democracy. The people merely request again of their new leaders that interference with their daily activities be minimized and their economic burdens lightened.

Except in countries taken over by Communism, life in Asia generally goes on just as it had before the transference of power, because the change is of men rather than policies. The number of men who have the capacity and opportunity to wield power in the country is limited. Consequently, the governing potential is a small group, consisting of those who have had similar economic and educational backgrounds and more or less follow the same policies in administering the affairs of government. The basic policy of most leaders is to preserve what is best in the culture and tradition of the people and at the same time advance along certain economic and social lines. A too radical change in the customary usages of the people might bring upon the government the wrath of the conservative peasant and military, and therefore the new leaders feel it is more expedient to channel their energies along accepted lines of action than to endanger their policies and positions by pushing the people impetuously into unfamiliar economic and social worlds. But too great an emphasis upon the preservation of the status quo may lead to stagnation and deterioration. Since it is necessary to conserve and advance at the same time, shifts in government are reflected more in the changing personalities of the leaders than in deviations in aims.

NEPOTISM

Under these circumstances, the character and orientation of the men in power become much more significant than constitutional provisions. It is more essential to know the views of the leader or leaders in a given situation than to understand the literal constitutional requirement. It is frequently better to be on the side of the right man than to be on the right side of the law. The ruler is prone to value loyalty and trustworthiness in his subordinates more than intelligence and competence. The former two qualities are indispensable; the latter are certainly useful but may prove harmful if loyalty is lacking. For this reason many leaders select their own relatives for government positions.

The families of this region have a strong tradition of mutual assistance. If a person is fortunate enough to become politically powerful or rich, his family and relatives naturally assume that they will share in his success. Because their fortunes are tied to his, they are his best source of trusted assistants. There are few sources from which the leaders of a particular country can recruit trained personnel to man the administrative posts of government. These leaders are very conscious of this deficiency and are spending much of their countries' resources in their efforts to increase the number of educated men and women. In the meantime, they are compelled by circumstances to rely upon a small coterie which includes their families, friends, and political colleagues.

The assumption of power by the friends and relatives of the leader sometimes results in their obtaining material rewards far beyond their salaries. They feel, and tradition often supports them, that a substantial reward for their loyal services is not an unreasonable expectation. Their new positions often have attached to them indirect benefits, which have been there for a long time and thus have become customary and accepted, though not legal. The more common sources of additional income are: favored treatment for certain business enterprises, the granting of import and export licenses—(these are very lucrative in countries where such licenses are difficult to obtain), manipulation of currencies, awarding of government contracts, and, in some instances, smuggling. The use of these avenues of income is condoned or overlooked if the bounds of propriety are not exceeded. If carried too far, however, these illegal practices may precipitate another coup or endanger the country's economy.

Some of the Southeast Asian leaders, mindful of the injurious consequences of this custom, have tried to inject a new attitude into their administrations. The late President Ramón Magsaysay of the Philippines was known and loved for his attention to the plight of the poor and for the absence of greed in his character. More recently, President Diosdada Macapacal of the Philippines disclosed his financial assets to the people and asked other government officials to follow his example.

POWERFUL MINORITIES

Most of the nations of Southeast Asia are troubled by sizable minority groups who demand special rights and at times carry on subversive activities. The activities of these minorities, who are sometimes of indigenous origin and sometimes of foreign extraction, frequently agitate the domestic political scene. In the early days of Burma's independence the Karens, the largest tribal group in Burma, fought fiercely for a separate state of their own. They were defeated, but the rebellion retarded Burma's economic and political progress. The people of Sumatra, Celebes, and other Indonesian islands have caused that government much mental anguish and material loss by their uprisings. The Chinese in Malaysia are trying to maintain the integrity of their schools and culture in the face of a determined government effort to bring about greater national unity through education in the Malayan tongue. Every country in Southeast Asia has its minority problems which, if not properly handled, could erupt in sudden bloodshed. These groups are also susceptible to the blandishments of subversive forces which, by the promise of greater autonomy, are attempting to align them in a front against the established government.

The Indians and the Chinese are the two most influential groups of foreign lineage living in Southeast Asia. Both nationalities have been in the area for a long time, and stories about these lands passed on by Indian and Chinese visitors and merchants are often the only eyewitness accounts of events that occurred in the ancient past of Southeast Asian countries. It was, however, under the favored treatment of the Western colonial regimes that these two foreign groups made extraordinary commercial gains in this region. After achieving independence, many countries promulgated laws to curtail the commercial holdings of these people and to limit their enormous landholdings, but they still dominate much of the economic life of the region either in their own names or in the names of citizens used as fronts.

Of these two minority concentrations, the Chinese are by far the larger and the more influential. They are found in every country of Southeast Asia, and their number has been estimated at about 12 million. This figure is subject to further scrutiny because the Chinese are loath to report the exact number of their group. There probably are many Chinese residing in these countries illegally who, if exposed by a census, would be deported. Most Southeast Asian citizens display a degree of antipathy toward these two minorities, which arises in part from their foreign origin and separateness from the community and in part from the sway they hold over the economic life of the country.

The leaders of Southeast Asian countries are suspicious of the Chinese living among them because their numbers and their strategic economic position, coupled with a strong attachment for their original homeland make them a potentially dangerous fifth column in each country. Both the Chinese Nationalists and the Chinese Communists view their people abroad as extensions of their power. The Chinese abroad generally think of themselves as part of the total Chinese community centered either in Communist China or in Nationalist China, from whom they are temporarily separated by space but permanently linked by blood and culture. The Chinese adapt easily to any environment, but they are rarely assimilated. They cleave to their culture wherever they may be and make great sacrifice to perpetuate it in their children. There is a tenacious quality in the Chinese character which enables them to carry on their characteristic way of life despite an alien land and culture.

The Chinese in Southeast Asia have traditionally looked to their embassy, whether Nationalist or Communist, for support and guidance in maintaining themselves on this foreign soil. The embassies have responded by assisting them in any way possible and have requested their assistance from time to time on projects of interest to the Chinese government. Thus the economic and political power of the Chinese group in each country is often at the disposal of the Chinese government to be utilized by it for such purposes as are deemed necessary and desirable.

This unpatriotic attitude on the part of powerful minorities poses grave problems for the governments of Southeast Asia. One of their primary aims is a unified nation-state which has the full allegiance of all who live within its borders. They need the loyal support of all their people if they are to achieve this goal, but some minority groups are not responding. For this reason, the Southeast Asian governments have promulgated laws on citizenship, land ownership, business enterprises, government employment, and even permissible living areas, all designed to reduce the economic power of these groups, to impel them into a closer relationship with their country of residence, and to mitigate any future harm to the country resulting from their activities. The Indonesians rounded up all the Chinese residing in the rural areas of the country and concentrated them in the cities.

In fairness to the Chinese in Southeast Asia it must be emphasized that many of them have intermarried with the inhabitants, entered into the life of the community, and merged their efforts with the majority to help build a viable state. The majority of them are more interested in making money than in advancing a political ideology, but threats of economic and political retribution compel them to support ideological and propaganda activities. It is also true that many of them are more interested in building up the economic power of their own families and groups than in contributing to the economy of the country itself. Obviously, this preference is not in the national interest of their adopted country.

IDEOLOGICAL AND INTERREGIONAL CONFLICT

There is a conflict of political and economic theories in this region which is causing the leaders and the people a certain confusion in their approach to the development of their country. A great many of the modern Southeast Asian leaders are attracted to the philosophy of socialism. They generally look to the West for models of socialism which will permit a combination of a planned society and the preservation of individual freedoms. But they also are impressed with the rapid industrial progress of China and Russia, and they want to emulate this advance in their own countries. They believe that the philosophy of these states has contributed to their successes, and thus the dogmas of Marx are rather popular in the thinking of many Southeast Asian leaders. But at the same time they are antagonized by the subversive activities of the Communists, especially the Chinese, in their own countries. On the one hand they are attracted by the idea of a planned economy; on the other they are repelled by the unceasing efforts of the Communists to subvert their countries.

The political problems of Southeast Asian countries also arise from external sources. Although the nations of this region are tied together by common religions, similar social customs, and in some instances a common ethnic origin, they are divided politically. A long history of invasions, seizures of territory, and rapine has left a residue of skepticism and animosity which still colors their relations with one another. The Cambodians abhor the Vietnamese, and view Thai activities with cynicism. Only recently they stopped all commercial air communication with South Vietnam over a fancied affront, and more recently gave political asylum to a South Vietnamese airman who bombed the presidential palace in Vietnam, killing some of its guards and residents. The North Vietnamese are fighting a savage war in South Vietnam in an attempt to make it a part of their country politically and ideologically, and they are abetted in this effort by a number of sympathetic Laotians. The Thais are skeptical of Cambodian intentions and fearful of a North Vietnam victory which would place a formidable enemy upon their borders. Thailand and Burma have not forgotten past wars between them which have ravaged their lands on a number of occasions. Malaysia is a recently created state which has had less time to build up memories of hate and rancor, but she was torn for years by a struggle with Communist invaders, mostly of Chinese origin, and therefore views with suspicion the present attempts of the Communists in Laos and South Vietnam to conquer these countries. She is also alarmed by the threat to her of growing Communist strength in the city of Singapore on her southern boundary. Relations between the Philippines and Indonesia are marked with some skepticism of each other's intentions. The Indonesians accused the Filipinos of aiding the rebels in their 1961 rebellion against the central government and feel that they are too closely allied with the United States. The Filipinos fear the rise of Communist strength in Indonesia and believe that the policy of President Sukarno has strengthened the Communist hand in Indonesia. They fear a Communist seizure of power in Indonesia which will bring great peril to them. The proximity of suspicious neighbors requires the constant attention of the Southeast Asian statesmen and further adds to the many political problems that are besetting them from within the nation by keeping them all in a state of suspense and uncertainty.

THE THREAT OF COMMUNIST CHINA

Finally, there is one nearby nation, powerful and aggressive, which is of more danger to many of them than their smaller neighbors—Communist China. Fearful and unnerving, Communist China looms over the people of Southeast Asia, an everpresent menace to their way of life and even to their existence as independent countries. For several thousand years China has been a factor in the external affairs of these countries, sometimes threatening, sometimes benevolent, sometimes imperialistic, but always important. Historically, many of the Southeast Asian countries have been influenced by the Chinese. The Chinese governed Vietnam for more than a thousand years, and the Vietnamese language and culture reflect the deep penetration of Chinese thought and practice during this long rule. Former political dominance by the Chinese in Burma is reflected today in the ethnic origins and spoken language of the Burmese people. Even after colonization by Great Britain, Burma acknowledged the overlordship of China by sending decennial tribute missions to Peking. The Thais and Laotians originated in South China and have long been susceptible to political and cultural currents flowing in from China. In their expansive periods, the Chinese ventured as far as Indonesia where they forced some kingdoms to acknowledge the sovereignty of China. They have long been in Malaysia and make up the great majority of the population of Singapore. The location of Luzon, the northern province of the Philippines, close as it is to South China has resulted in trade and cultural interchange between the two areas. There is no country of Southeast Asia where the existence of a belligerent China is not watchfully considered and thoroughly appraised.

Today, the gravitation of China toward the lands of Southeast Asia has been given added impetus by the proselytizing urge of the Chinese Communists and their fanatical belief that their dogmas will be accepted only after the application of force. This fundamental orientation of China, along with her proximity and military might and the presence of leftist subversive forces within their own countries, is proving a fearsome headache to the mainland countries of this region. This problem concerns the Indonesians and Filipinos also, but their water barriers ensure them a modicum of safety at this time. The struggle to impose Communism on the people of Southeast Asia is intensifying, and behind this mighty struggle are Russia and Communist China, but especially Communist China.

Red China supported the North Vietnamese in their successful effort to create a Communist state in North Vietnam and is cooperating closely with these Vietnamese to establish Communist states in Laos and South Vietnam. Laos has already been half-conquered by the Communists and is providing many avenues for the passage of Communist troops and guerrillas to South Vietnam. It is also serving as a base for the air-dropping and storage of arms and equipment for the Communist soldiers and terrorists in Vietnam. Laos was so hopelessly divided that the Americans agreed in 1962 to the establishment of a neutral government in Laos in order to forestall a complete Communist victory in that country. Some of the most savage fighting between Communists and the established government is taking place in South Vietnam.

THE VIETNAMESE WAR

On the body of a young North Vietnamese killed in battle this poem was found, written to his mother:

> *I began to look around and wondered
> what there was to liberate.*
>
> *The market was crowded with people
> in gay mood, the rice fields were
> green with rice plants.*
>
> *From a curved-roof pagoda came the
> sound of a worship bell. The class-
> rooms were full of cheerful children
> singing song in chorus.*
>
> *And in a plot of green the small but-
> terflies were busy on the yellow
> cabbage flowers.*
>
> *Peace and joy reigned throughout the
> country. But why—why did they
> order me to burn the villages, de-
> stroy the bridges, lay mines to sow
> death around?*

And then this soldier asked and answered the question whose blood it was that he had shed.

> *It was the blood of our people, those
> like mother and me.*
>
> *That night, my eyes were filled with
> tears and my sleep with nightmares.*

These words convey much of the doubt and distress that afflict the Vietnamese today. Who are these people whose troubles have drawn thousands of Americans to war for and against them, and threatened the world with a war that may spread beyond their borders?

The People and the Land. Some centuries before the beginning of the Christian era, the ancestors of the Vietnamese wandered from

China to the land around the Red River known as Tongking. This region is now the heartland of Communist North Vietnam. Gradually, the Vietnamese moved southward along the coast, and by about the fifteenth century A.D. they had occupied the delta of the Mekong River in the far south of the country. This area is the great rice-producing heart of South Vietnam and the scene of many skirmishes between the Viet Cong, the Communist-led forces, and the soldiers loyal to the government of Saigon, the capital of South Vietnam.

From around the third century B.C. until the tenth century A.D., the Chinese governed the Vietnamese. During a thousand years or more of close association it was inevitable that the Vietnamese should adopt many of the political, social, and cultural ideas and practices of the Chinese. Since the tenth century, the Vietnamese have been generally free of Chinese domination, but from time to time over the years the Chinese have claimed sovereignty over Vietnam and insisted that the Vietnamese pay tribute to the emperor. The desire of the Chinese Communists to play a dominant role in the affairs of the Vietnamese has a historical foundation. The Vietnamese, however, both North and South, do not relish the thought of Chinese influence, and they have sought to maintain their independence of policy and action.

The Vietnamese have had their share of war and civil struggle during their long history. They conquered their way southward; they have fought with the Cambodians, the Laotians, and the Thais; and they have made themselves feared in their region. In 1884, a French protectorate was established over the country, and in 1940 the Japanese occupied the land. During the Japanese occupation, nationalist forces grouped under the leadership of the Communist Ho Chih Minh and fought against the Japanese. Later, they continued the fight against the French, who tried to reassert their rule over the country at the conclusion of the Second World War in 1945. The French were defeated, and a settlement of the struggle was reached at Geneva on July 21, 1954, which divided the land into two separate countries—North Vietnam and South Vietnam. Today, there is war again in Vietnam as the Communist-led North Vietnamese endeavor to impose their ideology and rule upon the South Vietnamese.

The land is long and narrow, about 1,000 miles in length and from 30 to 300 miles in width. It has frequently been described as resembling a pole from the ends of which dangle two baskets of rice —slim in the middle and bulging at the extremities. The mountains sometimes run down to the sea itself, and endless pools of rice-fields reflect the glare of a burning sun. There are jungles and gloomy rain forests. The population is about 31 million: 17 million live in North Vietnam, and about 14 million live in South Vietnam. Some reside in large cities, in Hanoi, the capital of North Vietnam, and in Saigon, the capital of South Vietnam; but many more live in the farming villages of the countryside where comforts are few, the struggle to survive unrelenting, and knowledge of the world beyond the community very limited. The Tonkinese of the north and the Annamites of the center frequently show their scorn of the people who live in the southern portion, formerly called Cochin-China; and the southerners reciprocate with resentment and distrust.

Origins of the Present Conflict. Under the terms of the Geneva agreement of 1954, many thousands of Ho Chih Minh's supporters were repatriated from South to North Vietnam, but some thousands also stayed in South Vietnam and awaited the call for possible future action. The Geneva agreement also provided for free elections in both halves of the country for the purpose of uniting the country under one government by 1956. The President of South Vietnam, Ngo Dinh Diem, refused to hold elections on the grounds that no free election was possible in North Vietnam and that South Vietnam had not signed the agreement anyway. Ho Chih Minh had expected to win these elections; but when President Diem refused to hold them and began instead a rather successful policy—at least at first —of tightening his control over South Vietnam, Ho called upon his supporters in the South to act. A revolt started in South Vietnam which has not ended yet.

With persuasion and with force, the anti-government guerrillas gradually extended their control over the countryside. Many non-communists joined the "Front for the Liberation of South Vietnam," the formal name of the group which opposed the Saigon government, because they believed Diem's government was corrupt, unmindful of the needs of the people, undemocratic, and lacking social consciousness. Although those fighting against the Saigon government are called Viet Cong, or "Vietnamese Communists," it is reported that among the members of the Central Committee of the Front are non-Communist professional men, students, Catholics, Buddhists, and peasants. But many are also convinced that this is a Communist-front organization and that it is Ho Chih Minh, ruler of North Vietnam, who really controls and manipulates this organization for his own purposes.

By 1960, there was little doubt that the Viet Cong were winning the war in South Vietnam and that the statement of North Vietnam's Defense Minister, General Giap, "Thousands of small victories accumulate into a great success," was being proven true. The people of South Vietnam lived in the midst of chaos and terror. The Saigon government ruled by day in the cities and wherever it had soldiers; the Viet Cong covered the countryside by night. Nowhere was there safety; no man felt secure. It was dangerous to travel the roads by day without an armed escort. Ambushes, the burning of buses and automobiles, the mining of roads, and the murder of travelers were common occurrences. Every day the newspapers reported incidents ranging from pitched battles between large government and Viet-Cong forces to the kidnapping of individuals. The social, economic, and political life of South Vietnam was being slowly strangled. By 1961, it was apparent that the government of South Vietnam was near defeat. The United States became extremely concerned, and President Kennedy sent General Maxwell Taylor to the battle scene to investigate and recommend action.

U.S. Participation in the War. The Americans had been concerned with the Vietnamese war long before this time. In 1950, the United States started to support the French financially in their struggle against the Vietnamese, and it is estimated that a total of $1.2 billion was given by the Americans to the French in their attempt to reassert their dominance over the Vietnamese. When the French were on the edge of defeat in 1954, some American officials urged a military intervention in the war, but the idea was vetoed by President Eisenhower. After the partition of Vietnam, the United States sent 600 military advisers to South Vietnam, and by 1957 this number had risen to 800. After General Taylor returned to Washington with his recommendations, the number of American military advisers in South Vietnam increased to 11,000. At that time, the Americans also started to fly the Vietnamese into battle and to construct air-fields, port facilities, and other military installations. But the political and military situation continued to worsen. In November of 1963, the Diem government was overthrown and Diem himself was killed. Since that time there have been numerous coups and changes in government. The Viet Cong continued to grow stronger, and the number of American forces continued to grow to thwart them. It is now estimated that by 1966 the number of American forces fighting in Vietnam will increase to more than 200,000.

Why Are the Americans in Vietnam? On April 7, 1965, President Johnson gave the official reasons why the United States is in Vietnam. "We are there," he said,

> because we have a promise to keep. Since 1954 every American President has offered support to the people of South Vietnam . . . Thus over many years, we have made a national pledge to help South Vietnam defend its independence . . . To dishonor that pledge, to abandon this small and brave nation to its enemy—and to the terror that must follow—would be an unforgivable wrong . . . We are also there to strengthen world order. Around the globe—from Berlin to Thailand—are people whose well-being rests, in part, on the belief they can count on us if they are attacked. To leave Vietnam to its fate would shake the confidence of all these people in the value of American commitment. The result would be increased unrest and instability, or even war . . . We are there because there are great stakes in the balance. Let no one think that retreat from Vietnam would bring an end to conflict. The battle would be renewed in one country and then another. The central lesson of our time is that the appetite of aggression is never satisfied. To withdraw from one battlefield means only to prepare for the next. We must say in Southeast Asia—as we did in Europe—in the words of the Bible: "Hitherto shalt thou come, but no further."

U.S. Objectives in Vietnam. President Johnson in this same speech also stated the official objective of the United States in Vietnam. "Our objective is the independence of South Vietnam, and its freedom from attack. We want nothing for ourselves—only that the people of South Vietnam be allowed to guide their own country in their own way." He stated that we have increased our military support of the South Vietnamese government "in order to slow down aggression. We do this to increase the confidence of the brave people of South Vietnam . . . and we do this to convince the leaders of North Vietnam—and all who seek to share their conquest—of a simple fact: We will not be defeated. We will not grow tired. We will not withdraw, either openly or under the cloak of a meaningless agreement." He continued:

I wish it were possible to convince others with words of what we now find it necessary to say with guns and planes: Armed hostility is futile. Our resources are equal to any challenge. Because we fight for values and a principle, rather than territory or colonies, our patience and determination are unending. Once this is clear, then it should also be clear that the only path for reasonable men is the path of peaceful settlement. Such a peace demands an independent South Vietnam—securely guaranteed and able to shape its own relationships to all others, free from outside interference, tied to no alliance, a military base for no other country. These are the essentials of any final settlement . . . We have stated this position over and over again fifty times and more to friend and foe alike. And we remain ready, with this purpose, for the unconditional discussions.

Criticism of American Policy in Vietnam. There are those at home and abroad who criticize American policy in Vietnam. Some comment upon the apparent disregard of the political, economic, and social problems which are at the root of the Vietnamese conflict, and bluntly warn that these basic causes of unrest cannot be eliminated with guns. Some believe that a military victory in Vietnam is impossible in the long run and that the Americans should place more emphasis upon an economic and political rehabilitation of the country which will provide a lasting foundation for peace. Others state that the American bombing policy in Vietnam is making more enemies than friends and rendering a final political settlement most difficult. The critics generally agree that the United States is guided more by a strategy of war than a strategy of peace in Vietnam. Still others say that there is no stable government in South Vietnam, that the people give little loyalty to the government that is in power at any particular time; these people wonder whether a successful war can be waged under the guidance of an insecure and unstable political leadership. Some Americans in high position fear that American involvement in Vietnam could lead to an even larger struggle and eventually escalate into a nuclear conflict. Some of them state that the bombing of North Vietnam is hardening the Vietnamese against the Americans and may force them to turn to Red China for aid. They ask, Are the Americans really ready to engage in war with Red China? Finally, there are those who concede that the Americans may win the war, but they feel that in the process of winning a military victory, the Americans may lose the friendship of the Vietnamese people.

Conclusion. Few of those involved feel fully satisfied with the progress of the war in Vietnam, neither the North Vietnamese, the Viet Cong, the South Vietnamese, nor the Americans. Casualties are running high, and mostly it is the Vietnamese who suffer. Tons of bombs drop on jungle hideouts and villages thought to shelter the Viet Cong, and refugees throng in their thousands to camps hastily constructed and poorly maintained. Rice production has dropped, and many in this former rice-exporting region must now be supplied with foreign rice and foodstuffs. There is always the question, Can the fragile economic and social structure of the South Vietnamese survive much longer? All would like to see this war end quickly, but all know that it could continue for many years. Americans are finding the Viet Cong tough, shrewd, elusive, and the heat and terrain uncomfortable, unfamiliar, and dangerous. The threat of Chinese intervention and of nuclear warfare is always present, and frustrations abound for both sides. It is a war of sad ironies where women and children die with the Viet Cong in tunnels, bunkers, and peasant huts, and where a North Vietnamese soldier can write about the blood shed there:

> *It was the blood of our people, those*
> *like mother and me.*

> *That night, my eyes were filled with*
> *tears and my sleep with nightmares.*

EXTERNAL POLITICAL PROBLEMS

In addition to their fear of Communism, the people of Southeast Asia have an abhorrence of colonialism in any form. Since most of them were under the colonial regimes of Western powers for some years, the deep suspicion they developed of the intentions of the Western powers in Asia has not yet been completely dissolved. Anti-imperialism and anticolonialism are still shibboleths to arouse the emotions of the Asians and give them a will to fight. Until settled in 1962, the West Irian question was capable of firing the Indonesians into a high emotional flame, and Indians supported

Nehru wholeheartedly in his forceful seizure of Goa. The colonial regimes left a tainted heritage in the East which still conditions Asian feelings and attitudes toward the West.

The Southeast Asian countries are caught up in the great power struggle being waged between the blocs headed by the United States and Soviet Russia. International issues are constantly arising on which their moral support is sought, and their votes are wooed in the United Nations. It is sometimes extremely difficult for some of these small countries to take a stand, for they will be "damned if they do and damned if they don't." Some of them are extremely afraid of offending Red China because such action might bring upon them swift and terrible retribution. In their search for the safest path between these mighty forces some of them have adopted a policy of neutrality or nonalignment. They believe that holding themselves aloof and impartial with regard to the issues of the Cold War is the best way to ward off danger and to preserve the independent existence of their nations. Burma, Cambodia, Indonesia, and Laos, encouraged in this policy by India, Russia, and China, are trying to maintain neutrality on the international scene. Until their clash with the Chinese, the Indians believed that neutrality was in their national interest. They still hold to a policy of neutrality between the United States and the U.S.S.R. The Russians and the Chinese encourage neutralism because they have found that widespread neutrality works generally to their benefit; communist parties within neutral countries have greater opportunities to organize and expand than those within countries tied to the opposing bloc. Moreover, as the Communists know, many leaders of the Southeast Asian countries are oriented in their education and background more to the United States and Europe than to Russia, and if not neutral, would probably tend to join with these areas rather than with the Communists.

Other Southeast Asian countries have chosen to line up with one bloc or the other in the pursuit of security for their war-threatened region. South Vietnam, Thailand, and the Philippines are tied by treaties to the United States and other Western powers. Malaysia, although not linked by formal treaty to the Western bloc, in fact can be considered a member of the definite anticommunist bloc in Southeast Asia. North Vietnam is the only country formally linked to the Communist bloc, although Laos, if Laos falls to the Communists, will soon be the second one.

The political problems of Southeast Asia are many and pressing. Even the peaceful heritage of Buddhism, with its traditional co-operative spirit, does not appear capable of resolving the passionate hostilities that threaten to devastate this area. Freedom, independence, economic security, time-honored religions, traditions, and cultures, even existence itself, are in danger of being destroyed in Southeast Asia by war, the poisons of ideological suspicions, and the deadly erosion of the Cold War. It will require all the intelligence, courage, common sense, and dedication that can be mustered by the positively oriented people of Southeast Asia to check the negative, destructive forces that are besieging their land and people.

CHAPTER 40

ASIANS ARE PEOPLE
WITH A DESTINY

Now numbering over half the human race, the Asians of today have finally begun to assert the human right enjoyed by more fortunate people elsewhere to determine their own destiny. Refusing to continue the playthings of fate, absolute monarchs, and other nations, they are resolved to shape their own destiny to suit their own needs, their own wants, and their own ideals.

Asians are destined to eat better. Famine, for thousands of years a familiar guest in their homes, is no longer considered the decree of sadistic spirits and gods, or the inevitable response of a violated earth, to be passively accepted; it is now regarded as a community problem which can be understood in social and economic terms and solved by the joint efforts of human minds and human hands. Hunger, a state in which many Asians continually live, is no longer regarded as a natural condition, but a cause for active dissatisfaction, and Asians are resolved to remove it from their destiny.

Asians are destined to be better informed. Education and literacy have been idealized by countless generations of Asian people. The scholar stood at the apex of Chinese society, and only he could administer the affairs of state. The educated Brahmins were of the highest status in India. The Japanese hierarchy was dominated by the soldier-aristocrat, but tradition required that he be able to read and write. In Korea, Indo-China, Burma, Thailand, Indonesia, and the Philippine Islands, the educated man, one who could read and write, is the respected man. Today in Asia there is a tremendous drive toward the goal of universal literacy. Through literacy, Asians expect to gain access to the accumulated knowledge of mankind and thus build for themselves better and happier lives. Asian leaders are determined to industrialize their countries as fully and rapidly as possible; since modern industry requires workers who can read and write, these leaders are actively promoting mass education. Schools and village reading classes are springing up all over Asia.

Asians are destined to collectivize. Their leaders believe that they do not have the time to build up their industrial establishments in the same leisurely manner as did the great industrialized countries of the West such as Great Britain and the United States. They maintain that the quickening tempo of world events, the economic and political security of their countries, and the insistent demands of their people for a better standard of living require that they industrialize their countries at a breakneck speed, and they believe that this goal cannot be achieved without the collective organization of all the people and massive infusions of state aid.

Asians are destined to participate more in domestic politics. In non-Communist Asia people are becoming actively involved in the political life of their countries. The leaders think and speak of themselves as the elected leaders of the people, whether they are or not. Asian people are told that it is *their* government and *their* will that the government expresses. Elections are held in every country, and although the choice of candidates has usually been quite limited, most of the people do get a chance to express an opinion in a formal way. This is a new experience for them but one they have taken to with ease and enthusiasm. In Japan, India, Indonesia, the Philippine Islands, Malaysia, and Burma, the candidates have gone out among the people to woo votes and detail their platforms, and there have been enthusiastic turnouts at elections.

Never before in the history of Asia have the ordinary people been given the impression that they are important in the political life of the country. Never before have so many Asians had the experience of expressing a preference, though a limited one, for a political leader. Most leaders in the past came with the sword, and they did not seek the permission of the people to rule. That permission is now formally sought by most Asian politicians, and in some countries it has been refused.

Nehru was an excellent example of a leading politician who spent much of his time with his people. It was not uncommon for him to speak to a hundred thousand or more at one time, and it is reported that, on one occasion, he took a six-day motor tour in which he traveled over two hundred miles and made twenty speeches a day. He tried very hard to give his people a feeling of participation in government.

Participation by the people in politics will continue to increase in Asia as the people learn how to think and act in modern democratic ways. They are beginning to feel that they have importance as individuals and that this importance takes on added meaning when expressed in political action.

Asians are destined to be more respected. Perhaps nothing has been more resented by the Asian than the conception of him as inferior by the white Westerner, whether colonizer, missionary, businessman, or tourist. Clubs for white people only, in Bombay, Calcutta, Singapore, Hong Kong, Shanghai, Tokyo, Manila, and elsewhere, were and are hated symbols of white arrogance. City parks forbidden to natives by the British during their rule in Asia are painfully and bitterly remembered. A sense of elation spread throughout Asia, sometimes hidden, sometimes displayed, when the Japanese Asians defeated the whites in the early days of the Second World War.

Asians are determined to be respected. They feel that they are the equal of any other human group and the superior of many. Many of them are ready to forfeit law, order, and their own lives in order to obtain this respect.

The urge in most Asian countries to build up economic, political, and military power is in part motivated by the desire of these nations to be treated as equals of the Western nations. The reluctance to employ foreign personnel, the extreme sensitivity to any implied slur by white foreigners, the sometimes harsh treatment of white Westerners living in Asian countries, the desperate, defiant attitude shown when logic is sometimes on the side of the Westerner, the resentment at being forced by circumstances to accept charity from Western nations, the insistence on running their countries without support from foreigners, especially if it has been offered with any hint of foreign superiority, are all in response to offenses given by past and present generations of white foreigners.

Asians are destined to become more nationalistic. Nationalism is a creative emotional factor today in Asia. Westerners taught the Asian people to forge the bonds of a new loyalty—loyalty to a nation-state. Previously the Asian people gave their first loyalties to the family, the clan, the caste, the class, or to individuals, but seldom to a national entity. Patriotism, love of country, was not an important motivation as it was in the West. When the Westerners came to Asia, they brought the spirit of nationalism with them. Asians sharing the same territory and possessing characteristics in common which distinguished them from neighboring Asians, such as a common language, race, tradition, history, and religion, began to think of themselves as a separate and special body of people—as a nation. The leaders of the various Asian countries in order to foster internal unity, deliberately promoted this feeling of belonging to a special group. Japan is an outstanding example of a people deliberately infused with a feeling of national pride, centered in this case in an emperor alleged to be divine. Asians, following the example of Westerners, attempted, quite successfully, to express this cultural unity in the establishment of independent nations. Today patriotism is emerging as a strong motivation for the actions of the Asian people. The nation is replacing the family, the clan, the caste, the emperor, as the first loyalty of the people. The political and intellectual leaders of the Asian countries are using every device to bring about a more intense and devoted love of the nation-state. Asians are becoming like Western nationals in their response to a waving flag and a stirring national anthem.

Asians are destined to resist colonialism everywhere. The Asian people detest colonialism so much that they fight it not only on their own soil, but wherever it exists. Liquidating the remnants of colonial administrations, which are still scattered here and there in Asia, is the first concern of the Asian people. Indonesia fought bitterly to liquidate the Dutch colonial regime in New Guinea—Indonesians refer to this territory as West Irian—and replace the Dutch regime with an Indonesian government. India wrested Goa from the Portuguese.

The broader attitude of Asian hostility to colonialism was expressed before the United Nations General Assembly by Dr. Ide Agung, Indonesia's Foreign Minister, when he said:

> The problems of colonialism are, of course, of particular interest to us and to the peoples of Asia and Africa, in general. The Asian-African member states have this year . . . again brought before this Organization the colonial problems, such as the questions of Morocco, West Irian and, for the first time, that of Algeria. . . . Certainly, one cannot regard with equanimity the growing toll of lives lost every day in Algeria. . . . Nor can one calmly stand by and watch while the basic human rights, guaranteed in our Charter to all peoples, are relentlessly crushed and repressed in Algeria.

Asians are destined to resist external oppression. They have had their fill of foreign invaders who have lived off their land and dictated laws for them. Since the most recent oppressors in the long history of the Asian people were Westerners, Asian statesmen are particularly vigilant lest the great Western powers attempt to repeat their former successful invasions. The cry of "imperialism!" is still a familiar cry in Asia, and it conjures up vivid memories of Western administrators, Western soldiers, Western economic practices, Western exploitation, and Western arrogance. Imperialism is not a dead issue in Asia, but a vital one able to arouse the Asian people to intense and dedicated defiance.

But Asians are destined to engage in internecine conflict. The juxtaposition of three major powers in Asia—India, China, Japan —with a number of less powerful nations has already resulted in incidents, fears, border tensions, and conflicting spheres of influence. Nowhere are these problems more vividly illustrated than in the *White Papers* issued by the government of Pakistan entitled *India's War Propaganda Against Pakistan.* These documents charge that the Indian leaders have:

> never really reconciled themselves to the Partition of the Indo-Pakistan sub-continent and the creation of Pakistan. They hoped that it would prove a temporary phase and that Pakistan would soon be absorbed by India.
>
> The number of books and pamphlets which have been issued since the Partition in various Indian languages and advocating absorption of Pakistan into India must be running into hundreds.
>
> A study of the Indian press leaves no doubt that this absorption of Pakistan into India is to be brought about by means of force. In pursuance of this aim Indian leaders and Indian press have not only been urging the absorption of Pakistan by India but have seized every opportunity to preach war against Pakistan.

The feeling and spirit that pervade these official words of the government of Pakistan are reflected in the words of many of the other Asian nations with reference to their neighbors. The Nationalist Chinese government on Formosa conveys in even stronger language its hatred and suspicion of the Communist Chinese government on the mainland. South Korean spokesmen use very strong language when they speak of North Korean officials. Laos, Cambodia, and South Vietnam are extremely wary of the activities of the Communist officials of North Vietnam. Thailand, Burma, Malaysia, are all fearful of the colossus of Communist China on their northern borders. Some of the countries of Asia are suspicious of the intentions of the Japanese.

There is a new, dynamic spirit abroad in Asia. No longer the slow-moving, nonchanging Asia of storybook and movie, it is now a militant, demanding, searching Asia, prepared to fight for its future. The people of Asia now know that there is hope for themselves and their families. They have learned from Westerners, from Asians educated in the West, from Asians educated in their own schools, and from their leaders and neighbors, that they have the power and capacity to wrest a better living from the earth. The exciting idea that man is not fated to live desolate and insecure has aroused them to action and transformed them into crusaders marching toward a better world. The new revelation that poverty can be abolished, that man is under no cosmic necessity to suffer starvation at

The juxtaposition of India and Communist China has resulted in
continual tension between these two major Asian powers, a tension made more explosive by the long-standing border disputes
between India and Pakistan.

regular intervals, that living ill-housed and ill-clothed is not the decree of some incomprehensible fate, that freedom and good government are not only desirable but possible, has stimulated them to try to eliminate forever the shadows of political and economic uncertainty under which they have lived for thousands of years.

The Asians are dreaming of a future when they will have enough to eat, comfortable homes, education for their children, medical services and medicine for their sick, respect for themselves as individuals, freedom, peace, and political stability and security. They want these dreams realized, preferably within their lifetime. They place continuous and unyielding pressure upon their leaders to secure for them more and better opportunities for happiness. They champion those who earnestly seek the fulfillment of their dreams; they are sullen and threatening toward those who are obstructing their destiny, and their protest is sometimes written in their blood.

The goading challenge facing the Asians and the world is how to realize their impelling visions of a better life. Frustration, turmoil, and chaos will result from an unrealized destiny, for if they must to make their dreams come true, the Asians are destined to sacrifice themselves—and others.

SELECTED REFERENCES

It is not possible to list all the writings on Asia that can be read with pleasure and profit. The following books will lead the interested reader to other authors who can provide additional valuable and interesting information on the Asian people.

Those books and articles likely to prove especially valuable to the general reader are marked with an asterisk.

Asia

Ceadel, Eric B., ed., *Literatures of the East: An Appreciation* (London: John Murray, 1953). An introduction to the literature of Asia.

* Cressey, George B., *Asia's Lands and Peoples* (2nd ed.; New York: McGraw-Hill, 1951). An excellent general introduction.

* ————, *The Patterns of Asia*, edited by Norton Ginsburg (Englewood Cliffs, New Jersey: Prentice-Hall, 1958). Quoted on page 19.

Dean, Vera, and others, *The Nature of the Non-Western World* (New York: Mentor Books, 1957). The significance of nationalism and social change in Asia.

* De Bary, Theodore, ed., *Sources of Indian Tradition* (New York: Columbia University Press, 1958), *Sources of Chinese Tradition* (the same, 1960), and *Sources of Japanese Tradition* (the same, 1958). Three indispensable reference books on Asian thought.

* East, W. G. and O. H. K. Spate, *The Changing Map of Asia: A Political Geography* (New York: Dutton, 1950)

Fradier, Georges, *East and West: Towards Mutual Understanding* (Paris: Unesco, 1959).

Gunther, John, *Inside Asia* (New York: Harper & Bros., 1942). Informative and well written.

Michael, Franz H. and George E. Taylor, *The Far East in the Modern World* (New York: Henry Holt, 1956). A good introduction to contemporary Asian politics.

* Peterson, A. D. C., *The Far East: A Social Geography* (2nd ed.; London: Duckworth, 1951)

* Smith, Huston, *The Religions of Man* (New York: Mentor Books, 1958). A readable paperback with clear and concise accounts of the Asian religions.

Visser, H. F. E., *Art Treasures from the East* (Amsterdam: De Spieghel, 1954)

Ward, Barbara, *The Interplay of East and West* (New York: Norton, 1957). Deals with the problem of mutual understanding.

Yohannan, John, ed., *A Treasury of Asian Literature* (New York: John Day, 1956). An introduction to the literature of Asia.

India

* Basham, A. L., *The Wonder That Was India* (London: Sidgwick & Jackson, 1954). An excellent introduction to traditional India. Quoted on pages 93 and 108.

Brown, Donald M., *The White Umbrella: Indian Political Thought from Manu to Gandhi* (Berkeley: University of California Press, 1953)

Burlingame, Eugene W., *Buddhist Parables* (New York: Yale University Press, 1922). Quoted on page 71.

* Chandrasekhar, S., "The Family in India," *Marriage and Family Living,* Vol. 16 (November, 1954), pp. 336-42. A succinct account of the Indian family. Quoted on page 103.

* Dube, S. C., *Indian Village* (Ithaca: Cornell University Press, 1955). A good introduction to the village scene in India.

Dutt, G. S., *A Woman of Bengal, Being the Life of Saroj Nalini* (London: Hogarth Press, 1929). Gives valuable insight into the attitudes of the Indian woman. Quoted on page 99.

Emerson, Gertrude, *Voiceless India* (New York: John Day, 1944). A warm and engrossing book that sparkles with revealing descriptions of India's rural and social scene. Quoted on page 39.

Fisher, Louis, *The Life of Mahatma Gandhi* (New York: Harper & Bros., 1950). Covers various aspects of India's political life.

* Gandhi, Mohandas K., *An Autobiography or The Story of My Experiments with Truth* (Ahmedabad: Navajivan Publishing House, 1945). A candid account of himself and his times by a man whose name is synonymous with India's modern history and development.

Gates, Katherine, ed. and trans., *Ramabai Ranade, Himself: The Autobiography of a Hindu Lady* (New York: David McKay, 1938). Illuminates the attitudes of the Indian woman. Quoted on page 100.

Ghurye, G. S., *Caste and Class in India* (4th ed. in preparation; New York: Heinman). A competent study of the caste system.

Gist, N. P., "Caste in Transition," *Phylon,* Vol. 15, No. 2, pp. 155-64. An excellent account of the changing character of caste.

Griffiths, Sir Percival, *The British Impact on India* (London: MacDonald, 1952). Gives a good picture of modern India's political institutions and ideas.

Grousset, René, *The Civilization of India,* translated by Catherine A. Phillips (New York: Tudor Publishing Co., 1939). An informative and sensitive introduction.

————, *In the Footsteps of the Buddha* (London: Routledge and Kegan Paul, Ltd., 1932). Quoted on page 174.

Haigh, Sir Henry, *Some Leading Ideas of Hinduism* (London: Charles H. Kelley, 1903). Contains illuminating statements on this religion. Quoted on page 66.

Hamilton, Clarence H., ed., *Buddhism: A Religion of Infinite Compassion* (New York: The Liberal Arts Press, 1952). Quoted on page 173.

* Morgan, Kenneth W., *The Religion of the Hindus* (New York: Ronald Press, 1953). A good introduction. Quoted on page 63.

* Nehru, Jawaharlal, *The Discovery of India* (Calcutta: Signet Press, 1946). Strongly recommended as a basic book by India's key political figure.

Overstreet, Gene D. and Marshall Windmiller, *Communism in India* (Berkeley: University of California Press, 1959)

Spear, Percival, *India: A Modern History* (Ann Arbor: The University of Michigan Press, 1961). Solid, well organized, and well written.

Zinkin, Taya, *India Changes!* (New York: Oxford University Press, 1958). Points up the transitional social problems of modern India.

Pakistan

Bolitho, Hector, *Jinnah: Creator of Pakistan* (New York: Macmillan, 1955). One of the few good biographies about the "Father of Pakistan," who should be better known in the West.

* *Crescent and Green* (London: Cassell & Co., Ltd., 1955). Contains a number of solid essays by various authors on the life and culture of Pakistan.

Ikram, S. M., and Percival Spear, eds., *The Cultural Heritage of Pakistan* (New York: Oxford University Press, 1955). An informed treatment of the cultural background of the Pakistanis.

Iqbal, Sir Muhammad, *Poems from Iqbal,* translated by V. G. Kiernan (London: John Murray, 1955), and *The Secrets of the Self,* translated by Reynold A. Nicholson (Lahore: Muhammad Ashraf, 1955). The spirit of Islam and Pakistan glows in the lyrical verses of Sir Muhammad Iqbal.

Pickthall, Muhammad Marmaduke, *The Meaning of the Glorious Koran* (New York: Mentor Books, 1953). An inexpensive paperback translation.

The Holy Qu'ran, 2 Vols., translation and commentary by Abdullah Yusuf Ali (New York: Hafner Publishing Co., 1946). Copiously documented with commentaries and notes. Quotations from the Koran appearing in present volume were taken largely from this work.

Spate, O. H. K., *India and Pakistan* (New York: E. P. Dutton, 1953). The chapters on Pakistan are informative.

Ceylon

Bailey, Sydney D., *Ceylon* (London: Hutchinson's University Library, 1952). A good introduction.

East Asia

* Clyde, Paul H., *The Far East* (Englewood Cliffs, New Jersey: Prentice-Hall, 4th ed. forthcoming in 1963). A good general introduction.

Linebarger, Paul, Djang Chu, and Ardath Burks, *Far Eastern Governments and Politics: China and Japan* (2nd ed.; Princeton: Van Nostrand, 1956). An informative presentation of politics in East Asia.

MacNair, H. F., and Donald Lach, *Modern Far Eastern International Relations* (Princeton: Van Nostrand, 1955)

China

Barnett, A. Doak, *Communist China and Asia: A Challenge to American Policy* (New York: Vintage Books, 1960). An authoritative treatise on Communist China and its international activities.

Bonsall, B. S., *Confucianism and Taoism* (London: The Epworth Press, 1934). A helpful work on Chinese ideology. Quoted on pages 151 and 153.

Buck, Pearl S., *The Good Earth* (New York: John Day, 1949). A classic description of peasant life in China which can be read at one sitting.

Chiang K'ai-shek, *China's Destiny*, translated by Wang Chung-hui (New York: Macmillan, 1947). The thought of one of the living leaders of China.

Chinese Art, by many authors (London: B. T. Batsford, Ltd., 1952)

* Ch'u Chai and Wineberg Chai, *The Changing Society of China* (New York: Mentor Books, 1962). An excellent introduction.

* ———, *The Story of Chinese Philosophy* (New York: Washington Square Press, 1961). A basic work on Chinese ideology.

* Creel, Herrlee G., *Chinese Thought from Confucius to Mao Tse-tung* (Chicago: University of Chicago Press, 1953). A good introduction to Chinese ideology.

Duyvendak, J. J. L., trans., *Book of Lord Shang* (London: Arthur Probsthain). A helpful presentation of Legalism. Quoted on page 166.

Fairbank, John K., *The United States and China* (2nd ed.; Cambridge: Harvard University Press, 1958)

Giles, Herbert A., *A History of Chinese Literature* (New York: Grove Press, 1958)

Goodrich, L. C., *A Short History of the Chinese People* (3rd ed.; New York: Harper & Bros., 1959). A concise survey.

Hsien Chin-hu, *The Common Descent Group in China and Its Functions* (New York: The Viking Fund, 1948). A comprehensive work on the clan in China. Quoted on page 191.

Hsu, Francis, *Americans and Chinese* (New York: Abelard-Schuman, Ltd., 1953). A provocative interpretation. Quoted on page 152.

* Lang, Olga, *Chinese Family and Society* (New Haven: Yale University Press, 1946). Aspects of rural and social life.

* Latourette, Kenneth Scott, *The Chinese, Their History and Culture* (New York: Macmillan, 1950)

Lee Shao-chang, *Popular Buddhism in China* (Shanghai: The Commercial Press, 1939). The quotation from the Buddhabhasita-Anitayuh Sutra on page 175 was taken from this work.

Legg, James, trans., *Four Books, Chinese Classics,* and *Hsiao Ching* (London: Oxford, 1893-1895). These classic translations of Chinese philosophers were helpful sources for the original quotations used to illustrate Chinese ideology in the present volume.

Levy, Marion, *The Family Revolution in Modern China* (Cambridge: Harvard University Press, 1949). Aspects of Chinese rural and social life.

Liao, W. K., trans., *The Complete Works of Han Fei-tsu* (London: Arthur Probsthain, 1939). Quoted on page 168.

* MacNair, Harley, ed., *China* (Berkeley: University of California Press, 1946)

Mao Tse-tung, *New Democracy: Selected Works of Mao Tse-tung* (London: Lawrence and Wishart, 1958). The thought of one of the living leaders of China.

Redfield, Margaret, ed., *China's Gentry* (Chicago: University of Chicago Press, 1953). A somewhat controversial book but one containing many elements of truth about China's former upper class.

Smith, Arthur H., *Village Life in China* (New York: F. H. Revell Co., 1899). A classic description of the social and village life of the Chinese.

"Strategy and Tactics of World Communism," 81st Congress, House Document No. 154, Part 3 (Washington, D.C., 1949). Quoted on page 208.

The Asians: Their Heritage and Their Destiny

Sun Yat-sen, *Three Principles of the People,* translated by Frank Price (London: Routledge and Kegan Paul, Ltd., 1928). Gives valuable insight into the political thought of China. Quoted on page 208.

Snow, Edgar, *Red Star Over China* (New York: Random House, 1938). An enthusiastic and uncritical account which gives a favorable impression of Red China twenty years ago.

Tu Fu, China's Greatest Poet, translation and commentary by William Hung (Cambridge: Harvard University Press, 1952). Poems by one of the world's greatest poets. Quoted on pages 150-151.

Waley, Arthur, *Three Ways of Thought in Ancient China* (London: George Allen & Unwin, Ltd., 1936). A basic work on Chinese philosophy.

Wang, C. C., trans., *Dream of the Red Chamber* (New York: Doubleday, 1929). A good translation of a classic Chinese novel which graphically portrays social life in traditional China.

* Wieger, Fr. L., *China Throughout the Ages* (Hsien-hsien: The Mission Press, 1928). This excellent general work on China's culture and thought has withstood the passage of time.

Winfield, Gerald, *China: The Land and the People* (New York: William Sloane, 1948)

* Yang, Martin C., *A Chinese Village* (New York: Columbia University Press, 1945). Aspects of Chinese rural and social life.

Korea

Kyang Cho Chung, *Korea Tomorrow: Land of the Morning Calm* (New York: Macmillan, 1956)

McCune, George M., *Korea Today* (Cambridge: Harvard University Press, 1950)

Japan

* Benedict, Ruth, *The Chrysanthemum and the Sword: Patterns of Japanese Culture* (Boston: Houghton Mifflin, 1946). An informative study of Japanese social life.

Borton, Hugh, ed., *Japan* (Ithaca: Cornell University Press, 1951). A good general introduction.

* Embree, John, *Suye Mura: A Japanese Village* (Chicago: University of Chicago Press, 1939). A useful introduction to Japanese social life.

Gibney, Frank, *Five Gentlemen of Japan: The Portrait of a Nation's Character* (New York: Farrar, Straus, 1953). An excellent general introduction. Quoted on page 7.

Hearn, Lafcadio, *The Selected Writings of Lafcadio Hearn,* edited by

Henry Goodman (New York: The Citadel Press, 1949). Contains appealing descriptions of the Japanese people by a man who labored for many years to catch and convey their spirit and who loved them deeply. Quoted on page 259.

Ishimoto, Baroness Shidzue, *Facing Two Ways: The Story of My Life* (New York: Farrar & Rinehart, 1935). Yields insight into the domestic life of the Japanese and the attitudes of the women of Japan. Quoted on pages 254-55.

Keene, Donald, ed., *The Anthology of Japanese Literature* (New York: Grove Press, 1955)

* ———, *Living Japan* (London: William Heinemann, Ltd., 1959). A wonderful introduction.

Malm, William P., *Japanese Music and Musical Instruments* (Rutland, Vermont: Charles E. Tuttle Co., 1959). An introduction to the music of Japan.

Mears, Helen, *Year of the Wild Boar* (Philadelphia: J. B. Lippincott Co., 1942). Warm glimpses of the family and daily life of Japan and of the Japanese woman. Cited on pages 247, 257, and 260.

Michener, James A., *The Floating World* (New York: Random House, 1954). An interesting treatment of Japanese prints. Quoted on page 7.

Reischauer, Edwin O., *Japan: Past and Present* (2nd ed.; New York: Knopf, 1953). An excellent general introduction. Quoted on pages 273-74.

Sansom, G. B., *Japan: A Short Cultural History* (Rev. ed.; New York: Appleton-Century, 1944)

———, *The Western World and Japan: A Study in the Interaction of European and Asiatic Cultures* (New York: Knopf, 1950)

* Seidensticker, Edward, and the Editors of *Life*, *Japan* (New York Times, Inc., 1961). A beautifully illustrated and sensitively written introduction to Japan.

Webb, Herschel, *An Introduction to Japan* (2nd ed.; New York: Columbia University Press, 1957)

Southeast Asia

Benitez, Conrado, *History of the Philippines: Economic, Social, Cultural, Political* (Rev. ed.; New York: Ginn, 1954). Good general introduction to the Philippines.

Bernstein, David, *The Philippine Story* (New York: Farrar, Straus, 1947). A good general introduction.

Busch, Noel, *Thailand: An Introduction to Modern Siam* (Princeton: Van Nostrand, 1959). A good introduction to this country.

* Buss, Claude A., *The Arc of Crisis: Nationalism and Neutralism in Asia Today* (New York: Doubleday, 1961). Deals with the political aspects of South-East Asia at both the national and the international level.

Buttinger, Joseph, *The Smaller Dragon: A Political History of Viet-Nam* (New York: Praeger, 1958). A detailed history of this country from the earliest period to modern times. A mine of information.

* Butwell, Richard, *South-East Asia Today and Tomorrow* (New York: Praeger, 1961). National and international politics in South-East Asia.

Cady, John F., *A History of Modern Burma* (Ithaca: Cornell University Press, 1958)

Champassak, Sisouk, *Storm Over Laos: A Contemporary History* (New York: Praeger, 1961)

* DuBois, Cora, *Social Forces in South-East Asia* (Cambridge: Harvard University Press, 1959). Social life and social change in South-East Asia.

Fifield, Russell H., *The Diplomacy of South-East Asia: 1945-1958* (New York: Harper & Bros., 1958)

* Hall, E. G. E., *A History of South-East Asia* (New York: St Martin's Press, 1955). A good general history.

Herz, Martin F., *A Short History of Cambodia* (New York: Praeger, 1958). A good introduction to this country.

Kahin, George, *Nationalism and Revolution in Indonesia* (Ithaca: Cornell University Press, 1952). Deals with some important political features of this country.

Laos: Its Society, Its Culture, edited by F. M. Le Bar (New Haven: HRAF Press, 1960)

Pearson, Harold F., *A History of Singapore* (London: University of London Press, 1956). A quick but useful look at Singapore.

Purcell, Victor, *The Chinese in Malaya* (London: Oxford University Press, 1948). The great bulk of Malaya's population is divided between the Malays and the Chinese. *See* Winstedt below.

Thompson, Virginia, *Thailand: The New Siam* (New York: 1941). An older work on the prewar period in Thailand which is still useful.

Vlekke, Bernard H. M., *Nusantara: A History of Indonesia* (Rev. ed.; Chicago: Quadrangle Books, 1960). A recent solid history of this country.

Welty, Paul, "Viet-Nam Today," *World Affairs,* Vol. 125 (Spring, 1962), pp. 4-12. Provides some conception of the turmoil afflicting Viet-Nam at present.

Windstedt, Sir Richard, *The Malays: A Cultural History* (Rev. ed.;

London: Routledge and Kegan Paul, 1950). For the Chinese in Malaya, *see* Purcell above.

Woodman, Dorothy, *The Making of Burma* (London: Cresset Press, 1962). A fine survey of Burma.

————, *The Republic of Indonesia* (New York: Philosophical Library, 1955). A comprehensive work on this country.

INDEX

Absolutism: *See* Totalitarianism

Adoption: 193, 252-53

Age, reverence for: 30, 193, 200, 203-04

Agriculture: 23-25, 28, 36, 39-40; in China, 25-26, 140-41, 170, 182-83, 188-89; in East Asia, 139-40; in South-East Asia, 283

Akbar: 116, 121

America: *See* United States

Amitabha Buddha: 73, 147, 175, 244 (*see also* Mahayana Buddhism)

Analects, The: 149, 155 (quote)

"Ancestor worship": 94, 148, 178, 193, 197, 201, 203-04, 246

Ancestral hall: 192-97

Animism: 237-38, 284, 289, 290, 296

Arhat: 291

Arnold, Sir Edwin: 65 (quote)

Artisans: *See* Handicraft industry

Aryans: 81, 109

Asceticism: 58, 68, 72

Asia: 23-35; countries and territories of, 8-9 (map), 19; land area of, 19-22; population of, 20-21 (map), 22; religions of, 48 (map)

Asian continent: 8-9 (map), 19-22

Asoka: 60, 77, 112-14

Asramas: *See* Hinduism, beliefs of

Atman: *See* Hinduism, beliefs of

Atom bomb: 13, 321

Bhagavad-Gita: 62, 70 (quote), 102-03

Birth control: 249

Birth rate (Asia): 22

Bodhisattva: 173-75 (*see also* Mahayana Buddhism)

Book of Lord Shang: 166 (quote)

Brahman: *See* Hinduism, beliefs of

Brahmanism: 59 (*see also* Hinduism)

Brahmaputra River: 22

Brahmins: 319 (*see also* Caste system)

Brahmo Samoj: 117

British colonialism (in India): 116-18

British Commonwealth of Nations: 55, 57

Buddha, Gautama: 71-77, 112, 173-74, 232, 245-46, 291-92; life of, 71-72; teachings of, 73-77

Buddhahood: 245-46 (*see also* Zen Buddhism)

Buddha-nature: 245-46 (*see also* Zen Buddhism)

Buddhas: 174 (*see also* Mahayana Buddhism)

Buddhism: 59-60, 71-77; afterlife in, 74-75, 174-76; as vehicle of cultural diffusion, 173-77; beliefs of, 71-77, 245-46; compared with Chinese ideologies, 144, 147, 176-77; compared with Hinduism, 59; decline of, 246; ethics of, 74-76, 245-46; festivals of, 231-32, 293-95; gods of, 75, 77, 174-75, 241-42; influence of, 2, 10, 47-49, 77, 164, 176-77; monasticism in, 176-77, 241-42, 246, 292-96, 303; origins of, 71-72; political aspects of, 13, 241-42, 245-46, 269, 294-95; priesthood in, 176, 241-42, 246, 289-90, 292-93; psychology of, 74-75; schools of, 72-73, 77, 245-46, 284, 291-92, 298; scriptures of, 72; shrines of, 244; spread of, 48 (map), 60, 77, 146-47, 173-77; temples of, 242, 246; theology of, 59, 73-74, 76, 245-

343